PPL
32.00

Belling the Cat

Belling the Cat

Essays, Reports, and Opinions

Mordecai

Richler

Alfred A. Knopf Canada

PUBLISHED BY ALFRED A. KNOPF CANADA

Copyright © 1998 by Mordecai Richler Productions Limited

Canadian Cataloguing in Publication Data

Richler, Mordecai, 1931 –
 Belling the cat: selected essays and reports

ISBN 0-676-97152-0

I. Title

PS8535.I38A6   C814'.54   C98-930039-0
PR9199.3.R53S44 1998

First Edition

Cover design: Spencer Francey Peters
Cover photo: Gillian Edelstein

Printed and bound in the United States of America

In memory of Nick Auf der Maur
1942 – 1998

Acknowledgements

I HAVE DIVIDED the pieces selected for this collection into categories that speak to most of my interests: books, sports, travel, and politics. For something like ten years I wrote a monthly column entitled "Books and Things" for *GQ*, and that column has yielded most of the book pieces included here, while others were commissioned by *Saturday Night*, the *National Review*, and the *New York Times Book Review*. My essay on Mark Twain's *The Innocents Abroad* was commissioned as an introduction to that book by the Oxford University Press, but first appeared in the *New Criterion*. The sports pieces first appeared in *Maclean's*, *Inside Sports*, and the short-lived *New York Times* quarterly magazine supplement on sports. The political articles were originally written for *Saturday Night*. I am grateful to *Maclean's*, *Saturday Night*, the *New Yorker*, *GQ*, the *National Review*, *Playboy*, *New Criterion*, Oxford University Press, and the *New York Times Book Review* for permission to reprint these pieces here.

Contents

Belling the Cat

———

Writing for
the Mags

I FEAR I BELONG to the last generation of novelists who could supplement their incomes, earning life-sustaining cigar and cognac money, by scribbling for the mags. Between novels, I have been writing for magazines in Canada, the United States, and the United Kingdom for more than forty years now. It is no longer a growth industry, like, say, CD-ROMs, whatever they are; e-mail; nutter TV chat shows in which moms who have been screwed by their daughters' boyfriends are interviewed; talk radio; "artists" who spit mouthfuls of paint on their dipsy-doodle canvases for big bucks; blockbuster films that bring comic-book heroes to life, as it were; TV news documentaries (or, God help us, docudramas) that confirm everything you already knew; rock videos; and other modern horrors. So it is with an eye on history that I have compiled this collection of miscellaneous pieces that I wrote to support myself.

For openers, consider a list I have compiled of magazines of disparate quality for which I once wrote, which have expired long ago. In Canada, the *Montrealer*, *New Liberty*, *Tamarack Review*, *Weekend*, and the *Star Weekly* magazine. In the U.S., *Show*, *Signature*, the late Philip Rahv's *Modern Occasions*, *New American Review*, *Inside Sports*, *Holiday*, the New York *Herald Tribune's Book World*, and *Life* as it once was. In the U.K., *Town*, *Books and Bookmen*, *Twentieth Century*, *Encounter*, and *London Life*, the latter a promising magazine started by

Mark Boxer and Francis Wyndham that unfortunately folded after only a few issues.

The first thing I ever published in a magazine, back in the early fifties, was an embarrassingly sentimental short story, which I have since kept out of print, that was accepted by the *New Statesman*. It earned me a cheque for twelve guineas, signed by the legendary Kingsley Martin, who was then the editor.

Kingsley Martin once stopped at the desk of a recently hired young deputy editor and told him how pleased he was with his work. The young deputy, seizing his opportunity, complained about how difficult it was for him to support his wife and newborn child on a salary of fifteen guineas a week. "Good God," replied an astonished Martin, a lifelong socialist, "haven't you got a private income?"

In 1956, rooted in a London bedsitter without a private income, broke, I borrowed money for a return air ticket to Toronto and managed to sweet-talk CBC-TV into commissioning me to write a couple of plays. Out on the town one night, I met Frank Rasky, then editor of *New Liberty*, a magazine I much admired because each article it printed came with a challenging beat-the-clock headnote saying how long it would take to read it: for instance, four minutes and thirty-two seconds, or whatever. Rasky advanced me $250 against an article about what it was like for a novelist to write for TV. I churned out what I considered to be an erudite, insightful piece about the problems of addressing a large audience. Rasky liked it. "I'm going to put your name on the cover," he said. "We'll call your piece 'How I Hate Writing for Those TV Slobs.'"

Alarmed, I asked for the piece back, pretending I wanted to tighten it, and fled his office never to return. Back in London, I was hounded for months by indignant letters from Rasky, each one signed "Your Creditor," demanding his money back as well as reimbursement for the cost of printing a new magazine cover.

My Toronto money-grubbing excursion yielded a three-part piece about life in Canada for the London *Spectator*, which led to my becoming a more or less regular contributor, beginning with an assignment to turn out a monthly novel-review column. In those days, a reviewer could drop into the literary editor's office, take home twelve novels, and select four or five for review, skewering the last one in a brutal sentence or two. But there was a perk. Every Thursday, a Fleet Street bookseller would make the rounds of reviewers' homes and pay half the retail price in cash for the batch of twelve books. When the young Evelyn Waugh, wise beyond his years, was moonlighting as a reviewer, he usually insisted on the art books, which were the most expensive.

During my novel-reviewing stint for the *Spectator*, Arthur Koestler and Stephen Spender dug deep into their pockets and chipped in to offer a £100 prize for the best novel written by a prisoner. I was sent the first prizewinner for review, a nicely done coming-of-age novel set in Wales, with touching endpapers that showed how the prisoner in question had written his novel with a pencil in ruled exercise books. The prisoner, now released, was endearingly publicity shy, refusing an *Observer* request for an interview. At the time, I was sharing a flat with film director Ted Kotcheff, and I passed the novel on to him. He was so impressed that he forked out £500 for an option, and commissioned a mutual friend, Clive Exton, to do the screenplay. The author refused to meet with Kotcheff. In fact, once he had cashed the cheque, he did a flit, and with good reason. It turned out that he had taken a novel out of the prison library, about coming of age in Montana and Wyoming, and had reset it in Wales. Stung, Koestler and Spender did not offer the prize a second time.

A 1995 issue of that admirable literary journal *London Magazine*—which has now survived into its forty-fourth year, entirely due to the dedication of its editor, Alan Ross—featured an article on the troubled history of *Encounter*, concentrating on the scandal that broke in 1967. That was the year British intellectuals were shaken by the revelation that *Encounter*, edited by the brilliant Melvin Lasky, a New Yorker, and numbering among its contributors Koestler, Galbraith,

Nabokov, Dwight Macdonald, Ignazio Silone, Raymond Aron, and Isaiah Berlin, and just about every other member of the international liberal intelligentsia, had been clandestinely funded by the CIA since it was founded in 1953. Co-editors Stephen Spender and Frank Kermode both resigned, writing to the *Times* to protest that they had been deceived and ill-used. Isaiah Berlin ventured that Melvin Lasky, having failed to come clean about *Encounter*'s secret financing, had "compromised decent people." But the most amusing letter to the *Times*, so far as I was concerned, came from novelist Colin MacInnes, who, like me, was a sometime contributor. If this was CIA vigorish, he wrote, it certainly didn't amount to much. He was right. I was never paid more than £75 for two weeks' hard slog on an essay.

At this juncture in my magazine-writing career, I had learned to distinguish between those mags that paid munificently (*Life*, *Playboy*) but were read by nobody I knew, and those that offered me a pittance (*Encounter*, *London Magazine*, *New Statesman*, the *Spectator*, the *New York Review of Books*) but were read and commented on by people I respected.

Item: When the *New York Review of Books* was sold some years back, contributors were not enchanted to discover that its annual bill for courier services came to rather more than its budget for contributors.

The first time I was commissioned by *Life*, in 1970, the magazine flew me from London to Montreal, shortly after the murder of Pierre Laporte, who had been kidnapped by the FLQ (Front de Libération du Québec), to write an essay about our troubled country. In those days, the magazine suffered from a surfeit of editors, all of them intent on justifying themselves. My manuscript came back with irritating notations by various hands, and this led to a quarrel. In a list I had compiled of Canadians who had prospered in the U.S., I included "pitcher Ferguson Jenkins and catcher George Chuvalo." An editor protested, "I appreciate what you're saying, but we'll get hundreds of letters from readers saying Chuvalo is a boxer, not a ball player," and I had to yield.

I learned that even *Commentary* readers, whom I would have thought were a sophisticated bunch, could be Anti-Defamation-League quick to take offence. In a lighthearted piece I wrote about Jews in sport for that magazine in 1966, I speculated "it is possible that [Hank] Greenberg, [then] the only Jew in the Hall of Fame, was also tragically inhibited by his Jewish heritage. I'm thinking of 1938, when he had hit fifty-eight home runs, two short of Babe Ruth's record, but with five games to play, failed to hit another one out of the park. Failed . . . or just possibly held back, because Greenberg just possibly understood that if he shattered the Babe's record, seemingly inviolate, it would be considered pushy of him and given the climate of the times, not such a good thing for the Jews."

To my amazement, this provoked a spill of letters accusing me of tainting a great sportsman's reputation and of doing serious harm in the struggle against discrimination. Teasing or not, time proved me right for once. In 1974, when the splendid Hank Aaron hit his 715th dinger, overtaking the Babe's career record of 714 lifetime homers, he suffered something like a *fatwa*, requiring police protection against the many death threats he received in the mail.

Item: I became *persona non grata* at *Commentary* after I wrote a review in the *Nation* ridiculing *Making It*, an uncommonly coarse venture into autobiography by Norman Podhoretz, the magazine's editor. And ever since then, *Commentary* has celebrated the publication of each of my novels by running a lengthy denunciad in its pages. *Quid pro quo?*

Over the years, I enjoyed a far happier relationship with the old *Maclean's*, writing in turn for editors Ralph Allen, Blair Fraser, and then Ken Lefolii and Peter Gzowski, both of whom became cherished friends. Blair Fraser was a gentleman of the old school. He objected to an article I had written about life on the RCAF base at Baden-Sollingen, in Germany, because I included some embarrassing tittle-tattle I had picked up in the bar in the officers' mess, where, as he put it, I was a guest. However, he had no qualms about the fun I had at the expense of other ranks. The article was published as it stood, and an irate RCAF flack phoned *Maclean's* and said I would never be allowed to hang out on one of their bases again.

On another occasion, *Maclean's* allowed me to spend a week with wrestlers in Quebec and, years later, when I sat down to write my first children's book, *Jacob Two-Two Meets the Hooded Fang*, the Fang was modelled on an engaging wrestling "villain" I had spent time with on the road. My point is that not only do I enjoy writing for the mags, it has also been enormously useful to me.

I published my first novel, derivative beyond compare, when I was a mere twenty-three years old.

Item: In a little book the late George Woodcock wrote about my work, he ventured that I fled Canada because of the poor reviews *The Acrobats* received there. Actually, I quit Canada for England long before my first novel was published, and had I been inclined to flee every country where it was justifiably dismissed, I would still be a travelling man.

When *The Acrobats* was published in London in 1954, it was exhilarating to see it on display in Hampstead bookshops, alongside novels by real writers. With hindsight, however, I wish I hadn't published so early but had been obliged to endure a number of unsatisfactory jobs first, either in offices or on the factory floor. Then, like other novelists I know, I would now be able to send a bucket down such immensely valuable wells of experience. Deprived of such remembered sweet water, I owe it to the mags that I have been able to mix with wrestlers, RCAF-lifers, bush pilots, and other fauna, absorbing unfamiliar idioms that I could later put to use in the writing of novels.

Magazines have also rendered unto me assignments enabling me and my wife, Florence, to travel first-class at their expense, undertaking exotic trips we could otherwise ill afford. Unfortunately the business of getting from here to there has become increasingly frustrating, even infuriating, over the years, and I speak as someone who once adored travelling, the slap-happy sensation of traipsing down the twisting streets of a foreign city for the first time, your jaded senses heightened by what Gerard Manley Hopkins celebrated as "all things counter, original, spare, strange."

Of course, nowadays, disembark in Moscow, Barcelona, or Tel Aviv, set out for the main boulevard, and you are too often bound to be deflated by the familiar: a McDonald's, a Georgio Armani boutique, a Gucci, a pizza bar, and a shop called "Wyatt Urp" or "Doge City" (*sic*) specializing in designer jeans and hand-tooled western boots made by prisoners in China. Overpriced restaurants will welcome American Express, Visa, and MasterCard. CNN will be available on your hotel TV, and you can count on the indigenous channel to be showing reruns of "Dallas" or "Cheers," dubbed in Russian, Spanish, or Hebrew. Mind you these latter variations on the familiar can be inadvertently amusing. Case in point. In 1951, drifting down the Ramblas in Barcelona, somewhat footsore, I slipped into a cinema to catch a Joel McCrae western dubbed in Spanish and, lo and behold, good old reliable Joel moseyed up to the bar in Tombstone and demanded, *"Uno cognac, por favor."*

I first crossed the Atlantic, at the age of nineteen, in 1950, on board the *Franconia*, outward-bound from Quebec City to Liverpool. In those days everybody in tourist class on an ocean liner or propeller-driven airplane was equal, paying the same fare. Nowadays, however, after you have probably forked out something like a thousand dollars for your jumbo jet "hospitality" return ticket to Paris, Rome, or wherever, the odds are that the three-hundred-pound behemoth shoehorned into the seat beside you, having promised to fly on a rainy Wednesday while wearing his tracksuit with the Day-Glo stripes, most likely has acquired his ticket for $149.95, payable in twelve instalments. And if that isn't enough to put you in a yippee mood, it turns out that once he has stowed away a ton of "carry-on" luggage under his seat *and* yours, he happens to be a compulsive nose-picker or master of the silent fart, earning *you* dirty looks from everyone in the rows ahead and behind. And, naturally, he is a compulsive talker who wants to know how the world is treating you and where do you hail from?

Freeze out your seatmate, and he retaliates by fishing into one of his bulging flight bags and surfacing with the latest Garfield paperback, which has him quaking with laughter for the next four hours of flight time. The rest of the jet, it goes without saying, is usually filled with shrieking babes, kids playing tag, teenagers jerking their heads in time to the rock beat leaking out of the Walkman clamped to their ears, middle-aged wits who feel entitled to flirt with the stewardesses ("I've got the time, if you've got the place"), and battalions of Japanese tourists, laden with state-of-the-art camcorders, shooting film of cloud formations, of flight attendants propelling drink trolleys, and of each other standing up, sitting down, and performing other astonishing feats.

Then, after bouncing about at thirty-five thousand feet for seven hours, you land, ears throbbing with pain, and line up in an overheated hall to pass through immigration. This will take an hour, maybe more, because either you have arrived just after another flight from Colombia, every passenger a suspected drug smuggler, or there's an obviously impecunious African immediately ahead of you, who claims to be a citizen of Finland and is armed with an inch-thick passport that opens like an accordion and calls for a half-hour examination by a suspicious immigration officer.

Finally, smelly, eyes bloodshot, you reach your hotel, only to be welcomed by the news that they have no record of your reservation, or that your room, overlooking a parking lot, won't be ready for another four hours. Never mind. The bar is open, and there you can contemplate the ordeals that lie ahead: all those museums and churches and castles, as well as the snotty waiters you will have to tolerate in elegant restaurants. Because you are a North American, they will unfailingly check you out to make sure you are wearing shoes, and treat you as if you were about to sample your first glass of wine.

But the truth is I did enormously enjoy being sent on safari in Kenya, wandering about Marrakech with Florence, hunkering down at the Savoy in London and at the Crillon in Paris, and risking the temptations of the whisky trail in the Scottish Highlands, all in the line of duty. For these assignments I remain grateful to Art Cooper, editor of *GQ*, and to the late Horace Sutton of *Signature* magazine.

I was taken aback to read in the arts section of the Toronto *Globe and Mail* (May 2, 1992) that author Robert Mason Lee had said, "A good editor is like a lover. There's the tension that results in understanding; there's the sheer amount of time you spend together. A good relationship with an editor is a passionate one."

Nipping potential rumours in the bud, I must protest that would not be a fair description of my relationship with Bob Gottlieb, who has been my novel editor at Knopf for more than thirty years.

My first editor, whom I encountered in Paris in 1950, when I was a mere nineteen-year-old, was a man called Sinbad Vail. Sinbad, the son of Peggy Guggenheim and partner Laurence Vail, was the publisher of a little magazine called *Points*. We never met anywhere but in the cafés of Montparnasse and Saint-Germain-des-Près, to chat over snifters of cognac, instantly renewable and paid for by Vail. Young and callow as I was, I understood in a flash that I had stumbled on a vocation that would suit me to the end of my days.

My next editorial experience was a fortunate one. Diana Athill, of André Deutsch Ltd., nursed me and my first novel into print. The novel's publication earned me an introduction to the story editor of a London film studio. The day before we were to meet, I went window-shopping, pondering fire-engine red MGs, pausing before a real-estate agent's window in Belgravia to scan photographs of villas in Antibes and Saint-Paul-de-Vence. I met the editor, an emaciated sixty-year-old with a disconcerting facial tic, at a corner café in Soho, where we were served coffee in chipped railroad cups, with milk scum and soap bubbles floating on the surface. His hands trembling, he could not lift his coffee cup without splashing himself. An unabashed admirer of my first novel, he had not invited me out to make an offer for the film rights, but he did have work for me. Once a week, he said, he would send me a new novel. I would be expected to write a five-page synopsis, followed by my expert opinion on whether or not the book deserved to be filmed.

"Has your studio," I asked, "ever bought film rights to a novel on the basis of a reader's report?"

"Yes, only a few months ago, and the author was so grateful to the reader, he sent him a cheque."

"How much was it for?"

"Five guineas."

Editors can be helpful. Take the late Tony Godwin, for instance, who used to be my novel editor in London. Once, he tried to direct me towards big bucks. That was in the mid-sixties, when Florence and I were ensconced in a big, rambling house on Kingston Hill, in Surrey, and every evening at six served dinner to our then four children. I was helping Florence with this chore when, suddenly, our phone rang. "Hello," the woman on the other end of the line said. "Am I speaking to Mordecai Richler?"

"Yes."

"This is Sylvia Fine. Mrs. Danny Kaye."

Har, har, har was my response.

"Why are you laughing?"

"I am not laughing," I shot right back, but I still suspected it was my friend Jack Clayton having me on.

She and Danny were staying at the Savoy, she said. She wanted me to read Shaw's *The Doctor's Dilemma* and join her for drinks at five o'clock two days hence to discuss the possibility of my writing the book for the musical she had in mind. Sylvia Fine would be responsible for the lyrics.

"Who recommended me?" I asked, still suspicious. It was Tony Godwin. "Oh, right," I said, and as soon as she hung up, I phoned Tony. "Did you give my number to Sylvia Fine?"

"Yes."

So the next morning I hurried out to buy a copy of the Shaw play, read it, and turned up at the Kayes' Savoy suite at the appropriate hour. Muffled moans of pleasure came from the bedroom, where Danny was being attended by a masseur. Sylvia poured me a large

Scotch. "We wouldn't even be in London, with Danny playing at the Palladium," she said, "but Princess Margaret insisted on it."

"Ah."

"I greatly admire your work."

"I should warn you," I said, "that I have never written for the theatre."

Never mind, she said, refilling my glass. While Danny played out his date at the Palladium, she was going to Paris to visit various couturiers. I would accompany her, of course, and we could work on the project between fittings. "Now tell me what you thought of the play?"

Taking a long swig of my drink, I said, "I'm afraid I didn't like it."

"Good. Neither did I."

"Oh."

"We can scrap most of it," she said, tending to my glass again.

"Sylvia, I'm truly grateful for this opportunity, but I must say no. I'm working on a novel right now and . . ."

There was a long pause before she said, "Let's hope it's better than the last one," even as she screwed the top back on the bottle of Scotch.

"Hey, why don't you try Jonathan Miller?"

"I already have," she said, relieving me of my glass and showing me the door. "He recommended you."

I do have some pertinent advice for beginning magazine writers. In dealing with editors, a breed usually intimidated by the timorous libel lawyers their publisher employs, it is necessary to include two, maybe even three, redundant outrages in any article submitted. Then, when the editor pleads for five or six cuts of objectionable material, you, being a reasonable fellow, can agree to retract the two or three clangers you have included only for that purpose. Mag editors, to be fair, are not a totally useless breed, and I am pleased to pass on to young writers my own infallible formula for grading them. They are to be tolerated in direct proportion to how many long-distance calls you can make from their offices, where they take you to lunch, and whether they blink when you order your second double Rémy Martin VSOP with your cognac. With these criteria in mind, I am happy to award four stars to Art Cooper and to Graydon Carter, editor of *Vanity Fair*. The different editors of *Saturday Night* that I have dealt with over the years (Bob Fulford, John Fraser, and Ken Whyte) rate only three stars by dint of their being tainted by the Toronto disease, which is to say they have always felt honour bound to return to work in the afternoon, and that, inevitably, limits a guest's coffee-and-cognac time.

I have almost always enjoyed the company of other journalists and found them to be a generous lot, good companions, who are willing to share sources and their knowledge of the most agreeable watering holes, hotels, and restaurants if you are bound, for the first time, to a city they are familiar with. But, unfortunately, we are now ploughing a diminishing magazine field, writing for readers with an increasingly short attention span.

In 1950, Fleur Cowles launched two magazines. One of them, the monthly *Flair*, was truly elegant, its first issue featuring a story by Tennessee Williams. It didn't last. The other one, the weekly *Quick*, was no bigger than a pocket diary, and it ran no article longer than a hundred words. It also featured one-line reviews of novels, plays, and films, running the title and anything from one to four stars alongside, and that was it. *Quick* failed, but I fear it is an idea whose time has come. Relaunched today, I believe it would undoubtedly be a huge success.

I am responsible, to a degree, for the sad fate of Graydon Carter, who was born and bred in our nation's sophisticated capital. He would not have fallen on such degrading days, settling for the job of editing *Vanity Fair*, had he been admitted to my suspect creative-writing class at Carlton University, in Ottawa, in 1972. Alas, Carter applied too late, registration already closed. I have no doubt that had he come along earlier, in time to be enriched by my guidance, he might have gone on to become literary editor of the Sherbrooke

Record or possibly even the *Ottawa Citizen*'s entertaining columnist, instead of wasting under alien skies. Whenever we meet these days, I am still troubled by guilt.

Publication in a quality magazine is pleasing, but, on occasion, there is nothing to beat being commissioned, and paid, to write an article that is never written or published. I offer my experiences with *Vanity Fair* as a case in point.

Shortly after S. I. Newhouse, Jr., revived *Vanity Fair* in 1983, the title having been dormant since 1936, I dropped in to shoot the breeze with Richard Locke, the magazine's first editor. "What would you like to do for us?" he asked.

Thinking hard, I suggested that I would like to fly to London with Florence, spend a week there, and make the return crossing on the *QE2*, and write a piece about that legendary ship.

"That sounds like a good idea," he said.

I proposed that we not even discuss a fee, because I had no idea whether the article I had in mind would run to two thousand or eight thousand words.

"Okay," he said. "We can settle that later."

So Florence and I set out for London. On our last day in town, I took her to a restaurant in Fulham for lunch. Afterward, on impulse, I stopped a taxi outside and asked the driver what he would charge to take us to Southampton docks. "Fifty quid," he said.

"Let's go, then."

We stopped to pick up our luggage, and then, even as we tooled merrily down the motorway, I opened up my copy of the *International Herald Tribune*, and stumbled on a disconcerting item. Richard Locke had been fired.

A couple of weeks later, on a trip to New York, I went to lunch with Leo Lerman, the new editor of *Vanity Fair*. "Mordecai," he said, "you don't really want to write a boring piece about sailing on the *QE2*, do you?"

"It was Richard Locke's idea."

"We'll pay you, of course, but now I want to know what you will write for us."

We settled on an article about the little-known Canadian take-over of the American media: A. M. Rosenthal, then editor of the *New York Times*; Morty Zuckerman, publisher of the *Atlantic Monthly*; Morley Safer, a regular on "Sixty Minutes"; Peter Jennings, anchor of ABC-TV evening news; etc. et etc. Writing the piece turned out to be a grind, but I hand-delivered it, shame-faced, several months late. Leo Lerman lay in wait. "Mordecai," he said, "I want you to meet our new editor."

It was Tina Brown, and she didn't want the piece, for which I could hardly blame her. But I was paid again.

More than forty years of scribble scribble scribble, and I have been sued only once. Back in the sixties, when I was still rooted in London, the late Mark Boxer, who was then editor of the *Sunday Times Magazine*, planned a special issue on life in the north of England, and asked me to contribute an article about the Jewish community in Leeds. I was, at the time, bound for the all but contiguous city of Bradford with Ted Kotcheff, to hunt for locations for the film of *Life at the Top*, based on John Braine's sequel to *Room at the Top*. Kotcheff was going to direct and I had written the screenplay. So Boxer's proposal suited me just fine.

The old working-class Jewish neighbourhood of Leeds was now largely inhabited by Pakistanis, most of whom worked in the cotton mills, but we did find its one remaining Jewish restaurant. A poky little place now frequented, for the most part, by grizzly old men. The food was mediocre, the boiled beef that Kotcheff and I were served floating in a lukewarm, gluey sauce. But I liked it there. It was familiar. Describing it in the *Sunday Times*—affectionately, I thought—I noted that the place boasted all the traditional features of a struggling Jewish restaurant in a neighbourhood that was no longer thriving. The ancient waiters were ill-tempered. There were wine stains and crumbs on the white-linen tablecloth. Shortly after the piece appeared, the *Sunday Times* phoned to say that the restaurant was threatening to sue, claiming there had been no wine

stains or crumbs on the tablecloth. "How much do they want?"
I asked.

"Fifty pounds."

"Give it to them."

"They also want a retraction."

I couldn't agree to that. So, a couple of weeks later, I found myself on a train back to Leeds, accompanied this time by an intense,
upright WASP solicitor. He opened his file of correspondence, pondered it, and asked me, "How many crumbs were there on the
tablecloth?"

"I didn't count them."

"Quite."

We went to the restaurant for lunch, and no sooner did we sit
down than the solicitor said, "No crumbs."

"Quite."

"Or wine stains."

We hardly talked on the train back to London, but, on arrival, I
invited the solicitor to join me for a drink in the station's pub.
"Well," I said, "what do you think?"

"It's your word against his."

Kotcheff offered to back me up, but I wasn't going to court
against a struggling Jewish restaurateur. "Offer him a hundred quid,
but no retraction," I said. "Obviously the old boy wants to paint his
place."

It worked.

Sued only once, I also survived a picayune attempt to censor an essay
I wrote about the Mulroney years for *Saturday Night* in 1993. Mulroney tried to prevent its publication or, at the very least, to have it
blue-pencilled to suit his taste.

The afterlife of discarded politicians, their ability to put rejection
behind them and dazzle us with fresh, profitable identities, is a continuing source of astonishment to me. Mikhail Gorbachev, bounced
out of office, enjoyed a brief second coming as a boring syndicated

columnist and expensive after-dinner speaker in the freedom-loving West and, in 1997, was born yet again as a TV flack for Pizza Hut. A fulminating Margaret Thatcher, serving as her own wart-free Boswell, outsold just about everybody but Stephen King with her first book. Jimmy Carter, pure of heart, builds homes for the impoverished and is more highly regarded out of office than he ever was as president.

Then there is the business of our very own Brian Mulroney. Having flunked as a purveyor of second-hand furniture of dubious provenance, his first post-PM stint, Mulroney began to collect directorships like conkers, admirably determined to maintain Mila in the Tiffany style that Canadian taxpayers had accustomed her to. Happily, a 1994 appointment offered proof positive, if it were needed, that no sinner is beyond redemption. He joined the Freedom Forum, an American body dedicated to promoting freedom of the press. But instead of saluting Mulroney for his act of conscience, media cry-babies, like *Globe and Mail* columnist Robert Sheppard, have been characteristically snide.

According to Sheppard, the Freedom Forum, run by Allan Neuharth, founder of *USA Today*, is a suspect organization. Three of its directors (raking in between $51,000 to $81,000 a year) have quit, he wrote, and the New York attorney general's office confirmed that it was investigating the foundation for excessive spending (on itself) and possible financial improprieties. Furthermore, spoilsport Sheppard, bleeding envy, was displeased because, in the past, the foundation's executive committee met in Los Angeles during Super Bowl week, New Orleans during the NCAA basketball finals, and Rio de Janeiro during Carnival.

Obviously Sheppard would not pronounce the Freedom Forum pure until it elected to meet in Sudbury on Boxing Day. But I, for one, am proud that Mulroney was now going to swing his big bat in defence of ink-stained wretches. The truth is this represented a genuine change of heart, for in 1993, busy as he was still running our country, Mulroney found time to make editorial suggestions to *Saturday Night*. When he heard that I had been assigned to write an appreciation of his years in office ("So Long, Brian," June 1993), he phoned Peter White, his former principal secretary and a director of Hollinger Inc., primary owner of *Saturday Night*, to ask if they couldn't get somebody more objective to celebrate his contribution to Canada. Say, Mila.

Months later I phoned Peter White and asked, "Did Mulroney actually try to stop publication of my piece?"

"No," said White, "but he did object to certain phrases."

"Are you telling me that you showed him an advance copy of my article?"

"It's so long ago, um, I don't remember all the details. However, no editorial changes were made in your article."

True enough. But now I sleep better knowing that if another overreaching pol tries to tamper with something I've written, magnanimously offering his services as a freelance editor, I can always call on the press's born-again protector, freedom's champion, Sincerely Yours, Brian Mulroney.

Books
and
Things

───────

Mr.
Sam

———————

T HE MASS MIGRATION of East European Jews to North America—*de goldeneh medina*, "the golden land"—began in 1881–82, the reaction to a rash of pogroms in Russia. This migration accelerated when the Jews were run out of Moscow and other major cities in 1891, and became a veritable stampede in 1903, following the massacre in Kishinev, in southern Russia, in which forty-nine Jews were murdered and some five hundred mutilated.

Heroic is the *mot juste* for these impecunious, rough-and-ready migrants from the Pale of Settlement, these raw *shtetl* Jews who sailed steerage to "America, America" around the turn of the century. The most imaginative of these inspired ruffians founded RCA and CBS (David Sarnoff, William Paley) and literally invented Hollywood: Shmuel Gelbfisz, a.k.a. Sam Goldfish, but celebrated as Samuel Goldwyn; Lewis J. Seleznick (later Selznick); William Fox (formerly Fuchs); Louis B. Mayer, a failed New Brunswick junk dealer; Adolph Zuckor; and Harry Cohn, begetter of Columbia Pictures. Another child of the ghetto, Samuel Newhouse, laid the foundation for what would mature into an international publishing colossus, even as Helena Rubinstein started an enormous cosmetics business.

And here I must pause for a cherished anecdote, told to me by the curator of the Beaverbrook Museum in Fredericton.

Having commissioned Graham Sutherland to paint her portrait, Helena Rubinstein was so upset by the unforgiving result that she absolutely refused to pay for it. Years later she met Lord Beaverbrook at a party. "I bought that Sutherland portrait of you," he said.

Helena was outraged. "But I told him it was to be destroyed. *What have you done with it?*" she demanded.

"It's on view in my museum in Fredericton, New Brunswick."

"Oh well," she said, relieved, "I suppose that amounts to the same thing."

In the old days, the fast tracks out of the tenements and sweatshops led to either Tin Pan Alley (Irving Berlin, George Gershwin), vaudeville (Al Jolson, George Burns, Eddie Cantor, Fanny Brice, the Marx Brothers, Jack Benny, et al.), or the ring. Ah, and once we could boast some legendary pugilists, names that still resonate among those who retain an appreciation of the fancy: Abraham "the Little Hebrew" Attell, Reuben "Ruby, Jewel of the Ghetto" Goldstein, Maxie "Slapsie Maxie" Rosenbloom, Hall of Famer Benny Leonard, and the splendid Barney Ross. And, furthermore, most of these exemplars yearned to toil in Madison Square Gardens for Joe "Yussel the Muscle" Jacobs, the charm of their performances rated in *Ring* by Reb Nat Fleisher. While I'm at it, however, honour obliges me to note that, according to my indispensable *Encyclopedia of Jews in Sport* (the sole compendium of athletic achievement, I take it, that includes a section on chess), the *Yiddishkeit* of Maximillian Adelbert "Madcap Maxie" Baer was suspect:

The case of Max Baer and his brother, Buddy, also a heavyweight, is a confusing one. While there was a Jewish strain in the Baer family derived from the paternal grandfather, a Jew from Alsace-Lorraine, it seems that Jacob Baer, the father of the boys, was not a practising Jew and their mother was of Scotch-Irish descent. Despite this, Max did wear a Magen David on his trunks and proclaimed himself a Jew. However many believe this was merely for publicity purposes.

For those who couldn't sing or dance worth a damn and lacked a convincing left hook, there were alternative routes out of penury. Professional gambling (the brilliant Arnold Rothstein, the man who purportedly paid the Chicago Black Sox to throw the 1919 World Series, and who was the model for F. Scott Fitzgerald's Meyer Wolfsheim in *The Great Gatsby*), or the mob (Gyp the Blood, Kid Twist, Dopey Benny, Meyer Lansky, Dutch Schultz, Bugsy Siegal, Waxey Gordon, Longy Zwillman, Jacob "Greasy Thumb" Guzik, Moe Dalitz, Solomon "Cutcher-Head-Off" Weissman, and Max "Boo Boo" Hoff, as well as the good companions of The Little Jewish Navy and The Purple Gang). And then there was bootlegging—an interdisciplinary pursuit that, during the Prohibition years, married eager Canadian suppliers to American mobsters in the service of honest but thirsting citizens. This coming together, as it were, was later cited, by my Communist friends, as proof positive of yet another Karl Marx dictum: In the twilight of capitalism, entrepreneurs and the underworld would coalesce. Of course the Volstead Act of 1919, enshrining Prohibition in the United States, was monumentally stupid, a sop to grim rural puritans; and, with hindsight, those who conspired to contravene it can be seen as public benefactors, if not quite the performers of *mitzvoth*.

Mitzvoth, a Hebrew word, is the plural of *mitzvah*, which means a good work, expressing God's will. The *Sefer Mitzvoth Gadel* lists 613 possible *mitzvoth*, the first of which is "be fruitful and multiply." The great twelfth-century philosopher Moses Maimonides, in his *Book of the Mitzvoth*, argued, according to Leo Rosten in *The Joys of Yiddish*, that a man who performed in accordance with only one of the 613 deserved salvation, but this was followed by a kicker: "Only if he did so not out of self-interest, or to win credit, but entirely out of love and for its own sake."

Granted that bootleggers performed an admirable social service, they were unarguably into it for the fiduciary currency. And among the many morally flexible entrepreneurs who fattened on the trade, Jew or Gentile (Harry Hatch of Corby's, the Seagrams family, never mind those twice-removed Calvinist distillers in the Highlands who knew exactly where their joy juice was going), none was better at it than the Bronfman brothers and their brother-in-law Barney Aaron.

This Barney Aaron, incidentally, is not to be confused with his distinguished namesake, Barney "the Star of the East" Aaron, an East End of London fishmonger turned prizefighter in 1819, whose praises were once sung in a street ballad:

Houndsditch and the Lanes rejoice
    where the mart for clothes is;
Hebrew science lifts its voice,
    Aaron proves a Moses.
Barney Aaron! Barney Aaron!
    Through the Sin-a-gog and streets,
Rabbis with their oily 'air on,
    Shout his name and praise his feats.

The Bronfman family fortune, one of the most substantial in North America, was built on the rock of bootlegging. Instead of being defiant, or at least amused, about the gaudy origins of the family's billions, Sam in his time, and now his progeny, has remained unaccountably ashamed. Too bad. For the truth is the roistering Abe, Harry, Sam, and Allan sinned far less against the common weal than J. P. Morgan, John D. Rockefeller, or other robber barons. They did not put the lives of immigrants at risk, paying them a pittance to descend into extremely dangerous mine pits. They did not manipulate the stock market, wasting small investors, and neither did they hire goons to break strikes in their factories. All the same, the family is still trying to launder their early history, the only thing interesting about them, determined to render it as bland as possible, that is to say, squeaky-clean Canadian.

The most readable takes on Sam are to be found in James H. Gray's *Booze* and Peter C. Newman's *Bronfman Dynasty*, and the most embarrassing portrait, as maudlin as it is vacuous, emerged in 1982, in a privately printed memoir "by" Saidye Rosner Bronfman, Sam's widow. "He was a proud Canadian, loyal to his country in wartime and peace, and he attained high honours in his own country and abroad," wrote Saidye in a book that doesn't once mention bootlegging or the wounding social barriers raised against the Bronfmans by Montreal's unspeakably provincial high society. "But when his work day ended and the door to our home closed behind him, he became, simply, my husband, my darling, my Sam."

The books by Gray and Newman so dissatisfied the Bronfman family that they took to commissioning biographies. The first writer to be hired, Terence Robertson, completed a biography that was found wanting by the family and suppressed. The next writer to be employed, former *Time/Canada* editor John Scott, was yanked off the job after a few years of work. Finally the Bronfmans found themselves a house-broken academic who obliged them with a book-length tribute—*Mr. Sam: The Life and Times of Samuel Bronfman*—that managed the seemingly impossible feat of rendering this foul-mouthed buccaneer boring. On the other hand, the hungering Sam, who spent his declining years orchestrating paeans to himself, would undoubtedly have been pleased.

Ironies.

Bugsy Siegal and Dutch Schultz, both psychotic killers, have entered American mythology, undeservedly portrayed on film as less than contemptible by glamorous stars (Warren Beatty, Dustin Hoffman) at no cost to their heirs, if they had any. But Sam, who did so little mischief, and following Prohibition wiped his shoes clean and built a huge liquor empire, had to suffer his heirs forking out for a politically correct eulogy.

"My involvement in this project began in the spring of 1987," wrote Michael R. Marrus, "in a conversation with Charles Bronfman in Montreal. Two years later I agreed to write the book, supported by the Seagram Company under terms which kept the project's sponsors at a congenial arm's length. From those early discussions to the present, there has been complete agreement on one essential point: I was to have complete independence in the research and writing of the book. . . ."

This is self-deluding nonsense. Once having accepted such a bargain, aware of how touchy the Bronfmans are, Professor Marrus

would have needed to be a fool—and there is certainly no evidence
of that—not to have grapsed that the job called for a built-in censor,
and nicely, nicely was the only sure road to publication. Furthermore, Professor Marrus strikes me as sufficiently sophisticated
to know that any biography of a billionaire, paid for by a family
ashamed of its past, was irrevocably compromised even before the
first sentence was composed. Mind you, many years earlier, a better
writer, A. M. Klein, was hired to fill the humiliating office of Sam's
poet laureate. Degrading himself and his sullen craft, Klein obliged
with more than one hosanna in verse. Consider, for instance, an
acrostic bit of doggerel written to honour the reformed bootlegger's
fiftieth birthday, on March 4, 1941, and presented to him at a banquet as part of an illuminated address. The first stanza ran:

Sincere, laborious for the common weal,
Able, of heart capacious, broad of mind,
Militant for his country, of great zeal
Unto the human of earth's humankind,
Excellent in most wise philanthropy,
Leader well-chosen for his people's need.

Klein, a practising lawyer and editor of the *Canadian Jewish
Chronicle*, a socialist with real political ambitions, signed on with
Bronfman in 1939 and, come 1948, his half-time salary was $3,000,
sweetened by $1,000 in expenses. In return, the indentured poet,
wrote Professor Marrus, was to churn out speeches, annual company reports, "birthday and anniversary greetings Sam sent to friends
and family members, and even, in all likelihood, some highly personal correspondence, such as a long letter to his son Charles on the
occasion of his bar mitzvah." A. M. Klein addressed Sam as "mae-
stro," and, in 1957, already suffering from the nervous ailment that
would undo him, he was summoned to help his patron design his
personal coat of arms. Instead of falling about with laughter in the
face of such an outlandish conceit, Klein instructed the heraldry expert, "The ideal that is cherished is that of mankind throughout the

world, held together by pacts of friendship and loyalty." Klein was called upon again to write importuning letters when Sam was desperately pursuing a seat in the Senate. The poet, Joycean critic, and novelist was rewarded with the occasional *pourboire* for his efforts. In response, he grovelled. On March 24, 1941, he wrote Sam:

> I want . . . to thank you again for what you did for me last week, and how you did it. I may say now that I was so overwhelmed when I took a peak at that folded cheque as you were on the telephone, that my usual fluency of speech abandoned me, and I was all heart and no tongue. Your very candid letter—which you saw should reach me early in the afternoon, made me very happy indeed, and was reward enough; at the subsequent conversation, I said, "My cup runneth over." I was even then sorely tempted to persist in my arrogant gesture of refusal, but your charming separating of the letter from the cheque completely unarmed me. Moreover, I shuddered to reflect what would have happened to me had I come home that evening and told my wife that I was such a "knacker"—her vocabulary would have been very picturesque, indeed. And so my wife thanks you, and my son thanks you, and most certainly I do too.

Somewhere back there in the mountains and mists of Bessarabia, where the Bronfmans were rooted, there had to be—even then—an illicit still or village tavern, or both, tended by the family, otherwise owners of a tobacco farm. Bronf-man means "whisky-man" in Yiddish, and in those days, in the Pale of Settlement, Jews, more often than not, were issued surnames that identified them by their trades. In any event, in 1889, Yechiel Bronfman, then thirty-seven years old, sailed from Odessa (the port that spawned the great Isaac Babel) with his wife, Minda, and three children for the *goldeneh medina*. Yechiel was obviously far from impecunious because his party included his rabbi (with his wife and two children) and, according to Peter Newman, a maid and a manservant as well. Soon enough life in a sod hut in the sheer wintry hell of the farm development of Wapella, Manitoba, was sufficient to strip Yechiel of his money. The resolute Bronfman patriarch, about whom so little is known, was reduced to selling firewood and peddling frozen fish in order to provide for a brood that now also included Sam. By dint of what must have been backbreaking hard work, Yechiel was able to move everybody into a real house in Brandon in 1892, and eleven years later the family bought its first hotel in Emerson, Manitoba. Next they acquired the Balmoral, in Yorkton, Saskatchewan, where fifteen-year-old Sam put in time as a bellboy and began to sharpen his skills at the pool table. Abe, the chronic gambler, and Harry and Barney Aaron did well enough in their various hotels (rooms a buck a night in 1905, with "special attention given to commercial travellers") to buy one for hot-to-trot twenty-three-year-old Sam in 1912: the Bell, in Winnipeg. Many years later, in 1951 in fact, a small-time hoodlum, testifying before Senator Estes Kefauver's Special Committee to Investigate Organized Crime, volunteered that the Bronfmans' prairie railroad hotels were actually a chain of whorehouses. Confronted with this story in the last years of his life, Sam countered, "If they were, they were the best in the West."

This jaunty riposte, nicely larded with ambiguity, is also revealing of the Bronfman family's disconcerting weakness for propriety. Just about every time Professor Marrus delivers one of Sam's tart comments, there is a footnote, crediting the quote to Terence Robertson's suppressed biography, which makes me suspect that the latter was altogether too lively for the family taste.

Three years after Sam acquired the Bell Hotel, the Bronfman brothers experienced their first epiphany. In 1915, in Winnipeg, Harry fell in with a rabbi's son who had invented a "medicated" wine, and one-two-three he and Barney Aaron were in partnership with him, peddling the stuff in dry Saskatchewan. Next we were into those goofy years when the nectars that did more than Milton could to justify God's way to man were available only in drugstores, going by such wink wink names as Liver and Kidney Cure, Dandy Bracer, Zig Zag, Rock-a-Bye Cough Cure, and Ayers Sarsaparilla.

Then, in 1919, with the advent of Prohibition in the United States, the Bronfmans began their bumpy ride into Canadian mythology. The most capable of all the bootleggers, they owned half of the twenty-odd liquor-export houses along the Saskatchewan border. Out of bonded warehouses in Saint John and Halifax, they shipped schooners full of booze, with documents claiming the cargos were bound for Cuba, Nassau, or Honduras. On bottles of liquor that came out of the same casks, they slapped labels that read Johnny Walker (*sic*), Hague and Hague (*sic*), and, most endearingly of all, Glen Levitt.

The prudent Professor Marrus writes of these halcyon days, "It is possible that the Bronfmans, or at least Sam, tried to keep relations with important American bootleggers at arm's length. Long afterwards, Sam claimed he warned Harry to steer clear of criminal elements. Sam himself cultivated the American market through an agent, a former Winnipeg bartender. . . ." Marrus is caught trying to sanitize events yet again: "On March 10, Sam dropped in on *what has been called* a bootleggers' 'open convention' in Seattle . . ." (italics mine). But, in *The Rest of Us: The Rise of America's Eastern European Jews*, Stephen Birmingham wrote, "Sam Bronfman came down from Canada and wooed [Meyer] Lansky with lavish dinners. Lansky responded by getting Bronfman tickets to the heavyweight 'prize fight of the century,' between Jack Dempsey and Luis Angel Firpo in 1923. A deal was struck, and the two men became partners, a relationship that lasted through Repeal and after." The story about the prizefight tickets was confirmed by Robert Lacey, author of *Little Man: Meyer Lansky and the Gangster Life*, in an interview with the *Toronto Star*. "How do I know? Lansky's widow swears to this." But Lacey also noted, "The Bronfmans are Canadian and saw the obvious. They didn't actually break the law but they did profit from the folly across the border and sold their booze through Lansky." And Birmingham wrote, "What impressed Lansky most was that what Bronfman was doing was all perfectly legal—in Canada, that is. . . . In fact, the Ottawa government actually encouraged the export of liquor to the United States, by refunding the nine-dollar-a-gallon tax that it imposed on all liquor sold for consumption within Canada."

Through the good offices of Joe Reinfeld, a powerful New Jersey bootlegger, Sam also got to cut a deal with Abner "Longy" Zwillman of Newark, the man who was Jean Harlow's lover and one of the Big Six that included Lansky, Frank Costello, Bugsy Siegal, Joe Adonis, and Charles "Lucky" Luciano. According to Mark Stuart, author of *Gangster #2*, a biography of Zwillman, Reinfeld once said, "My biggest mistake was sending [Longy] to Montreal to meet Sam Bronfman. Now he's got the connection, too."

Then Reinfeld's brother Abe is supposed to have said: "And Sam really admires the kid. Last time I was there, he kept telling me how well behaved Longy is, how studious-looking. 'You'd never guess he was a *shtarker* [a strong-arm man],' Sam tells me. 'Also he has a head on his shoulders,' Sam said. Sounded to me like he was ready to marry off one of his daughters to Longy."

The fastidious Professor Marrus does reproduce the same Abe Reinfeld quote in his biography, but the last sentence is excised, possibly in the interest of economy. Proving himself a more proficient advocate than biographer, he continues to waffle: "Sam's association with prohibition-era criminals follows this pattern: a link is imputed through a rumoured meeting or indirect contact, without anything more substantial on the relationship." And again: "Sam's association with Joe Reinfeld may have brought him into occasional contact with some high-ranking American bootleggers, including perhaps Longy Zwillman, but the connection does not seem to have gone further than that." Or, put another way, Sam never met his customers. Possibly he didn't even know who they were.

Bootlegging, which made the Bronfman brothers millionaires, also dealt them embarrassments. Paul Matoff, married to one of their sisters, was gunned down at their export house in Bienfait, Saskatchewan, in the autumn of 1922, and rumour had it that Harry Bronfman was the intended hit. Then there was the Cyril Knowles affair. One day in Regina the obdurate Knowles, a customs and excise inspector who was obsessed with putting the Bronfmans behind bars, arrested three American rum runners and impounded their cars. The men cited Harry as their protector. And then Harry, claimed Knowles, offered him a $3,000 bribe, which he promptly refused. Harry denied the charge, countering with an unconvincing tale of a misunderstanding. Next the grimly upright Knowles found himself summoned to Ottawa, where he had to wait in a corridor for two hours while Sam and Allan conferred with the customs minister, the Honourable Jacques Bureau, who later had to resign in disgrace, but not before, wrote Peter Newman, destroying nine filing cabinets full of incriminating documents. Knowles, once admitted to Bureau's office, was told that he had exceeded his authority and would not be returning to Regina. "The Bronfmans had evidently pulled some strings," wrote Professor Marrus, "[but] did cash or favours change hands? Knowles believed so, but no conclusive evidence has ever come to light," which is to say Bureau failed to give the Bronfman brothers a receipt.

In Prohibition's whoopee days, American bootleggers loaded up at one or another of Sam's export houses and then took to dirt roads in their Hudson Sixes, trailing thirty-foot chains to throw dust in the face of pursuers. My impatience with Professor Marrus does not stem from any objection to his prose style, which is lucid and refreshingly free of clichés, but from his attempt to duplicate that feat seventy years on. Sam Bronfman, unarguably a *grauber* (uncouth, vulgar), was a Canadian original. One of the few. So Professor Marrus has erred in obliging the old pirate's misguided family, stifling the roar of the bootlegging years in 100 of his book's 470 pages, and then allowing *Mr. Sam* to dwindle into a conventional corporate history, emphasizing Sam's Jewish community work and philanthropy. To be fair, however, these pages are redeemed from time to time by tales of Sam's pathetic social pretensions and lust for honours and tributes.

Late in life, Meyer Lansky was obviously envious that two former bootleggers he had dealt with, Sam Bronfman and Lewis Rosensteil, had emerged from Prohibition to become legitimate liquor magnates.

"Why is Lansky a 'gangster,'" he asked, "and not the Bronfman and Rosensteil families?"

The answer, surely in Sam's case, was that he was considerably more intelligent than Lansky; a driven man who, in the words of Tennyson, his favourite poet, was always ready to seize "the skirts of happy chance." And certainly Sam did achieve respectability for his children, though nothing approaching the success of the progeny of another reformed bootlegger, the odious Joe Kennedy.

Early on Sam showed promise as a forgivable fibber and an audacious, if seldom successful, social climber.

In 1921, writes Marrus, "the Zionist leader Chaim Weizmann travelled through Canada and the United States to drum up support for the Jewish colonization of Palestine. . . . Sam later claimed to have met Weizmann in Montreal and to have travelled on the train with him all the way to Winnipeg, having extensive discussions of Zionist affairs." If that was the case, Sam couldn't have made much of an impression on Weizmann, because he doesn't even rate a footnote in Norman Rose's definitive biography of Israel's first president. However, Professor Marrus did unearth one Bronfman in the Weizmann papers—a reference to Sam's younger brother in a letter dated March 18, 1927: "Allan's request for the Zionist leader's advice on shares in Commercial Solvents Corporation, the firm that held the licence to Weizmann's chemical patents."

Sam moved to Montreal in 1924 and four years later was perched in a mansion on Westmount's heights: No. 15 Belvedere Road. Rich as he was even then, it could not have been easy for him, an alien in WASP heaven, a man twice-tainted: not only a bootlegger, but a Jew. And those, those were the days of rampant anti-Semitism in Canada.

John Buchan, who would become governor-general in 1935, the first Lord Tweedsmuir of Elsfield, had already written *The Thirty-Nine Steps*, wherein a brave and good spy explains to the thriller's hero, Richard Hannay, that behind every financial conspiracy there was "a little white-faced Jew in a bathchair with an eye like a rattlesnake."

R. B. Bennett, who would become prime minister in 1930, had, in his Saskatchewan days, been a warm supporter of the Ku Klux Klan, its prairie slogan: "One Flag, One Language, One School, One Race, One Religion." And in 1935 Bennett yielded to Mackenzie King, who was terrified that Jews might buy property adjoining his Kingsmere estate.

If, in the twenties and thirties, bigotry was the unhappy rule in Canada at large, it was most acute in Quebec. There a Union Nationale backbencher could rise in the provincial legislature and quote, with impunity, from *The Protocols of the Elders of Zion*. And, in Montreal, the Abbé Groulx, Canon Emile Chartier, rector of the University of Montreal, Cardinal Villeneuve, and other insidious clerics could rage against Jews and praise fascism, their crude racism amplified in the pages of *Le Devoir*, *L'Action Catholique*, *Le Patriote*, and other publications. Of this time, and that place, Professor Marrus, his grasp of Montreal rudimentary, writes, "[the city] had . . . a live-and-let-live ethnic environment in which Jews and other minorities had little trouble feeling at home."

Ostracized by both WASP and francophone society, denied entry to the clubs favoured by their richest tradesmen (the Mount Royal, the Mount Stephen, the St. Denis), Sam responded by becoming a cartoon laird. This inspired lout out of Bessarabia, this child of the prairie sod hut, began to think of the Old Country not as the Pale of Settlement, but as the Scottish Highlands. In lieu of the Wailing Wall, Culloden; and, no doubt, the novels of Sir Walter Scott doing more to evoke his origins than the stories of Sholom Aleichem. Returning home from trips to London or Scotland, where he had gone to ingratiate himself with the liquor barons, the foul-mouthed and touchingly unselfconscious Sam took to sweetening his speech with the occasional "I say!" or "Fancy that!" Suits of armour found their way into the ancestral home on Belvedere Road. The family's chauffeur was dressed in a dark navy uniform, with a double-breasted jacket, britches, and boots. Jensen, the butler, was a veteran of the Danish Royal Guard. Poor Sam never ate at home without his jacket and insisted that his sons do the same. The Distillers Corp. headquarters he built for himself on Peel Street, opposite the once-fashionable

Mount Royal Hotel, was a toy-size version of a sixteenth-century
Scottish castle, complete with battlements, turrets, and spiked
portcullis. And then Professor Marrus goes on to quote somebody
identified only as "an unfriendly critic" on the nature of the building:
"the worst of Tudor and Gothic with early Disneyland." Checking
out the chapter notes in *Mr. Sam*, I discovered that Unfriendly Critic
was none other than Terence Robertson, author of the suppressed
Bronfman biography, who is leaned on for some twenty-four more
lively quotes in Marrus's book.

Recalling the Bronfmans' early days on Belvedere Road, his
daughter Phyllis Lambert told Professor Marrus: "There was a constant dichotomy between our Jewish upbringing and the life of the
upper class . . . a style that probably came from British royalty.

"We had Danish, Canadian, French nurses and governesses, who
meted out cod liver oil and some form of punishment every day
(mostly spankings), Milk of Magnesia once a week, and insisted on a
bland diet and keeping neat and clean and doing our homework."

Shunned by the *goyim* he was trying to emulate according to his
limited understanding, Sam, in his turn, was disdainful of the Jews of
St. Urbain Street. "Poorer Jews, and the East European immigrants
who flocked to Montreal during the 1920s, were entirely outside the
Bronfmans' social circuit, and Sam sometimes felt uncomfortable in
his encounters with them. 'Loud talking, gesturing with hands when
speaking' were habits he found embarrassing, Phyllis recalls. 'Awful,
just awful' he would say, seeing immigrant Jews relaxing on their
front porches when driving with his children through a Jewish
neighbourhood on his way to the family's country home in Ste-
Marguerite. It was 'awful, just awful for our people' to behave that
way. 'Gradually he took on the role of a judgemental paterfamilias
responsible not only for his own immediate family and wider family
group,' Phyllis observes, '. . . he was also concerned about these out-
ward signs for "our Jewish people".'"

Of course had Sam ordered his chauffeur to slow down on St.
Urbain Street, and had he then eavesdropped on those loud-talking
Jews who gestured with their hands, he might have discovered some

were pedlars with an eye on the main chance, others were as obsessed with moneymaking and social position as he was, but that
many more were tossing about names and ideas—disputing their
merit fiercely—that were now and forever beyond his shallow vision
of the bounties this world had on offer. What some of them were ar-
guing about out there on the front porches was Hillel versus Shamai,
the show trials in Moscow, Dante's debt to the Rambam, Mel Ott's
batting stance, Tolstoy's views on education and pacifism, Trotsky,
Hank Greenberg's chance of breaking Babe Ruth's home-run
record, the validity of Kafka's vision, Dostoevsky's Grand Inquisitor,
Mahler's conversion to Christianity, the sayings of Rabbi Akiba, and
so on. He also might have found out that St. Urbain Street's Jews
would have been astonished to learn that Bronfman had the gall to
take himself for their paterfamilias. Many considered Sam *prost* (vulgar, unlearned) as well as a bit of a *gonif*. While others, who scorned
him with equal fervour, were actually burning with envy over his
riches. In any event, in 1939—notwithstanding the indignation of
many a Labour Zionist—Sam was thrust into the presidency of
Canadian Jewish Congress. The reasoning of Moshe Dickstein and
other lamentably innocent socialists was that Bronfman, albeit an
ignoramus, now enjoyed such economic clout that he would be an
effective advocate in Ottawa for Europe's menaced Jewry. Voting
for an Elijah who would shriek to the heavens, they elected an Uncle
Tom who would toady to those who had already rejected him. This
rapscallion, bloodied in the Prohibition wars, who could fly into a
legendary rage when his own profit or loss was at risk, cursing like a
longshoreman, ripping telephones out of the wall, turned out to be a
paterfamilias who could only muster a whimper in the cause of his
people. Accepting his high office, Sam told the delegates, "If I might
define the aims and objects of this Congress, I would say that they
were to make our people a better people. . . . It is the responsibility
of Congress to see that Jews are good citizens in their respective
communities across Canada, and so to conduct themselves that they
will gain the respect of their fellow citizens—the non-Jewish citizens. We have got to be just that much better to gain this respect."

Later, instead of denouncing Ottawa's shameful immigration policy, one that denied Jewish refugees entry into an all but empty country, Sam continued to flatter and fawn. "Canadian Jews are, or should be, first of all, Canadians," he said, as if it had ever been otherwise. And, he added, "If you draw up a list of countries and nations that deal fairly with all the different groups within their realm, the name of the British Empire would head the list."

Jewish leaders who were fighting for the admission of refugees to Palestine, then under a British mandate, were outraged, but Sam, who was never without his own agenda, did earn the praise of both the Montreal *Star* and the *Gazette*. Bronfman, noted the *Star*, had made an "eloquent tribute to British liberty and to the freedom which is enjoyed by the Jewish people under the British flag." And so far as the *Gazette* was concerned, "Bronfman has said what too many people in these days are inclined to take for granted."

Sam's public pronouncements were not always pompous. With hindsight, it must be allowed that he could be inadvertently funny on occasion. Pledging his support for war bonds, he said Canada must aim to "build a Maginot Line on the economic front against Nazi barbarism." But Saul Hayes, a Canadian Jewish Congress official, was concerned. Years later, he recalled that Sam "was a man of consummate ambition, with an inordinate quest for publicity." However, it should be noted that he was also a literary patron of sorts. In 1940, he commissioned Stephen Leacock to write a boosterish history, *Canada: The Foundations of Its Future*, that would be distributed by Seagram, once cleansed of certain Leacock dictums; i.e., the one warning a postwar Canada against welcoming "all the mongrels of unredeemed Europe" as immigrants. Complimentary copies of Leacock's *Canada* were sent to George VI Rex Imperator, Haile Selassie, Jack Benny, and Marshall Joseph Stalin, each with a handwritten dedication composed by A. M. Klein and signed by Sam. The dedication to Stalin read:

To Marshall Joseph Stalin,
mighty leader, of mighty peoples, in war

so vigorous as in peace far-seeing,
whose hammer pounds Fascism, and
whose scythe reaps freedom, this
history of his ally and neighbour is
respectfully inscribed.

In 1948, the Université de Montréal, obviously in lieu of a re-
ceipt for a donation, awarded Sam an honorary degree, Monsignor
Olivier Maurault singling out "the people of the Bible's" commitment to "mutual aid" as well as their "genius for business," at which
point Sam should have taken his scroll and shoved it up that obnox-
ious cleric's arse, but of course it was not to be. Seven years earlier,
Sam had already displayed an insatiable appetite for tributes and
honours. Professor Marrus writes:

> . . . Sam revelled in the ritualistic praise and admiration he
> received at the staff parties and tributes that were part of the
> rhythm of life at Seagrams. In March 1941, in celebration of
> Sam's fiftieth birthday, the company staged one of the earliest
> and most elaborate of these tributes, without concession to
> wartime austerity. Across the Seagram empire, more than 4,000
> employees attended birthday banquets in fifteen cities. Three
> days after attending Canadian dinners at the Waterloo and Ville
> LaSalle plants, Sam sat at the head table of another gala affair,
> at the Starlight Room of the Waldorf, and addressed the thou-
> sands across the United States using a "revolutionary telephone
> hookup." "All of you I consider part of one business family,"
> Sam told his employees that evening with genuine feeling, using
> one of his favourite metaphors for the company.

By 1948, Sam was the "universally acknowledged leader of
Canadian Jewry." But Professor Marrus's claim could also have been
made for the chief rabbi and one or two others. The truth is that
the Canadian Jewish Congress, now as then, does speak for rather
more Jews than does the Lubavitcher Rebbe or the Jewish Defence

League, but I'm surprised that Marrus subscribes to the canard that there is a homogeneous Jewish community represented by a single voice.

In any event, come 1949, Sam was dissatisfied with his Canadian Jewish Congress flock, which had failed to honour his tenth anniversary of service with fireworks or whatever. Never mind. Seagram catered a spiffy sixtieth birthday bash for him at the Waldorf, attended by two thousand admirers, even as his name was being taken in vain by witnesses appearing before Senator Kefauver's committee looking into organized crime, among them, one Niggy Rutkin, an embittered old associate.

Rutkin: They own little hotels up there. Now, if you want to find out more about the hotels, you can ask the Canadian Mounted Police, and they will tell you about the little hotels, and you can use your imagination.

Kefauver: Is it like certain types of tourist camps down South? Is that the kind of hotels they were?

Rutkin: Well, I don't know how they are there, but only from what I read of hotels, that people sleep very fast, they rent them quite a few times during the night.

Kefauver: I want to explain that I did not mean to disparage all of the tourist camps, but there are some very few that are alleged to do that sort of thing.

Frank Costello told the committee: "I want to make it specifically on record that I bought in New York, whether it was from Bronfman or anyone else, and if Bronfman shipped it to anyone else, I bought it from someone else."

In 1953 Sam and Saidye were invited to attend the coronation of Queen Elizabeth II. The seats they were allocated in Westminster Abbey were behind a giant pillar, but they were able to trade up. Sam's exposure to royalty clearly gave him ideas. It was around this time that he first began to style himself "King of the Jews," happily unaware of the fate of the last Jew to make that claim.

The ultimate *goyish* honour Sam craved, and paid for many times over, was that dubious patronage plum: a seat in the Senate. But this so-called Jewish seat was denied to Sam and his heirs, in both cases going to family retainers who had campaigned for it just as assiduously: in the first instance, Laz Phillips, and in the second, an out-of-breath Leo Kolber. It is a pity that the Canadian establishment was so mean-minded, for Sam was undoubtedly more accomplished and deserving than many a dolt sitting in the Senate, and he had also done more for Canada. Unlike many of today's entrepreneurs, whining about the free-trade deal, Sam had welcomed a chance to compete in the bigs, and had forged an international liquor giant. He had a magic touch. Texas Pacific, an oil company he bought for $50 million in 1963, was sold by his heirs in 1980 for $2.3 billion. It should also be remembered that Sam contributed millions not only to Jewish causes at home, or in Israel, but also to McGill and the Université de Montréal and other institutions. In his declining years there was also something endearing about the old pirate. The driven social climber who had once tarted up his speech with "I say!" and "Fancy that," now seemed to enjoy nothing more than getting together with old cronies to sing Yiddish songs.

In 1971, a spill of events was organized to honour Sam's eightieth birthday, including a "Gay Nineties" evening at the Sha'ar Hashomayim Synagogue. Congratulatory telegrams and greetings were solicited from notables around the world. He was presented with a special commemorative medal. And at a dinner for two hundred and fifty people, Saidye rose to croon "their song" to him:

Baby face,
You've got the cutest little baby face.
There's not another one could take your place.

Baby face,
My poor heart is jumpin',
You sure have started somethin'.
Baby face,
I'm up in heaven when I'm in your fond embrace.
I didn't need a shove,

'Cause I just fell in love
With your pretty baby face.

Later that year, on July 10, Sam Bronfman, one of the most successful tycoons this country has ever produced, died at home, proof
positive that, contrary to report, an unexamined life can be worth
living.

The
Reichmanns

I N THE 1980s, their halcyon years, the ultra-Orthodox Reichmann brothers—led by the supremely confident Paul, his
judgement once reckoned to be infallible—were perched atop
a family nest egg estimated to exceed $10 billion. Sole proprietors of
the largest property company in Western history, they were ranked
among the world's ten richest families, only a hop and a skip behind
the British royals, who enjoyed the advantage of a bit of a head start.
Even so, as Anthony Bianco reports in *The Reichmanns: Family,
Faith, Fortune and the Empire of Olympia and York*, most of them continued to live modestly in a far from fashionable Toronto suburb
favoured by Orthodox Jews. They built the seventy-two-storey
First Canadian Place in Toronto, went on from there to New York
to create the World Financial Center, and then mortgaged their
bundle, betting everything on a grandiose idea ahead of its time, the
multibillion-dollar development of Canary Wharf on a stretch of
abandoned docklands on the Thames.

The yeshiva-educated Reichmanns were the stuff of legend.
Their word, it was said, was their bond. They wore yarmulkes everywhere, ate only *glatt* kosher and, at considerable cost, shut down
their construction sites during the Sabbath and the Jewish religious
festivals—a total of sixty-four to sixty-five days of the year. Impressed
Presbyterian brokers in Toronto were reported to be spending their

lunch hours studying the Talmud in the hope of cracking the Reichmanns' secret. (For instance, in 1977 the Reichmanns acquired eight
New York City skyscrapers for a cash outlay of a mere $46 million. A
decade later, those properties were worth $3 billion.)

And they did have a secret. If they had cracked a biblical injunction—enabling them to prove enormously efficacious at serving
both God and Mammon—it was with a little help from the Supreme
Architect, who had been quick to show His displeasure with the
Tower of Babel. In the 1980s, Paul confided to a young relative,
Morris Brenick: "What multiplied my initial success by a factor of a
hundred had nothing to do with my own efforts. It was God's will
that I was successful on such a scale."

The humble egg was the rock on which the family fortune was
founded. Back in Beled, Hungary, in the 1920s, Samuel Reichmann just
about cornered the egg market, selling to Austria, Germany, and England. Ironically, the resolutely Orthodox Samuel, who loathed Godless
communism, owed his early wealth not to the Almighty's favour but
to Bolshevik-induced chaos. Traditionally, Russian exporters con-
trolled the European egg market, but, following war and revolution,
they were no longer up to the job. Samuel stepped into the breach.

Truly rich before the Depression began, the perspicacious Samuel
moved the family out of Hungary in the early 1930s, beginning the
peregrinations that took them to the International Zone of Tangier
in 1940, where the Reichmann history becomes somewhat murky.
Samuel, already conversant with international currency deals, became a money changer, playing the market with such élan that he
was said to have accumulated $20 million in nine years. His name
turned up in a number of raw o.s.s. reports, possibly unreliable, that
purported to implicate him in trafficking with the Germans. Anthony Bianco doubts the veracity of these charges, but does allow
that Samuel did considerable business with the notorious Albert
Grebler, who was blacklisted by the Allies for dealing with Nazi
Germany. "Reichmann's unholy association with Albert Grebler
continued well into the 1950s," he writes, "long after his family's
financial security had been assured."

In Tangier, it was the dominant family matriarch, Renée, who, with the help of her daughter, Eva, cajoled Franco's officials into issuing protective visas to Jews in Nazi-occupied Budapest, helping to save several thousand lives. Renée also sent tens of thousands of food parcels, under the aegis of the Spanish Red Cross, to the inmates of Auschwitz and other concentration camps. The mind boggles at the numbers. I certainly do not recall Primo Levi or Eli Wiesel ever writing, Oh boy, it's Thursday, and this afternoon those ss charmers will be distributing food parcels from Renée Reichmann. One day, during a lull in the packing, a troubled Sephardic youth did confront Mrs. Reichmann: "What's the use? Do you really think the Germans will allow the Jews to eat?" Mrs. Reichmann replied, "If just one Jew eats the chocolate, I am satisfied." And nearly fifty years later, Isaac Klein, who had been in the slave-labour camp of Kaupfering during the last months of the war, did remember receiving a food parcel that could have come from Tangier. And other parcels, he said, were distributed to the women in the camp.

Paul has been notably quick to defend his mother's honour— once, memorably, while pursuing a libel suit against *Toronto Life* magazine, which had published an article about the Reichmanns full of innuendoes about their Tangier years (and which later apologized after an out-of-court settlement). But on another occasion he seemed ambivalent about her commanding nature, incidentally revealing a rare flash of humour. Renée succeeded Samuel as head of Olympia & York. A few years after her death in 1990, Paul recalled that Prince Charles had stopped by Olympia & York's office in London to inspect the scale models of Canary Wharf. "I understand that your mother is the chairman of your company," he said. "How does that work for you?" In lieu of disclosing his reply to Mr. Bianco, Paul Reichmann observed, "You could say we had the same problem."

In the mid-1950s, the Reichmanns quit the balmy Tangier honey pot for the tundra, arriving in Canada with a rumoured $30 million and settling in both Montreal and Toronto, where they established floor- and wall-tile companies. (Olympia & York was not created until 1964.) The eldest brother, Edward, at once the only flamboyant Reichmann and the least successful, chose Montreal, but failed to understand the *belle province*. When he bought the Canadian branch of Pilkington's Glass from Lord Pilkington in 1961, he decided it should be renamed in deference to the growing militancy of French-Canadian separatists. So he dubbed it Maple Leaf Ceramics, unaware that, insofar as the separatists were concerned, he was now brandishing in their faces the hated symbol of what they saw as the conqueror's flag.

(I am not qualified to fault the accuracy of Mr. Bianco's take on the Reichmann's Tangier, New York, or London years, but in each case he strikes me as fair-minded, as well as commendably knowledgeable about recherché Jewish religious matters. However, his Canadian pages are tainted by boners small and large. Montreal is not "the separatist capital of Canada," and did in fact vote against separation in the 1995 referendum, the second in what threatens to be a continuing series. In the mid-1950s the Jews of Montreal were no longer "scattered along the length of" Boulevard St-Laurent (not St. Lawrence Boulevard, as he has it), but had moved on to the suburbs of Côte-St-Luc, Hampstead, and Ville St-Laurent. Allan E. Gotlieb, our former ambassador to Washington, spells his name with one *t*, not two. Far from supporting the aspirations of French Canadians "as unobtrusively as possible," the Jews of Montreal, who have always identified with the English-speaking community, fear the new nationalism. Thousands have quit the city, and those who have stayed on remain resolutely federalist. And while there was an infamous "national socialist party" in Germany, there isn't one in Canada. Our social democrats call themselves the New Democratic Party [NDP].)

The Reichmanns have been prodigiously generous to their fellow ultra-Orthodox. They have lavished hundreds of millions on yeshivas in Israel, Canada, and the United States. But they did not endear themselves to Canada at large when they took advantage of an arcane tax loophole (the "Little Egypt Bump," named after a Chicago stripper) in their $2.8-billion purchase of Gulf Canada in 1985. The tax break, which saved them $500 million, led to questions in Parliament. The Tory government's deputy minister of finance, Marshall "Mickey" Cohen, who had monitored the sweetheart deal, was hired by the Reichmanns two months later. Whether the timing, Mr. Bianco writes, was "an example of naiveté or Machiavellian calculation remained open to debate. . . . At a minimum, Cohen and the Reichmanns had flouted proscriptions against the appearance of conflict of interest."

Anthony Bianco, a senior writer at *Business Week*, spent four years working on *The Reichmanns*. The usually reclusive Paul Reichmann granted him five long interviews, and he was helped by other family members, but the result is far from hagiography, if that's what the hypersensitive family expected. If it was once said of the Reichmanns that their word was their bond, Mr. Bianco writes, as the empire crumbled not even Paul's signature was his bond. "In his increasingly desperate efforts to save Olympia & York from bankruptcy while maintaining his domination of the company, Reichmann dissembled and connived in ways that left all sorts of people feeling ill-used, including many of Olympia & York's most valued employees."

The Reichmanns, a nicely balanced study, tells you everything you want to know, and then some, about the family's convoluted real-estate deals, but Paul Reichmann, a man charged with contradictions, remains an enigma. He lost Canary Wharf in 1993, as well as the family's immense natural resource holdings, in what was arguably the largest corporate bankruptcy in Canadian history. Then in 1995 he regained a toehold on the project, and now owns 5 per cent of it. Mr. Bianco concludes on a grace note of sorts. He says Paul Reichmann "appears now to have a decent chance of going down in history not as the Man Who Blew $10 Billion but the Man Who Blew $10 Billion and Changed the Face of London."

Lansky

RGUABLY, the enduring American pop myth is not the cowboy but the gangster. But surprisingly, the noun "gangster" is not to be found in my 1961 edition of the *Oxford English Dictionary*, which skips from "gangsman" (defined as a dock porter) to "gang-tide" (the three days preceding Ascension Day). Eric Partridge, in *Origins*, traced the word back to the Old English *gangsweg*, a "going away," a passage, but then lost me in a deluge of abbreviations, saying it was "akin to syn Ofris, OHG–G, MD–D, Da *gang* . . ." Finally I found gangster in my 1972 A–G supplement to the *OED*. First usage, in 1896, is credited to the *Evening Dispatch* of Columbus, Ohio: "The gangster may play all sorts of pranks with the ballot box, but in its own good time the latter will get even by kicking the gangster into the gutter." Until 1925, according to the *Dictionary of American Slang*, "gangster" was another word for politician, not criminal.

My personal experience of gangsters has been slight. There was a gangland killing in my old Montreal Jewish neighbourhood in 1934—Max "King of the North" Feigenbaum was gunned down in front of his house at 4510 Esplanade—but we had to wait another twelve years for our next Jewish gangland slaying, that of "sleek and well-groomed" Harry Davis, who was said to be in cahoots with Pincus Brecher of Brooklyn's "Murder Inc.," a corporate title attributed to Harry Feeny of the *New York World-Telegram*.

So, like most members of my generation, I had to count on the movies for my knowledge of gangland etiquette—say, Paul Muni in *Scarface*. For the most part, I relied on the celebrated Warner Brothers company of players of the thirties and forties: Edward G. Robinson reaching for his gat in *Little Caesar*, John Garfield, Humphrey Bogart as Sam Spade, and, of course, Peter Lorre and Sydney Greenstreet. And what an enviable bunch of molls these ruffians could count on as resource persons: Mary Astor, Ida Lupino, Claire Trevor, Joan Blondell, Ann Sheridan, and Barbara Stanwyck. And, above all, in those days, there was the incomparable James Cagney, his gangster shoulder-shuffle impeccable.

Who can forget Cagney in *Angels with Dirty Faces*? A murderous bum, he is nevertheless a hero figure to a group of misguided tenement cherubs with shining morning faces, namely Leo Gorcey and the Dead End Kids: Bim, Hunky, Patsy, and Crab. This situation understandably grieves Pat O'Brien, Cagney's boyhood buddy who is now the neighbourhood priest. When Cagney is inevitably sentenced to fry, his young admirers know that he will strut that last mile to an inspiring hero's death. However, O'Brien intervenes. And Cagney, obliging him, pretends to be a yellow rat who has to be dragged screaming to the chair. Happily, this self-sacrifice (the noblest in art since Sydney Carton was guillotined in *A Tale of Two Cities*) leads to the salvation of Bim, Hunky, Patsy, and Crab. Eschewing the gangster life, I assume that they matured into junk-bond mavens, defence contractors to the Pentagon, or the founders of savings and loan societies.

Following the Warner Brothers days of glory, there has been a second generation of gangster movies, spawned by the hugely successful *Godfather* series. Dustin Hoffman has portrayed Dutch Schultz in *Billy Bathgate* and Warren Beatty has obliged us with his take on Bugsy Siegal. As we continue to look to the movies for our knowledge of gangster behaviour, I was delighted to learn, in Robert Lacey's entertaining biography *Little Man: Meyer Lansky and the*

Gangster Life, that gangsters themselves also turn to Hollywood for helpful hints on deportment. "[The] 1946 season at the Colonial Inn was a succession of surprises. When George Raft, the film star, arrived in [Florida] to spend some time with Benny [Bugsy] Siegal and his other friends, [the public-relations man] assumed that the actor would take advantage of his visit to study the originals on whom his gangster roles were based. But the reverse proved the case. It was the gangsters who spent their time studying Raft, trying to find out the name of his tailor, and who made his elegant, hand-crafted shoes."

Then, in an endearing scene in the final pages of this impressively researched biography, Mr. Lacey describes Meyer Lansky, then seventy-nine years old, and some twenty surviving cronies gathered round a television set in Miami, in 1981, to watch the opening episode in "The Gangster Chronicles," an NBC miniseries based on the lives of Lucky Luciano, Bugsy Siegal, and Meyer Lansky. Vincent Alo, a.k.a. Jimmy Blue Eyes, was unhappy with a scene that showed Siegal driving a convoy of bottleg liquor down from Canada, toting a machine gun. "When a *Yiddisher* boy goes into that sort of business," he said, "he is not going to work as a truck driver."

Benny Sigelbaum, another member of the group that night, wanted NBC to be sued for portraying Bugsy Siegal as a violent and unthinking thug.

"What are we going to sue them for?" asked Lansky. "In real life, he was even worse."

The women were entranced with the handsome young actor who was playing Luciano, who, in his halcyon days, wanted to organize prostitution nationwide: "The same as the A&P."

Lansky was not a great believer in the so-called Honored Society. "They were so honorable," he once said, "that nobody in the Mafia trusted anybody else."

He could give as good as he got. "If Socrates and Plato had trouble defining what morality was," he once said, reminiscing about the days when he owned an opulent gambling casino in Batista's Cuba, "how can people come along, just like that, and lay down that gambling is immoral?"

Another time, trying to comfort Frank Costello, who worried about gamblers being confused with gangsters and hoodlums, Lansky told him: "Don't worry, don't worry. Look at history. Look at the Astors and Vanderbilts, all those big society people. They were the worst thieves—and now look at them. It's just a matter of time."

In one of the many unexpected comic anecdotes that enrich *Little Man*, Mr. Lacey reports that an FBI bug placed in Lansky's room at the Volney Hotel in New York, in 1962, failed to yield any incriminating detail. However, it did establish that his taste ran to matzohs, sardines, Jell-O, Irish stew, and ham, and that, at the time, he was reading a history book, a grammar, and a book of French quotations. According to an urgent FBI teletype, Lansky stated: "These are things you need with no education, because you can get mixed up."

Alert FBI snoopers also recorded for the ages one of Lansky's *pensées*: "Some people never learn to be good. One quarter of us is good. Three quarters is bad. That's a tough fight, three against one."

Mr. Lacey's biography both dispels and confirms various gangster myths. Lansky never did say of organized crime—as credited by *Life* magazine in 1967—that "we're bigger than U.S. Steel." So Hyman Roth, his alter ego in *The Godfather, Part II*, got it wrong.

I am pleased to report, however, that there does seem to be honour at least among some thieves. Other gangsters welcomed partnership deals with Lansky because he was not greedy and had never been known to hoodwink an associate. Lansky was proud of the fact that knowledgeable gamblers had never doubted the integrity of the tables in either his Florida or his Cuban casino. "Everybody who came to my casino," he said, "knew that if he lost money, it wouldn't be because he was cheated."

Bugsy Siegal and Joe Adonis, both partners of Lansky in the forties, were proud to be associated with such an intellectual. "That Meyer!" one of them once said. "Can you believe it? He's a member of the Book-of-the-Month Club!"

In later life, Lansky was envious of famous distillers who had founded their family fortunes on the solid rock of bootlegging, primarily Sam Bronfman and Lewis Rosensteil of Schenley's. Both had supplied him with booze during the Prohibition years, and both had gone on to become respectable businessmen. But Mr. Lacey's Lansky is far from being a financial genius. He lost money on most of his legal ventures and held on to his oil shares far too long. And when the man who came to be known as the Chairman of the Board, and who was reputed at one time to be worth $300 million, died, he left his wife and three children less than a million to split among them, according to the best evidence that Mr. Lacey could assemble.

When Fidel Castro seized Lansky's opulent Riviera Hotel in Havana, the Little Man took an estimated $9-million bath. "Don't expect a lot of money," Uncle Jake warned his niece and two nephews, the younger one a West Point graduate. "If your father died today, he's broke."

Astonishingly, there is no index entry for Meyer Lansky in Irving Howe's splendid but possibly too fastidious *World of Our Fathers*, and neither does he make any mention of Kid Twist, Big Jack Zelig, Gyp the Blood, Dopey Benny, Waxey Gordon, Bugsy Siegal, Dutch Schultz, Philip "Little Farfel" Kovolick, Little Hymie Holtz, and other East End hoodlums, easily the most colourfully named bunch of bandits this side of the Newgate Calendar. It is no knock on Mr. Howe to say that what is called for to complete the story of our American Jewish heritage is a writer of the stature of Isaac Babel.

In his absence, and in the face of Mr. Howe's opting not to embarrass us before our Gentile neighbours, I have had to make do with *The Rise and Fall of the Jewish Gangster in America*, by Albert Fried, as well as other studies usually written in a style bound to provoke unintended hilarity. Take, for example, Mark Stuart's *Gangster #2: Longy Zwillman, the Man Who Invented Organized Crime*, which contains a memorable description of his hero's backstage encounter with the young Jean Harlow: "Her large nipples seemed to be forcing their way through the cheap fabric [of her filmy dressing gown] as if gulping for air."

Meyer Lansky was born Meyer Suchowljansky some time around 1902 in Grodno, on the border of Russia and Poland. In this city of forty thousand souls, 70 per cent of the population Jewish, he attended *cheder* (Hebrew school) until he and the rest of the family followed his father to Brooklyn in 1911. In 1914, the Lanskys moved to Grand Street in Manhattan, and Meyer attended the Educational Alliance School. Other Alliance School students of his generation included Davis Sarnoff, founder of NBC; Eddie Cantor; Jan Peerce; Rabbi Hillel Silver; and Louis J. Lefkowitz, who went on to become attorney general of New York State.

When he was still a boy, Lansky got to know both Bugsy Siegal and Salvadore Luciana, a.k.a. Lucky Luciano. He was already a young man on his way when he met the legendary Arnold "the Brain" Rothstein, who ran a sort of one-man foundation for neophyte gangsters. Numbered among Rothstein's alumni were not only Lansky, but also Luciano, Jack "Legs" Diamond, Dutch Schultz, Longy Zwillman, and Francesco Castiglia, who became Frank Costello.

Meeting daily with his associates at Ratner's kosher restaurant on Delancey Street, Lansky chain-smoked over endless cups of coffee. Soon he and his first wife were living in the Majestic, the same apartment building as Walter Winchell, on the Upper West Side. By the mid-thirties, he had graduated from Ratner's to the Norse Grill in the Waldorf Astoria, where Luciano and Siegal kept apartments.

Lansky hopped, skipped, and jumped from casinos in Saratoga Springs, N.Y., through Florida and Las Vegas, to Havana. Thomas Dewey tried to collar him and so, later, did Estes Kefauver, with equal lack of success. Each time he shook off prosecutors, the legend grew. Lansky was untouchable. He was, however, deported from Israel when he was an old and ailing man; this, even though he had undeniably helped with money and arms during the Israeli War of Independence. On the other hand, Lansky was able to see the last of his would-be prosecutors, Attorney General John N. Mitchell, end up in the slammer. This had to be gratifying to a seventy-five-year-old man who walked his dog down Collins Avenue in Miami every day, stopping for a gossip with old cronies at Wolfie's or in the coffee shop of the Singapore Hotel. In the words of one FBI agent in Miami, "He was able to go to his grave laughing that he whipped us all."

In his last days, this sometime associate of mob killers might have felt at home at a Republican convention. One afternoon on South Beach, his grandson recalled, Lansky caught sight of a long-haired and grubby hitchhiker. "Grandpa rolled down the window," Meyer 2nd remembered. "Get a haircut and take a bath," he yelled, "and I might give you a ride next time."

In the mid-seventies, Mr. Lacey writes, his days of big money and power long past, Lansky "collected his Social Security check regularly. A member of the American Association of Retired Persons, he received his monthly copy of *Modern Maturity*, an anthology of helpful bran recipes, advertisements for large-print books, and cheap deals at Holiday Inns."

Meyer Lansky died of cancer in the Mount Sinai Hospital in Miami on January 15, 1983. His last coherent words to Teddy, his second wife, were: "Let me go! Let me go!"

Woody

This essay was first published in Playboy *(December 1991), long before Woody Allen's troubled private life attracted so much media attention. I have not brought it up to date, as it were, as a matter of principle. Woody Allen's private life is his business, not mine.*

WOODY ALLEN is the survivor, by my count, of no less than sixteen book-length studies, as well as reams of critical essays in publications ranging from *People*, through the *New York Review of Books*, to the *West Virginia Philological Papers*. He has, over the wasting years, been accused of "high school existentialism," "a failure to transcend the values of John Wayne," of churning out "films that exemplify the inauthenticity and self-absorption that he appears to criticize," and of using trick photography to "invent a non-existent past." It has also been charged that in real life that deceitful bastard is not "the half-pint of neurosis" or "rabbit in flight" or "little mouse with eyeglasses" that he portrays on the screen. *Au contraire.* That on the evidence, Woody is a fake *schlemiel*. The truth is that, by 1991, the real Woody Allen was ensconced in a duplex penthouse apartment on Fifth Avenue that offered a 360-degree view of Manhattan through floor-to-ceiling wraparound windows; he owned four courtside seats to Knicks basketball games, tooled around town in his very own Rolls-Royce, was a regular at Elaine's, and the rumpled *shmattes* he wore were in fact designed by Ralph Lauren.

Shame, shame.

But it should also be allowed that, between 1968 and 1990, Woody Allen had written and directed an astonishing twenty-one films, acting in most of them as well. These films have often been outrageously witty, refreshingly funny, original, and, on occasion, inspired.

In *Hannah and Her Sisters*, the death-obsessed TV producer, Mickey Sachs, played by Allen himself, turns briefly to the Catholic church for answers to the Big Questions. He is seen explaining himself to a priest and then peering into the window of a religious bookshop. Then we cut to his apartment and a close shot of Sachs emptying the contents of a brown paper bag on the table. Out pops a framed print of Christ wearing his crown of thorns, then a crucifix, and on top of both goes a loaf of sliced Wonder Bread, clearly a saucy Jewish take on the spiritual offerings of the outside world. Or what film scholars mean when they say somebody has made a visual statement.

Hannah and Her Sisters is one of Woody Allen's most satisfying films, an all but seamless stitching together of the author's comic and angst-ridden voices until we get to the final moments, a family Thanksgiving dinner. It's something of a cop-out, veracity being sacrificed on the altar of neatness, enabling audiences to file out of the cinemas feeling good inside rather than being troubled by unwanted recognitions. What happens is that Hannah's husband (Michael Caine), who has lusted for and had an affair with one of Hannah's sisters, is suddenly and unconvincingly reconciled with his wife. And that bundle of anxieties, Mickey Sachs, Hannah's first husband, has surprisingly stumbled on the yellow brick road to happiness by marrying Hannah's other, most vacuous sister. Then, yielding a yippee in the film's dying moment, Sachs—hitherto ostensibly sterile—is told by his wife that she is preggers by him. His joy is unconfined. But, much more likely, the self-doubting Mickey

Sachs that we have come to know would have reacted differently. The news would have confirmed that his wife had been unfaithful to him.

Whatever the flaws of *Hannah*, I must hastily add that Woody Allen has never given us a film that insults the intelligence. Even his failures, however portentous, are interesting. Looked at another way, nobody can really be dismissed as a high-school existentialist who has been quoted as saying, "I don't want to gain immortality in my works. I want to gain it by not dying."

I have not ploughed through all or even most of the books about Woody Allen's oeuvre, but I have endured one of the most pretentious, *Woody Allen* by Nancy Pogel, from which I have plucked at least two zingers that I would like to see adorn the newspaper ads promoting his next flick in lieu of the increasingly tiresome two thumbs up from Siskel and Ebert.

1. Allen's films "carry on debates between fabulation and realism, between illusionism and anti-illusionism."
2. "Mikhail Bakunin's discussion of intertextuality and the dialogical imagination provide a spacious framework for interpreting Allen's densely allusive, inclusive films."

Her manifest virtues as a prose stylist aside, Nancy Pogel has some imposing credentials, including professor of American Thought and Language and teaching in the Film Thematic program at Michigan State University. Dr. Pogel's latter office, which I take to be that of glorified projectionist, establishes an unbridgable generation gap with me. In my student days, films (thematical, dialogical, or filled with fabulation) were something we saw when we skipped a seminar on Spinoza or Whither Canadian Multiculturalism. Of course this rendered matinees far more enjoyable, enriched by dollops of guilt. On one of the most memorable of those afternoons I skipped Psych 104 to see *Love Happy* with the Marx Brothers. To digress briefly, some twenty-two years later, at the 1972 Cannes Film Festival, I had lunch with Groucho and Anthony Burgess, among others, at the Carlton Hotel. An ebullient Groucho offered Burgess a Montecristo and was somewhat miffed when, instead of lighting up like the rest of us, he stuffed the cigar into a shirt pocket. "Aren't you going to smoke it?" Groucho demanded.

"No, I'm going to keep it as a souvenir," said Burgess, and then he went on to describe a scene from *Love Happy* that he still cherished. "Harpo is leaning against a brick wall," he said, "and when you drift past you ask him, 'What are you doing, holding up the wall?' He nods yes and when he lets go the wall collapses."

"You remember that," said Groucho, astonished.

"Indeed, I do."

"My God, I've had three wives and I can't remember any one of them."

When somebody at the table asked Groucho about today's comics, he replied that the only one he had time for was Woody Allen.

Some years earlier a friend of mine had caught Allen on the Johnny Carson show: "Carson was gabbing away with this skinny little stand-up comic, I had no idea who he was, and he told Carson that he had recently married and now rented a cottage in the country as well. Next he fished out photographs of both for Carson to look at. 'My wife,' he said, 'is the one with the shingles.' I've been a Woody Allen fan ever since."

Woody Allen, *né* Allen Stewart Konigsberg, was born in Flatbush in 1935, the son of Martin and Nettie, both of whom he said years later were "into God and carpeting." At one time or another Martin worked as a jewellery engraver, an egg candler, a cab driver, and a bartender at Sammy's Bowery Follies in Manhattan. Nettie was employed as a bookkeeper in a Brooklyn floral shop. The Konigsbergs were observant Jews, which meant that Woody attended Hebrew school, or *cheder*, after classes at P.S. 99, and there he must have studied Talmud, an early encounter with the absurd:

Janni went to an inn and asked for water, which they brought him. He noticed the women muttering, so he threw some away and it turned into snakes. He said to them, "I have drunk of your water and you will drink of mine." He made one of the women drink and she turned into an ass. He mounted her and rode into the marketplace. Her companion came and released her from the spell, so that he was seen riding a woman.

Surely it was based on the memory of such studies that Woody Allen later concocted his parody for the *New Yorker*, "Hassidic Tales, with a Guide to Their Interpretation by the Noted Scholar," from which I will quote just one story: "A man journeyed to Chelm in order to seek the advice of Rabbi Ben Kaddish, the holiest of all ninth-century rabbis and perhaps the greatest *noodge* of the medieval era.

"'Rabbi,' the man asked, 'where can I find peace?'

"The Hassid surveyed him and said, 'Quick, look behind you!'

"The man turned around, and Rabbi Ben Kaddish smashed him in the back of the head with a candlestick. 'Is that peaceful enough for you?' he chuckled, adjusting his yarmulke."

In his commentary on this tale, Woody Allen's noted scholar asks why has the man journeyed to Chelm to bother Rabbi Ben Kaddish. "The Rabbi doesn't have enough trouble? The truth is, the Rabbi's in over his head with gamblers, and he has also been named in a paternity suit by Mrs. Hecht. No, the point of this tale is that this man had nothing better to do with his time than journey around and get on people's nerves. For this, the rabbi bashes his head in, which, according to the Torah, is one of the most subtle methods of showing concern. In a similar version of this tale, the Rabbi leaps on top of the man in a frenzy and carves the story of Ruth on his nose with a stylus."

Following the publication of "Hassidic Tales," the *New Yorker* received many letters accusing it of anti-Semitism and Woody Allen was singled out as a self-hating Jew, one of that notorious literary band that—in the minds of some, at least—includes Philip Roth and Stanley Elkin, and others too numerous to mention here.

Some years after his *New Yorker* piece appeared, Woody Allen, writing in *Tikkun* magazine, a bimonthly Jewish critique of politics, culture, and society, noted, "Now, I have frequently been accused of being a self-hating Jew, and while it's true I am Jewish and don't like myself very much, it's not because of my persuasion. The reasons lie in totally different areas—like the way I look when I get up in the morning, or that I can never read a road map."

Predictably, an irate *Tikkun* reader responded, "You tell us that being Jewish has nothing to do with why you don't like yourself very much. Fine. But why, in every single movie you've produced in which you appear, do you portray yourself to some degree as a self-mocking, self-degrading Jew? You're lying to yourself and your audience if you say that your 'persuasion' has nothing to do with it."

If one of the movies the irate *Tikkun* reader had in mind was *Hannah and Her Sisters*, then she clearly got things wrong. Allen, in the worried shape of Mickey Sachs, far from being a self-mocking, self-degrading Jew, is, if anything, altogether too adorable. In fact, if there is a charge to be made against Woody Allen, it is that he sometimes seems too ingratiating, his appeal for love embarrassingly naked. Take that *Tikkun* piece, for instance. It dealt with Jewish Holocaust guilt (". . . I, who was a small boy during World War II and who lived in America . . . never missed a good meal with meat and potatoes and sweet desserts . . ."), reflections on the wives of both Lot and Job, and his Israeli problem, which had led him to write a piece for the *New York Times* op-ed page, saying he "was against the practice of Israeli soldiers going door-to-door and randomly breaking the hands of Palestinians as a method of combating the *intifada*." He was "for a more flexible attitude on negotiating land for peace." But his essay was disingenuously titled "Random Reflections of a Second-Rate Mind," which struck me as an appeal for readers to write in protesting no, no, first-rate. Honestly, Woody.

In the event, the *Tikkun* piece provoked a note from a certain Rabbi Jack D. Spiro of Norfolk, Virginia: "The only thing defensible about Woody Allen's article, 'Random Reflections of a Second-Rate Mind,' is the title." A more scholarly rabbi than Spiro would have recognized in Woody a disciple—filtered through S. J. Perelman, mind you—of the twelfth-century philosopher Maimonides, author of *The Guide for the Perplexed*, wherein, possibly anticipating the theme of *Crimes and Misdemeanors*, he wrote:

> Men frequently think that the evils in the world are more numerous than the good things; many sayings and songs of nations dwell on this idea. They say that a good thing is found only exceptionally, whilst evil things are numerous and lasting. Not only common people make this mistake, but many who believe they are wise. Al-Razi wrote a well-known book, *On Metaphysics*. Among other mad and foolish things, it contains also the idea, discovered by him, that there exists more evil than good. For if the happiness of man and his pleasure in the times of prosperity be compared with the mishaps that befall him—such as grief, acute pain, defects, paralysis of the limbs, fears, anxieties, and troubles—it would seem as if the existence of man is a punishment and a great evil for him.

Another of Woody Allen's biographers, the French film critic Robert Benayoun, once asked him, "Do you believe in Jewish comedy, born from fear, aggressiveness, exaggeration, self-defence?"

He replied, "The truth is I grew up in a very Jewish neighbourhood, yet I never experienced in my life any kind of anti-Semitism, I was never bullied at school because I was Jewish, I suffered no incidents, was never refused admittance, contrary to Groucho Marx in his well-known joining-a-club joke. I'm always surprised to meet someone who says I'm a Jewish comedian. In over a hundred jokes I do, there may be one Jewish joke; it's like adding spice to a meal, but people will always say: you do so many Jewish jokes."

Well now, although a twenty-one-year-old Woody Allen did work a holiday camp in the Poconos in the summer of 1956 (Tamiment, where his predecessors included Danny Kaye, Sid Caesar, Imogene Coca, Carl Reiner, Mel Brooks, and Neil Simon), nobody can accuse him of over-indulging in blatantly Jewish jokes with a built-in wink to the *landsman* in the audience. Clearly he is above such shtick. However it is also fair to say that just about everything Woody Allen has produced has been enriched by his experience of having been born and raised an urban Jew in America, as witness some of his most novelistic films: *Annie Hall*, *Hannah and Her Sisters*, *Crimes and Misdemeanors*. Furthermore, the perplexed and endearing fumbler he had played in so many of the twenty-one films he had written and directed by 1991 obviously did not study at Andover or Groton, going on from there to Yale, the Skull and Bones, and then maintaining a sailboat convenient to his summer cottage on the Maine coast. Then, of course, there is the undeniably Jewish triumph of *Oedipus Wrecks*, Woody Allen's part of *New York Stories*, the other two segments of the trilogy being directed by Martin Scorcese and Francis Ford Coppola. This explosively funny piece was surely the ultimate film take on the possessive, smothering Jewish mother, who in this case disapproves of her son's *shiksa* fiancée, played by Mia Farrow. The son is a bumbling insecure lawyer called Sheldon Mills (Woody Allen). One day Sheldon and his girl take mum to a magic show where she disappears in a magician's Chinese box, only to suddenly loom very large indeed in the skies over Manhattan, remonstrating with her son whenever he dares to emerge from his apartment. *Oedipus Wrecks* boasts at least one inspired moment. As the magician on stage drives a sword through his Chinese box to prove that Sheldon's mother, whom we have seen enter the box a moment earlier, has really disappeared . . . there is a cut to a reverse-angle reaction shot of Sheldon, his face suffused with joy, a Jewish son's epiphany time. "This film," Woody Allen told Eric Lax, "will resonate in Israel. It will be the *Gone with the Wind* of Israel."

In 1952, when Allen Stewart Konigsberg was a mere sixteen-year-old junior at Midwood High, in Brooklyn, he was born again as

Woody Allen and began to peddle one-liners to Nick Kenny, Earl Wilson, and other newspaper columnists. "Enclosed," he would write to one columnist or another, "are some gags for your consideration and sent exclusively to you." This juvenilia, for which he will be forgiven, ran from "It's the fallen women who are usually picked up" to "Woody Allen boasts that he just made a fortune—he was downtown auctioning off his parking space." Soon enough he graduated from planting freebies in the columns to acquiring an agent and being paid to write knee-slappers for Guy Lombardo, Sammy Kaye, and Arthur Murray. From there it was a hop, skip, and a jump to signing with the William Morris Office and writing skits for Buddy Hackett, Herb Shriner, and Peter Lind Hayes. In 1953, he joined Larry Gelbart and Mel Brooks, among others, writing for the legendary Sid Caesar TV specials, earning $1,500 weekly. Five years later he left the William Morris Office and began his association with Jack Rollins and Charles Joffe, who produce his films to this day. In a world not noted for its loyalties, where "intimate" friendships seldom outlast a film's shooting schedule, it speaks eloquently for Woody that he never graduated from the professional partners who had such faith in him when he was young and unknown. Mind you, they are an effective pair who managed to secure a unique film contract for Woody with Orion Pictures. Providing he does not exceed a certain budget, Woody Allen has total control over his films, everything from costumes to casting subject to his approval. Reportedly he works for minimum fees as director, writer, and actor, his modest stipend sweetened by a reasonable percentage of the box-office gross. This is to say that Woody Allen, just like those crazies who write books or labour in the theatre, wagers on his own worth, settling for a royalty rather than demanding obscene millions up front.

It was the perspicacious Rollins and Joffe who first encouraged Woody Allen to perform his own material, nourishing their all but pathologically shy stand-up comic through some iffy years. Woody, who had chucked $1,700 a week as a comedy writer to risk appearing as a performer for a mere $75, had never forgotten that the clubs

were cleansed of out-of-town Rotarians for him by the first of the
new-style intellectual comics, Mort Sahl, who broke in at the "hungry i" in San Francisco in 1953. The revolution launched by Sahl,
bearing a rolled newspaper in his fist, also yielded Nichols and May,
Shelley Berman, and Lenny Bruce, as well as Woody slipping into
his famous moose routine, wherein he takes a live moose to a costume party only to have it come in second to the Berkowitzes, a
married couple dressed as a moose.

I recently saw for the second time the first film Woody Allen
wrote (with Mickey Rose), directed, and starred in, *Take the Money
and Run*, wherein he plays the feckless thief Virgil Starkwell, and it is
still refreshingly funny, especially that memorable scene where Virgil
slips a bank teller a stick-up note:

> TELLER: What does this say?
> VIRGIL: Um . . . can't you read it?
> TELLER: Um . . . I can't read this. What's this . . . "act natural"?
> VIRGIL: No, it says, "Please put fifty thousand dollars into this
>   bag and act natural."
> TELLER: It does say "act natural."
> VIRGIL (looking at note): Uh . . . "I am pointing a gun at you."
> TELLER: That looks like "gub," that doesn't look like "gun."
> VIRGIL (studying note with teller): No, that . . . that's "gun."

I assume that Virgil Starkwell was Woody Allen's first tentative
pass at the persona perfected in *Annie Hall* and carried through in
Hannah and Her Sisters, among other films. My problem with this
character is that we are asked to accept him as the quintessential
fumble-fingers, the loser who will never win the girl or the job, but
he is obviously too witty, too original, to be convincing in that role.
On reflection, however, this lack of credibility is a pittance to pay in
return for the enjoyment that caricature has given us over the years.

The best of the comic pieces Woody Allen wrote between 1966
and 1980 have been collected in three volumes: *Getting Even*, *Without Feathers*, and *Side Effects*. One of the most magical of these pieces,

"The Kugelmass Episode," was the story of a bored college professor who is told by the Great Perksy, a magician, that he "can meet any of the women created by the world's best writers." Kugelmass selects Madame Bovary, drifting in and out of Flaubert's novel so that soon "students in various classrooms across the country were saying to their teachers, 'Who is this character on page 100? A bald Jew is kissing Madame Bovary?'" This manner of fantasy was given another spin in *The Purple Rose of Cairo*, wherein the glamorous Depression-era film star steps down from the screen to court downtrodden housewife Mia Farrow. Allen, who taught himself magic tricks when he was a boy growing up in Brooklyn, flirts with fantasy again in the uneven *Alice*, the story of an insufferably affluent New York matron, much given to shopping and body care, who falls in with a Chinese herbalist who puts her on a diet of drugs. Some of it is funny, but there are also uncharacteristic lapses into a level of humour more appropriate to *Porky's*. Take, for instance, the scene where Joe Mantegna, sharing a drug with Mia Farrow that renders them both invisible, slips into a department store changing room to ogle a gorgeous model trying on garments.

In a conversation with biographer Eric Lax, Woody Allen said that "he would love more than anything in the world to do a murder mystery," but he feels it is too trivial. "I'm torn," he said, "because I think I could be very funny in a comedy mystery and it would be enormously entertaining in a totally escapist way for an audience. But I can't bring myself to do that. This is a part of my conflict. My conflict is between what I really am and what I would really like myself to be. I'm forever struggling to deepen myself and to take a more profound path, but what comes easiest to me is light entertainment. I'm more comfortable with shallower stuff." Then, with a laugh, "I'm basically a shallow person."

It strikes me that this, like calling his *Tikkun* essay "Random Reflections of a Second-Rate Mind," is yet another plea for reassurance. In no danger of being mistaken for Dostoevsky, neither can he

be dismissed as shallow. In fact, he is one of the most gifted of contemporary filmmakers, astonishingly prolific, hopelessly hankering
after perfection, which is available only to those with more limited
artistic ambitions. Clap hands for Woody.

Just Find
a Million
Readers and
Success Will
Surely Follow

S UMMONED to New York in May 1990 to pitch my new novel, I managed, between interviews, to meet my wife for a quick drink in the upstairs bar at Sardi's. There were two women seated nearby. One of them complimented Florence on her appearance and then turned to me. "I know you," she said.

A Canadian born and bred, I continued to lower my eyes modestly.

"Who *were* you?" she demanded.

Once a writer, I could have told her, but now a pedlar, condemned to zip from one bookshop to another, lining up with other writers contending in the summer sweepstakes to autograph copies of my latest effort. Hitting the road, flying off to a reading and signing in Washington, I was in such need of sales guidance that I turned to a current best-selling how-to book, Harvey MacKay's *Beware the Naked Man Who Offers You His Shirt.*

"LESSON 22: HARVEY'S ODDS ON BEATING THE COMPETITION.

"*Just show up* . . . You're a winner *80 percent* of the time. Most accounts are won because nobody else is calling on them.

"*Show up on time* . . . What could be more annoying to a salesperson who can't deliver the first thing he's promised to deliver, his or her own body?"

Harvey's Lesson 20 was even more instructive.

"THE MOST VALUABLE TOOL A SELLER CAN HAVE.

"More than one buyer."

That struck home, let me tell you. Danielle Steele already had over 125 million satisfied customers and Tom Clancy, a maven of "knife-edge suspense," had over 15 million of his novels in print. Of course, Mr. Clancy is also unequalled at illuminating character through dialogue. Take, for instance, this telling exchange from his blockbuster, *Clear and Present Danger:*

"'Two-Six Alpha, this is Eight-Three Quebec, do you read, over?'. . .

"'Eight-Three Quebec, this is Two-Six Alpha. I read you five by five, over.'. . .

"'We have a target on profile, bearing one-nine-six, range two-one-zero your position, Angels two. Course zero-one-eight. Speed two-six-five. Over.'. . .

"'Roger, copy. Out.'"

On book-tour flights to Washington, Miami, Seattle, and San Francisco, I devoured recent best-sellers, shamelessly searching for hints on how to do it. I studied books by Danielle Steele, Tom Clancy, Robert Ludlum, Janet Dailey, Harvey Mackay, Stephen King, and Barbara De Angelis, Ph.D., among others.

A born snoop, I turned first to Dr. De Angelis's *Secrets About Men Every Woman Should Know.* Babs came with imposing credentials. She had not only appeared on "Sally Jessy Raphael" and "Geraldo," but was also executive director of the Los Angeles Personal Growth Center, as well as the creator of a "relationships seminar" called Making Love Work. Her new book, also available on video ("Your very own private seminar!") promised to reveal everything you ever wanted to know about women who are excessively needy and clingy, talk too much in bed, or *suffer from chipped fingernail polish.*

The perspicacious doctor, who claims to have worked with tens of thousands of men and women over fifteen years, was willing to make risky pronouncements based on that experience—pronouncements like "The differences between men and women have existed throughout the ages." Elsewhere, however, I had to grapple over and over with De Angelis's sentences, without ever quite getting the hang of them. Take this one, for instance: "*Until the introduction of birth control*, women's and men's roles were determined by the simple fact that women could get pregnant and bear children, and men could not" (italics mine).

Obviously no Woody Allen fan, the author sees contemporary man as "the Solitary Hunter" or "the Displaced Warrior." Me, I respond to that, but I do hope the good doctor will amend an offensive colonialism before the inevitable United Kingdom edition of her book. I am thinking of the passage that reads: "Up until not very long ago, man was still hunting and killing the food for his family; he had to be ready to defend them physically, whether against the Indians or against the British."

Some of Dr. De Angelis's advice is exemplary. "TURN-OFF 18" advises women not to talk about former lovers: "It's time to face the truth—your partner doesn't want to hear about the men you've been with before him." On the other hand, I fear she can mislead women who, "IN AN ATTEMPT TO BE 'NICE GIRLS'. . . HIDE THEIR MAGNIFICENCE." "Make a list of all your talents," she recommends, "abilities, honors, accomplishments and good qualities, and share the list with your partner."

Dr. De Angelis's secrets about men, it should be noted, are not only based on her labours with tens of thousands, but also on sad personal experience. For as long as she can remember, she has always chosen men "who needed fixing in a particular area of their life." Some, for example, needed to get organized and "use their talents to make money." Until recently, she had given her power away to every man with whom she'd been in a relationship, allowing herself to be unappreciated. Sitting down at her computer to compose Chapter 3 ("Filling in the Emotional Blanks: How to Stop Giving More Than You Get in Love"), she wept, tears streaming down her face. "It was the pain of my own broken heart, the pain that comes from having given so much more in love, so many times in my life, than I was given back."

In the summer of 1956, when Terry Southern, Mason Hoffenberg, and I were all rooted in the cliff-top town of Tourette-sur-Loup in the Alpes-Maritimes—driven by greed, consumed with envy at the commercial success of others—we tried to concoct the ultimate *Reader's Digest* story, something the editors couldn't refuse. Unfortunately, the deeper we dug into it, the funnier and more scatalogical it became.

My point is that although many an impecunious literary man thinks that if only he held his nose long enough he could turn his hand to churning out a blockbuster, the truth is—as Tug McGraw once observed in a different context—you gotta believe. And none, it strikes me, is more sincere than sudsy Danielle Steele. One of her recent novels, *Daddy*, is heartwarming beyond compare, and thus has sold in the millions. It tells the story of the admirable Oliver Watson, a forty-four-year-old advertising executive, ostensibly the happily married father of three, who is shocked to discover that Sarah, his wife for eighteen years, has decided to abandon him and her comfy suburban home to go back to Harvard for a master's degree and just possibly to write a novel.

"You need a good shrink, that's what you need," Oliver says. "You're acting like a bored, neurotic housewife." To which Sarah replies: "You don't know anything about me. . . . You don't know what it's like, giving up everything you've ever dreamed of. You've got it all, a career, a family, a wife waiting for you at home like a faithful little dog, waiting to bring you the newspaper and fetch your slippers. Well, what about me, God damn it! When do I get mine? When do I get to do what I want to do? When you're dead, when the kids are gone, when I'm ninety? Well, I'm not going to wait that long. I want it *now*, before I'm too old to do anything worthwhile, before I'm too old to give a damn any more, or enjoy it."

Soon enough, however, for all her bold, modish talk, the selfish Sarah reveals her true colours. She begins an affair with a twenty-five-year-old student in Sodom-on-the-Charles, a Frenchman wouldn't you know, named Jean-Pierre, who is eventually killed off in a car accident. The lending library wages of sin.

Meanwhile Ollie's troubles, like Job's, multiply. His mother develops Alzheimer's and is also killed in an accident. His randy seventy-two-year-old father marries again. His eighteen-year-old son falls for a mindless young thing and soon enough impregnates her. The next thing you know Ollie is seduced by yet another selfish, sex-crazed book editor. Finally he finds truth and beauty in Beverly Hills, of all places. It comes in the delectable shape of prime-time television star Charlotte Sampson—Charlie to her pals. Charlie, obviously made of the right stuff, gives up a shot at the lead in a Broadway play to become homemaker to Ollie and his troublesome brood, who, I take it, will live happily ever after. Ollie, we read on the last page, "had it all, the life he had wanted, and a woman who made it all worthwhile. And he knew, without a doubt, that he was the luckiest man alive."

Ms. Steele's prose is penny plain, functional, its vocabulary limited, not given to surprising metaphors or stylistic flourishes. But when she's overwhelmed by emotion, her sentences, like those in an old Walter Winchell column, tend to suffer from highly charged ellipses, as in "until finally he slept in her arms . . . Oliver . . . the boy she had loved long since . . . the man he had become . . . the love that had begun and now might end at Harvard."

Though she is resolutely on the side of good housekeeping versus careers for women, Ms. Steele, no prude, is also given to steamy passages. Nothing, mind you, to rival the heat of Janet Dailey's *Masquerade*. ("Masks hide," the blurb writer notes. "They also enhance, tantalize, intrigue—and deceive.") Especially when "beautiful Remy Jardin, the daughter of a prominent New Orleans family, tangles with headstrong Cole Buchanan [who] has fought his way out of a life of poverty and despair . . . to become president of the Crescent Line." Cole, let's face it, is a male bimbo. "[Remy's] hands moved freely onto his bared chest, all hard, bronzed flesh over sinewy muscle, smooth and hot to touch, like satin over sun-baked steel."

I wasn't shocked by the titillating passages in either *Daddy* or *Masquerade*, but I was deeply troubled by the fact that in both novels men, no longer in the first flush of youth, are given to lifting their lady loves off the floor, scooping them into steel-like arms with a satin finish, and carrying them off to the boudoir, *more often than not on the second floor.* This is dangerous stuff, raising expectations among women that will be largely unfulfilled by middle-aged men like me and my bunch, who tend to suffer from disc problems.

Bouncing high in the skies on a flight from Washington to Seattle, mindful of one of Harvey Mackay's more sagacious admonitions—"LESSON 61: DON'T TRY ON THE PANTS UNLESS YOU'RE READY TO BUY THE SUIT"—I had to admit that I was incapable of composing such dulcet concoctions as *Daddy* or *Masquerade*. But, mining my rich experience as a high-school air cadet, possibly I could enhance the sales allure of my fiction by gilding it with military detail, like the superstar Tom Clancy, a man's man. On the evidence, however, Tom Clancy's macho novels are not meant so much for men as overgrown boys. The sexiest items in his novels are the pieces of military hardware, which are unfailingly described in loving, sensuous detail.

Reading a writer for the first time, searching for ideas I can steal for profit, I like to sniff out the early influences. The author's debt to, say, Henry James, Conrad, Joyce, or Hemingway. In the case of Mr. Clancy's *Clear and Present Danger*, the formative influences are obvious: *Popular Mechanics*, *Jane's Fighting Ships*, John Wayne's movies, and *Action Comics*. His machines are three-dimensional but his characters are wooden. Their dialogue, such as it is, would be more appropriate rising out of comic-strip thought balloons than enclosed by quotation marks. But he can spin a yarn, as they say, and he flatters sedentary civilians with Inside Military Dope, or IMD, as he would surely have it.

Harvey Mackay, the author of *Beware the Naked Man Who Offers You His Shirt*, is determined to help not only us, but obviously himself as well. Incredibly, his book opens with ten pages of endorsements from, among others, Roger A. Enrico, president and chief executive of PepsiCo Worldwide Beverages; Rabbi Harold Kushner; Al Neuharth, founder of *USA Today*; Pat Riley, head coach of the Los Angeles Lakers; Bob Ulrich, chairman and chief executive of Target stores; Donald Trump; and Gloria Steinem. Most sections of the book, no longer than a couple of pages, will not tax anybody with sufficient attention span to take in a television commercial. There are "Self-Inventory" and "Personal Profile" tests to fill out and an endless spill of inspirational anecdotes. My favourite reads:

"The successful people I know always have a carrot in front of them, slightly out of reach, no matter how many carrots they already have. When he was thirty, Lou Holtz wrote down a list of 107 lifetime ambitions on a slip of paper. They ranged from owning a 1949 Chevy to being invited to the White House for dinner. By the time he was fifty-two, he had achieved 86 of them. Do you want to bet whether he'll make the other 21? And when he does, if he'll tear up the original list and write down another 107?"

Flying home at last, suffering from too many club sandwiches consumed on the trot between radio interviews, but my arm not exactly sore from signing books, I finally turned to Stephen King, the prolific author of perennial best-sellers, who can write very well indeed. In *Misery*, his extremely clever and witty 1987 novel, the protagonist is Paul Sheldon, an author of romance novels whom I take to be Mr. King's alter ego. At one point Sheldon muses: "There are lots of guys out there who write a better prose line than I do and who have a better understanding of what people are really like and what humanity is supposed to mean—hell, I know that . . . There's a million things in this world I can't do. Couldn't hit a curve ball, even back in high school. Can't fix a leaky faucet. Can't roller-skate or make an F-chord on the guitar . . . But if you want me to take you away, to scare you or involve you or make you cry or grin, yeah, I can. I can bring it to you and keep bringing it until you holler uncle. I am able. I CAN."

Misery is Stephen King's horrific variation on the theme of Scheherazade. In it, Sheldon tires of writing his best-selling novels about a bosomy, nineteenth-century heroine named Misery Chastain, so he kills her off in one last novel and retreats to the Rockies. One day he crashes in his sports car on a wintry mountain road and wakes up in a secluded farmhouse in a thinly populated part of Colorado. He is heavily drugged: his pelvis shattered, his knee crushed, both his legs broken. He is also the captive of an enormous, goofy former nurse, equally proficient with the reward of pain-killing drugs or the punishing blow of an axe.

Smiling down on her helpless prisoner, Annie Wilkes lets him know that she is his number-one fan. She absolutely adores Misery and wants Sheldon to bring her back to life; it wasn't fair for him to kill her off in the first place. He is to begin writing a new Misery novel for Annie *starting right now*. "So you just sit there," she says, "and you think about who is in charge here, and all the things I can do to hurt you if you behave badly or try to trick me. You sit there and you scream if you want to, because no one can hear you. No one stops here because they all know Annie Wilkes is crazy, they all know what she did, even if they did find me innocent."

Misery, like all good novels, has a subtext. Obviously Annie Wilkes, not one to hide her magnificence, is an astute take on the relentless muse that continues to inspire Danielle Steele, Janet Dailey, and many another indispensable novelist. Or, *pace* Harvey Mackay, she is the carrot, always slightly out of reach, that prods best-selling authors to scale the literary heights. Roger, copy, out, as Tom Clancy would say.

Mencken

O LD JOKE.

A Jewish boy, determined to become a TV anchorman, is sent to the best elocution teacher money can buy. Handsome, impeccably groomed, he goes on to dazzle Harvard political science professors with his acumen, but he is then turned down in succession by CBS, NBC, and ABC. "How come?" his exasperated mother asks.

The young man replies, "B-b-because th-th-they're a-a-anti-Semites, a-a-all of th-them."

I am repeating this old chestnut only to illustrate that I have no patience with Jews who blame all their inadequacies on discrimination. Or who unfailingly label a bigot anyone appalled by the intransigence of successive Israeli governments. Or who invoke the Six Million glibly, trivializing the Holocaust. However, the real thing does occasionally surface in the most unfortunate places, which brings me to the sad case of H. L. Mencken, a hero of mine.

Mencken, justifiably the most revered of iconoclasts, pitiless tormentor of the American "booboisie," has, on the evidence of *The Diary of H. L. Mencken*, edited by Charles A. Fecher, turned out to be something of a boob himself, deeply prejudiced against blacks and Jews. "It is impossible," he ruled, "to talk anything resembling discretion or judgement into a colored woman. They are essentially child-like, and even hard experience does not teach them anything."

Elsewhere, the nicest thing he has to say about the "dreadful kikes" is that they are smart cookies.

Poor Hank. As early as 1931, his once *Judenfrei* street in Baltimore was threatened. The neighbourhood, he moaned in his diary, was fast declining. "There is no sign of a Negro invasion," he wrote, "but the neighbors grow progressively poorer. . . . At 1528 some Jews have the old Schlens house, with various ratty tenants." Ten years later, Sinclair Lewis lets him down, his latest girlfriend being "a young Jewess rejoicing in the name of Marcella Powers," who is "a completely hollow creature—somewhat good-looking, but apparently without intelligence." Then, in 1942, the historian Samuel E. Morrison, who was then lecturing at Johns Hopkins, tells Mencken that his students are mainly Jews, and that few of them show any capacity.

One of the most offensive passages in the diary, an entry dated "Baltimore, December 2, 1943"—a time when the Jews of Europe were being systematically exterminated—deals with the election of a man called Winter, ostensibly "a presentable fellow," to the Maryland Club, after which the new member took a room in the joint and appeared to spend all of his time hanging about the place. "One day," Mencken writes, "he was seen entertaining an elderly and palpably Jewish gentleman in the dining room, and someone asked who his guest was. It turned out that the guest was his father."

It was then discovered that Winter's real name was Winternitz and that he was, in fact, the brother of one smart kike, Dr. Milton C. Winternitz, dean of Yale medical school. Presented with the damning evidence, Winter/Winternitz did the decent thing. He promptly resigned.

Mencken writes, ". . . there was no objection in the board of governors to bringing an occasional Jew to a meal in the club, but . . . this applied only to out-of-town Jews, not local ones. There was a time when the club always had one Jewish member, but the last was Jacob Ulman. Ulman was married to a Christian woman, a great-granddaughter of Thomas Jefferson, and had little to do with the other Jews of Baltimore. When he died the board of governors decided that he should be the last of the Chosen on the club roll. There is no other Jew in Baltimore who seems suitable."

In defence of such outlandish prejudice, William Manchester—whom Mencken brought to the *Baltimore Evening News* in 1947—wrote in a letter to the *New York Times Book Review*: "In all our thousands of hours together I never heard Mencken insult Jews or blacks." Furthermore, he noted, racial slurs that are now taboo, even shocking, were actually set down by Mencken in private, at a time when such epithets and jokes were commonly heard in polite society." Mencken, he goes on to argue, is the victim of generational chauvinism—the judging of the past by the standards of today. "If we are going to adopt generational chauvinism as dogma, many past heroes will be diminished, including liberal heroes. The kind of anti-Semitism that appears in Mencken's private diary may be found elsewhere: for example, in the early letters of Eleanor Roosevelt and Adlai Stevenson."

It can also be found in Harry Truman's letters to his wife, Bess; the correspondence of Ernest Hemingway; the poetry of T. S. Eliot and Ezra Pound; as well as in the diaries of Virginia Woolf, who was married to a Jew. Virginia didn't care for her sister-in-law Flora, writing in her diary, "I do not like the Jewish voice; I do not like the Jewish laugh."

The argument that anti-Semitism must be forgiven Mencken, and other gifted people, because it was commonly held, even trendy, in polite society at the time—like rumble seats or the foxtrot—is hopelessly asinine. What was acceptable on the walls of public toilets, or among the booboisie, was not to be expected among people of so-called sensibility. So, yes, they are diminished for conspicuously failing to rise above the deplorable biases of their time.

H. L. Mencken's prejudice against Jews for, among other things, knowing the price of everything but the value of nothing is charged with irony. On the evidence of his largely mean-spirited diary, Mencken was himself obsessed with money matters. Take the entry of September 22, 1932, for example: "During the past ten or twelve years [Sinclair Lewis's] earnings have probably run beyond $600,000, but all he has to show for them is his place in Vermont, which would probably not bring $15,000. The $30,000 advance that he drew on

'Ann Vickers' . . . is gone. He is trying to sell the movie rights . . . but so far without success. The Jews have offered him $30,000, but he is holding out for $50,000."

Elsewhere, we are told that Zelda Fitzgerald's illness has been an enormous expense for Scott, "and he has been forced to plug away at stories for the *Saturday Evening Post*. . . . He told me that [*Post* editor George Horace] Lorimer had reduced him from $4,000 to $3,500 a story." Then, when we get to January 10, 1935, we learn that Louis Untermeyer, the poet and anthologist, averages about $100 a lecture. "Sometimes he gets $125, but probably more often he has to take $75."

Another financial entry, inadvertently amusing, has to do with Theodore Dreiser, also an anti-Semite. It seems that Dreiser was complaining to Mencken about his old publishing house, Liveright, then under the "control of a Jew named Pell, who by Dreiser's account is a fearful swine." The same year, Dreiser received $100,000 from another Jew, Jesse Lasky, for the movie rights to *An American Tragedy*. Mencken writes: "After Lasky had bought the rights, Will H. Hays (of the film censorship office) made objection to his doing the book as a movie, and it was laid on the shelf. When the talkies came in Lasky got it down and finally induced Hays to give him permission to produce it. But when Dreiser heard of this he demanded an additional fee of $60,000. His contention was that he had sold the movie rights, not the talkie rights. He told me that Lasky protested bitterly, but finally paid the money."

Or, put plainly, the anti-Semitic Dreiser managed, as they say, to jew Lasky.

The wittiest line in the diary cannot be credited to Mencken himself but to a lawyer, Moorefield Storey. When William Randolph Hearst's name came up, Storey said, "Hearst married a prostitute, and then gradually dragged her down to his own level."

For all my objections, Mencken remains a delight to read and to read about. In a story about him that I cherish, he was seated at his desk in the newsroom of the *Evening Sun* when a reporter asked, "Who was Von Kleist?"

"The Chinese saviour," Mencken shot back.

Morley Safer's Vietnam

T HOSE WHO HAVE READ *The Powers That Be*, a study of the
rise of America's media empires by David Halberstam, will
recall that Morley Safer was not Lyndon Johnson's favourite
correspondent in Vietnam. The morning after the CBS "Evening
News" broadcast Safer's devastating 1965 report on the burning of
the hamlet of Cam Ne by marines, Frank Stanton, then president of
CBS, took an early phone call.

"Frank," said the caller, "are you trying to fuck me?"

"Who is this?" asked the still sleepy Stanton.

"Frank, this is your president, and yesterday our boys shat on the
American flag."

LBJ, convinced that the amiable Safer was a red-hot Commie,
launched an investigation by the FBI, and the CIA, and the Royal
Canadian Mounted Police, an investigation that proved Safer a
Canadian, to which LBJ responded, "Well, I knew he wasn't an
American."

It didn't end there, either.

In the early 1980s, when a team of researchers interviewed the
last American ambassador to South Vietnam, Graham Martin (a man
Safer had never met), he told them, "The question of Morley Safer
is interesting. I knew him well. I also knew he was a KGB agent—so
did the White House. . . ." A few years later, Dean Rusk, who was

LBJ's secretary of state, said that it was "common knowledge at the White House that the reporter was a questionable character with ties to the Soviet intelligence apparatus . . . the White House had its own intelligence on him but for reasons I can't recall, they never used it."

I used to see something of Safer in London in the sixties and never suspected him, but since then I have had second thoughts. When we had lunch together in New York, a few years back, it was at the *Russian* Tea Room. By his own admission, he reads novels by foreign intellectuals. Something else. *He paints.*

Readers, now that you have been warned, I must also allow that Safer's *Flashbacks: On Returning to Vietnam*, a journal of a trip undertaken in 1989, is at once poignant, intelligent, evocative, and very readable indeed. There are some nicely turned portraits to be found in these pages. Here, for instance, is Dan Rather introducing himself in the bar of the Caravelle in Saigon: "A stream of admiration poured from his lips. A touch excessive, I thought, nevertheless very nice to hear. The man was trying very hard to be courtly, but the effect was destroyed by the strange way he was dressed. It was not the green army fatigues and combat boots—though it was most unusual for correspondents to be dressed for war in Saigon—it was the leather shoulder holster and nickel-plated Smith and Wesson .38 caliber revolver strapped to the outside of his clothing that gave an otherwise friendly encounter an edge of menace. I could not imagine who he might have to shoot in the Caravelle. The service was always quite good."

Safer reports that Rather, for his part, has no recollection of that particular conversation and maintains he has never carried a gun.

The previous year, in 1965, there was Barry Goldwater, defeated in the presidential election the year before, holding forth drunkenly in the same bar: "I'd like to see you pansy reporters out there in the boondocks getting your asses shot at. No guts, no guts . . . I wish they would let me have my way out here. There wouldn't be a gook or fucking reporter left in six months . . . our kids are dying out there right now while you guys are up here getting pissed . . . you're nothing but a bunch of yellow bastards."

Safer served as a correspondent in Vietnam through most of 1965 and 1966 and was there again in 1970 and 1971, but he didn't get to Hanoi until eighteen years later: January 18, 1989. ". . . A furtive, unapproachable city," he describes it, "[the] faces of the people resemble the façades of the shabby state shops. Shutters drawn, protecting empty shelves." However, he had only been there for a day when he was allowed to visit with the legendary General Vo Nguyen Giap, now just short of eighty years old, nominally the deputy chairman of the Council of Ministers for Science and Technology, with little, if anything, to do. Giap told him, "I once met Brzezinski, President Carter's National Security Advisor in Algiers, and he took me in both his hands and said, 'I have long admired your courage, General Giap.'"

The story is plausible, Safer ventures, as Brzezinski would never lose an opportunity to ingratiate himself.

A far more sympathetic veteran of the conflict was Bui Tin, age sixty-two, colonel, People's Army of Vietnam (retired). Wounded in the battle of Dien Bien Phu, during the French war, and again at Khe Sanh, during the American war, he recalled the difficulties of the Ho Chi Minh Trail: "A man could lose two hundred grams of blood every day from leeches . . . many of the men bled to death," he told Safer. "Food was a constant worry, especially for the big units. I remember we shot an elephant once, and for five days we had meat. Men drowned; they fell off cliffs; they died of malaria and snake bites. I used to look up in the sky and envy you in those helicopters."

Meanwhile, some twenty-six thousand American support troops were ensconced in the Long Binh army post, some sixteen miles from Saigon, equipped with eight Olympic-sized swimming pools, ranges for archery and skeet shooting, a couple of bowling alleys, putting greens and driving ranges for golf, four football fields, and two whorehouses run by outside contractors. "Twenty-two thousand Vietnamese workers," Safer writes, "were brought on the base each day to service the needs of the 26,000 American support troops. Support troops for the support troops."

In Saigon, now reborn Ho Chi Minh City, Safer met with Dr.
Duong Hoa, a woman who was one of the sixteen founders of the
National Liberation Front, the political arm of the Vietcong. During
the war, Hoa, ostensibly friendly with Ambassadors Henry Cabot
Lodge and Maxwell Taylor, was actually serving as a spy, but, she
told Safer, "[The Americans] were still my friends. The English and
French ambassadors too."

Hoa, who now runs a maternity clinic, quit the party in 1979.
"Something goes wrong at a certain age," she said. "You stop seeing
things as clearly at forty as you did at twenty-one. I thought I was
making a revolution for the people . . . I know that sounds very
idealistic, but you must understand how determined we were. I discovered that I made a revolution for a cause, for a discipline, for an
ideology. The people had nothing to do with it. I have no regrets
because it was necessary above all to get the foreigners out of our
country."

Hoa was also disillusioned with the northerners now in power in
Ho Chi Minh City, where it was rumoured that party officials were
selling exit visas and that the children of Politburo members were
importing expensive European and Japanese cars. "[The northern-
ers] have no idea how to function in peace," she said. "The people
they sent down here were military. All they know is war and political indoctrination."

Safer, a first-rate reporter, had the good sense to ask all the right
questions of the survivors. One of the most interesting of them,
surely, is Pham Xuan An. During the war An was a popular and indispensable part of *Time*'s Saigon bureau, and he still remembers all
the American correspondents with enormous affection, even though
he was an agent of the Vietcong all along, with the rank of regimen-
tal commander. Now sixty-two years old, "emaciated, almost cadav-
erous," the scholarly An lives modestly, his living room overflowing
with books in English, French, and Vietnamese.

How, Safer asked, did his double life start?

"It was the most natural thing. In 1944 the Japanese were still
here. I joined the Viet Minh with most of my classmates. It was not

a matter of choice; it was the only thing to do. We were patriots. Then, when the French came back, nothing had really changed, just the enemy. I did nothing very brave; I ran a few errands."

But, like so many others, An now feels the revolution has failed miserably. Why, Safer asked.

"Ignorance. Willful, mean-spirited ignorance. They called it a *people's* revolution. But of course the *people* were the first to suffer; the *people* were immediately forgotten. They still haven't remembered the *people*. Have you been in the streets at night? That is where to find the people. Asleep in the streets . . . that is the bed that the revolution has made for them. The men who run this country, I don't think there are two of them who have even a high school diploma. All that talk of 'liberation,' twenty, thirty, forty years ago, all that plotting, and all the bodies, produced this, this impoverished, broken-down country led by a gang of cruel and paternalistic half-educated theorists."

Safer asked An if he regretted what he had done, now that he had seen the results.

"I hate that question. I have asked it of myself a thousand times. But I hate the answer more. No. No regrets. I had to do it. This peace that I fought for may be crippling the country, but the war was killing it. As much as I love the United States, it had no right here. The Americans had to be driven out of Vietnam one way or another. We must sort this place out ourselves."

Supersex

I BELONG TO A GENERATION brought up to believe that masturbation was risky business. It could lead to blindness. The first time my mother heard me utter "a dirty word," she washed my mouth out with soap. When my friend Jack Rabinovitch came home one day and told his mother, "Izzy Fogelman says babies are born coming out between their mother's legs," his mother said, "You mustn't play with Izzy Fogelman any more."

We were, in current parlance, a prudish bunch. Sexually deprived. As teenagers, we demonstrated affection for our dates by holding hands. Taking in a double feature at the neighbourhood Rialto, we hoped to benefit by a little necking with proscribed limits, but afterwards we did not go on to discuss multiple orgasms or, as Dr. Ruth has it in her *Guide for Married Lovers*, speculate on the fun to be had with velvet ropes: "Bob had tied Ann to several beds since they first tried bondage. . . . The easiest bed is, of course, one with posts or legs, so he can spread-eagle Ann, tying her wrists and ankles to the four corners. Additional criss-crossing and half-hitching binds her down by the thighs, midsection and diagonally between her breasts. Then Bob teasingly begins to draw a velvet rope end across her erogenous zones until she is excruciatingly aroused. . . ."

In those days the men's toilets in Montreal bars did not yet stock machines that coughed out strawberry-flavoured condoms for a

couple of bucks. But strolling downtown these hallelujah days, I can
pass several strip clubs, a couple of sex-novelty shops, with specials
on handcuffs or spiked leather belts, and maybe three porn cinemas
and a couple of peep shows before I find the places that cater to my
particular perversions: say, a reliable cigar emporium or a deli that
stocks decent pickled herring. Speaking of herring, although I consider myself an expert on its many varieties, I have yet to feast on a
specialty recommended by Germaine Greer in the London *Spectator*
(February 13, 1971), a fish that is marinated "between the vulvae to
make a delicacy for a lover."

Simultaneous with sex becoming ubiquitous, adolescents are becoming increasingly inarticulate. Witness one of the fabled Lake-
wood, California, Spur Posse gang, as quoted by Joan Didion in a
1993 *New Yorker:* "There's the girls that, you know, that you have
respect for and that you'll romance, you know, you'll take them out
and it's like the romance scene, it's not like, you know—and then
there's these other girls, you know, you're going to drive over there,
you already know what's going to happen, you know, it's no romance, you know, it's just—wham. You know, three and out."

Bear with me. Assuming that Homo sapiens has not yet attained
a state of perfection and that evolution is a continuing process, I will
now venture into Wellsian and Huxleian territory, anticipating a different Brave New World. Taking the idiot idiom and sexual thug-
gery of so many into account, I expect that thousands of years from
now the new mutants will have their heads where their genitals used
to be, and vice versa. If this seems far-fetched, remember that hawks
were once dinosaurs. In any event, this evolutionary process will
come as a blessing to our species. It will enable the readers of Dr.
Ruth, Rachel Swift, Dr. Sandra Scantling, Sue Ellen Browder, and
other illuminati to jump one another on impulse, say, as the lights
change on Third Avenue, without having to endure the tiresome
business of learning first names or even undressing. Wham. You
know, three and out.

These dark thoughts about our future were triggered by two
relentlessly silly and insufferably earnest sexual self-help books, both

of them calculated to squeeze all the pleasure out of lovemaking, describing it as if inspired by *Popular Mechanics* or a plumber's trade journal: *How to Have an Orgasm . . . as Often as You Want*, by Rachel Swift, and *Ordinary Women, Extraordinary Sex*, by Dr. Sandra Scantling and Sue Ellen Browder.

Rachel Swift is the pseudonym of "an average woman in her thirties" who, having finally had her first orgasm during sex, decided to publish a step-by-step self-help book for others who were missing out. Practise control, she advocates. Prepare yourself by becoming proficient at masturbation. "Your own hands," she writes, "are the most useful tool . . . [because] they are warm as well as uniquely sensitive." But she also recommends rolled-up socks, or the arm of a teddy bear, which is soft *and* firm.

Once, she writes, while she was staying in a hotel room in Bali, "the waiter knocked on the door with a dish of exotic fruit. Feeling horny, I sized up the man—and decided his bananas looked more appetizing than he did. When he had shut the door, I unpeeled a not-too-ripe banana and used it to great effect."

My considered advice is that if you are invited to Ms. Swift's home for dinner, turn down the fruit salad.

Among the various life-enhancing exercises advocated by Ms. Swift, my favourite is "Class C: Masturbation in Public!

"*Exercise 7.13.* For the really daring: if you can do this at will, then you're a star pupil. Of course nobody will know what you're doing. The trick is to exert some pressure where it matters, without seeming to be doing so. I've done it on the subway timed to the rhythm of the train. More than once I've . . . used my heel while kneeling on the floor talking about the state of the nation. But if you're at this stage, you don't need me to point out the possibilities."

At her most romantic, Ms. Swift does not recommend roses, Mozart, or Dom Perignon but an exercise devised by one Dr. Arnold Kegel in 1952 "for women who needed to improve urinary control by strengthening the pubococcygeal or p-c muscle, which controls the size and tension of the vaginal opening. Much to his patients' delight, the exercises increased their ability to have orgasms," as well as, it is to be hoped, decreasing any chance of pissing on their partner, which can be a turn-off for some.

Ordinary Women, Extraordinary Sex is the book that answers the questions, "Why is one sexual moment a turn-off and another seemingly similar time a tremendous turn-on? Does enjoyment of peak sex depend on your partner, the setting, your frame of mind, or something else?" Dr. Scantling, a *certified* sex therapist who has treated thousands, is certainly qualified to answer these queries, and her findings have been rendered readable, as it were, by the redoubtable Sue Ellen Browder, a contributing editor of *New Woman*. These two searchers-after-truth settled on a study of 86 women, selected out of 536, who struck them as "high-absorbers," most likely to have experienced "supersex."

Supersex, so far as I can determine, involves travelling in place, enabling women to float in space, to witness liquid fireworks and spectacular displays of light.

Supersexers, regardless of race, colour, or creed, sometimes feel as if their mind could envelop the whole world. They like to watch cloud shapes and changes in the sky. They can be deeply moved by a sunset. Their altered state during supersex, it seems, resembles the overwhelming sense of oneness the great Hindu, Christian, and Jewish mystics have reported feeling when communing with God or nature.

"It was like flying," said Catherine, a thirty-nine-year-old court stenographer, who might just possibly be an unconscious racist. After making love for three hours straight, she transcended the physical, report Scantling and Browder. "It was like everything was involved: my mind, my body, my whole spiritual being. That's when I thought I saw God. What did God look like? White."

Another supersexer, this one a forty-two-year-old executive, rhapsodized about a man ten years her junior: "I'd never made love with a man so *verbal* during sex. . . . It was a real turn-on for me . . . right in the middle of lovemaking he sat up straight in bed and shouted, 'Holy shit! This is so much fun!'" (italics mine).

To each her own epiphany.

Saul
Bellow

H E HAS BEEN HEAPED with honours. Justifiably so. But, in 1993, at the age of seventy-eight, Saul Bellow was being circled by intellectual picadors, intent on lowering the old bull's head, making him bleed. Alfred Kazin, writing in the *New Yorker*, accused him of being a "university intellectual," this child of the Depression and Marxism now moving in the company of "conservative Big Thinkers at the University of Chicago." Hilton Kramer, pronouncing in *Commentary*, adjudged him still one of "that dwindling remnant of homeless liberals," his most recent work disappointing, as a consequence of his "acquiring the smug and apodictic tone of a writer whose celebrity was now a refuge from experience and a barrier to any direct engagement with the world."

Michael Jackson is a celebrity. So is Oprah Winfrey. But Saul Bellow's fame, let me hastily point out, does not necessarily extend even as far as Montreal's old working-class Jewish quarter, where he spent his early childhood, and about which he wrote memorably in *Herzog*. As I wrote in *This Year in Jerusalem*, I once went to meet a friend for lunch at Moishe's steakhouse on Boulevard St-Laurent, or the Main, as we always called it. While I waited for my friend, a waiter came over to chat about the old days when we had all lived in the neighbourhood.

"Remember Sid Horowitz?" he asked.

"I don't think so."

"Sure you do," said the man at the next table. It was Marty Hoffman, Baron Byng High, class of '48. Now sole proprietor of Pantalon Picasso—Picasso Jeans. "*Langer loksh* Horowitz. He was with the Y basketball team the year they won everything."

"He came in here yesterday with his new wife," said the waiter. "A *shiksa*. Maybe twenty-five years old. He was wearing a rug."

Marty wanted to know if I remembered Shloime Scheiderman.

"Sorry, no."

Then the waiter recalled more names from the old days. Charna Rosen. Moish Bercovitch, who was doing time. Dr. Phil Gold, a credit to us. Foolishly, I tried to trump that last name. "Do you know who used to live right around the corner from here on Napoleon Street?"

"Sure. The Kushners. They were in footwear. Retail."

"Saul Bellow," I said. "Right around the corner from here. When he was a little boy."

"Bellow?" the waiter asked, puzzled. "Now you've got me. What was his father in?"

Bellow has been accused of being a misogynist. And now he has been branded a racist by Brent Staples, a talented young black journalist on the editorial board of the *New York Times*. The blacks portrayed in *Humboldt's Gift*, he wrote, were unfailingly "sinister" and, in *Mr. Sammler's Planet*, given to gratuitous violence. But in the same *New York Times Magazine* article, plucked from Staples's then soon-to-be published memoir, *Parallel Time*, only two black characters are dealt with at length: Staples's murdered brother Blake ("Blake was a drug dealer; he was known for carrying guns and using them. His killer, Mark McGeorge, was a former customer and a cocaine addict") and Stephen Dale, a friend from junior high school ("Stephen was found dead, shot four times in the head and face. In the pocket of his overcoat were $100 in cash and seven glassine packets of heroin"), which is not to say that Staples is also a racist or, worse news, a self-hating black.

In a singularly nasty description, included in the *New York Times Magazine* excerpt, Staples, who once caught a glimpse of Bellow in broad daylight, ventures that possibly, just possibly, the Nobel laureate has become a dirty old man: "He moved through the crowd looking downward, hungrily scanning hips, crotches, and legs. This was how he did it. The rest of us were a junkyard where he foraged for parts."

Most recently Bellow got into hot water for remarking to a journalist in passing, "Who is the Tolstoy of the Zulus? The Proust of the Papuans?" While he was at it, he might have added, "And where is the Canadian Mozart?" Mind you, he couldn't have tossed that out with impunity, either. Where I come from, it would only have added to his charge sheet.

P.C.'s brackish waters have polluted even Canada's once pristine shores. W. P. Kinsella, author of *Field of Dreams*, has been found guilty of "cultural appropriation" for daring to write about natives in his Hobbema stories. Then, at a recent meeting of the Writers' Union of Canada, black, native, and authors of Asian origin, claimed that they were being discriminated against by ofay publishers and that their few books in print were seldom reviewed. They announced that they wished to convene a conference, paid for by the government, from which white union members would be excluded. Pierre Berton, the popular historian, his liberal credentials impeccable, was sufficiently intrepid to protest that this would amount to intolerable discrimination, but the wimp in the chair, appropriately obsequious, allowed that as "a writer of pallor" he understood the minority group's special problems. Oh dear, oh dear, once I was a Jew, born and bred in Montreal, but, in the new nomenclature, I find myself reduced to "a non-visible minority member," and now "a writer of pallor," narrowly Eurocentric for that matter.

"'Eurocentrism' has become a terrible reproach," Bellow noted in a lecture delivered at the Mozart Bicentennial in Florence, in 1991. "We reproach ourselves even for the few decencies, bourgeois relics, with which we cover our shame. We hear from all sides that we are 'inauthentic' and that we are, every one of us, imposters."

Hilton Kramer made a valid point in *Commentary* when he argued that a sadly defensive Bellow waffled in his *New York Times* op-ed response to the kerfuffle created by his off-the-cuff remarks about Zulus and Papuans. Bellow refers to his zinger "as alleged" before he owns up to it, saying that he was merely trying to make a "distinction between literate and preliterate societies," and then, making nice, he added, "Preliterate societies have their own kinds of wisdom, no doubt, and primitive Papuans probably have a better grasp of their myths than most educated Americans have of their own literature." But in the end the major novelist so many of us cherish did not fail us.

"Righteousness and rage threaten the independence of our souls," he wrote. Then, without actually naming the odious, but increasingly menacing Louis Farrakhan, he went on to say, "The rage of rappers and rioters takes as its premise the majority's admission of guilt for past and present injustices, and counts on the admiration of the repressed for the emotional power of the uninhibited and 'justly' angry. Rage can also be manipulative; it can be an instrument of censorship and despotism."

Elaborating on this theme in an interview with a *New Yorker* "Talk of the Town" reporter, he said, "P.C. is really a serious threat to political health, because where there is free speech without any debate, what you have is a corruption of free speech, which very quickly becomes demagogy. People in general in this country have lost the habit of debating questions. TV does it for them."

It All Adds Up: From the Dim Past to the Uncertain Future is Saul Bellow's collection of what Philip Larkin once dubbed Required Writing. It's a compelling grab bag of non-fiction pieces by a novelist who is also a wise man, which does not necessarily follow. Okay, a grumpy, somewhat mournful wise man, but—to borrow from the current vernacular—the author of *The Victim, Seize the Day,* and

Herzog is entitled. Bellow's collection is made up of memoirs, essays, lectures, complaints, an interview with himself, and farewells to contemporaries; ". . . trifles I wrote to support myself," Bellow notes in his introduction.

What is astonishing about this collection, in the first place, is Bellow's stubborn, touchingly mistaken belief that he is now addressing a literate rather than today's largely post-literate audience. Bellow, who sprang to manhood in a more cultured and civil time, makes the risky assumption that there is still a sizable community of voracious readers out there who have absorbed not only Tolstoy, Dostoevsky, Stendhal, and Balzac, but also Wyndham Lewis, Herzen, Trotsky, Nietzsche, Marx, Ruskin, and Ortega y Gasset, among others.

I have just been correcting proofs of a book of my own in which I made a passing reference to "the children of Sarah and Hagar," only to have the phrase flagged by my copyeditor, requesting me to i.d. both names. To begin with, I was irritated, but then I grudgingly had to allow that she was right. It was no longer a given that even readers of so-called serious books were familiar with the Bible. Bellow, made of sterner stuff, makes no such concession to the new illiteracy, dropping French aphorisms here and there and only condescending to translate one of them. Interestingly enough, Hilton Kramer, or his *Commentary* copyeditor, was more realistic. Kramer's quotation of Bellow's use of "*On ne donne rien si libéralement que ses conseils*" is immediately followed in parenthesis by "One is never so generous as with advice."

In his essay on Mozart, a celebration of the mysteries of genius, Bellow rebukes Edmund Wilson for having written, in 1931, that in the Soviet Union he felt that he was "at the moral top of the world, where the light never really goes out," but he also admits to dissatisfaction in rereading some of his own earlier judgements, because of radical changes in his point of view. Bellow, who was a Trotskyite in 1933 ("How could I forget that Trotsky had created the Red Army," he writes), now describes himself as "some sort of liberal, but I don't know where liberalism has gone in this country in the last twenty years." He was in Mexico in 1940 and had arranged to meet Trotsky in Coyoacan. Alas, we have been deprived of a record of that meeting, because Bellow's appointment turned out to be set for the very day that Trotsky was assassinated. Mistaken for a foreign journalist, Bellow was taken to view the body in the hospital: "He had just died. A cone of bloody bandages was on his head. His cheeks, his nose, his beard, his throat, were streaked with blood and with dried iridescent trickles of iodine."

In "Facts That Put Fancy to Flight," Bellow, taking the novel's faltering pulse, bemoans today's terrible insistence on factual accuracy. "How many storeys does the Ansonia Hotel really have, and can one see its television antenna from the corner of West End Avenue and Seventy-second Street? What do drugstores charge for Librium?" The movies, he justifiably observes, have already got the wrong end of the stick. Producers consult archaeologists in the making of Roman spectaculars. "As long as the chariots are faithful copies . . . it seems to make little difference that the dialogue makes you clutch your head. . . ." While he salutes Mark Twain's knowledge of navigation and "the descriptions of process" in Hemingway's fishing stories, he fears that in "the U.S.A., today, the facts appear to have it all over the imagination," and that the American desire for the real "has created a journalistic sort of novel, which has a *thing* excitement, a glamour of *process*; it specializes in information." True, as far as it goes, but James Joyce, in exile, wrote home to determine the exact placement of a tree on St. Stephen's Square.

Bellow is absolutely right to insist that "in every case it is the writer's excitement that counts," but unfortunately the mundane facts are also necessary. Auden understood that. In his astute poem "The Novelist," he wrote that the poet "can amaze us like a thunderstorm," but the novelist must "learn to be plain and awkward."

> For to achieve his lightest wish, he must
> Become the whole of boredom, subject to
> Vulgar complaints like love, among the Just
>
> Be just, among the Filthy filthy too. . . .

Happily, Bellow is convinced that the teaching of literature in the universities has been a disaster, the instructors "interpreting" masterpieces, explaining what Ahab's harpoon symbolizes, but instilling no passion for novels or poetry. "What people learn is how to conduct a cultured conversation for a few minutes without betraying ignorance or stupidity."

Bellow, a big cultural fisherman, casts his line both high and low, covering all the water, reeling in not only Tolstoy and Mozart, but also Chicago's Yellow Kid Weil, Bathhouse John Coughlin, and Facts-and-Figures Taylor. Far from regarding the rest of us as a junkyard where he forages for parts, he has, to my mind, always approached his world with morally informed appetite, and a sense of irony, providing in abundance the excitement that counts, and celebrating what is enduringly beautiful in the human spirit. Osip Mandelstam, he notes, quoting the murdered poet's widow Nadezhda, always carried a pocket edition of *The Divine Comedy* with him, "just in case he was arrested not at home but in the street."

Chicago belongs to Bellow now and forever, as surely as Yoknapatawpha County does to Faulkner or nineteenth-century London to Dickens. It should come as no surprise, then, that a couple of the most enjoyable pieces in *It All Adds Up* are, in fact, memoirs of Chicago. His prodigious gifts as a novelist beyond dispute, Bellow turns out to be a first-rate reporter as well. His collection is enriched by splendid accounts of Paris, circa 1948; a journey through Franco's Spain; and reports from Tel Aviv and Sinai in the aftermath of the Six-Day War.

I was pleased to see Bellow scornful of Sartre's political posturing in the immediate post-Second World War period ("Reading [him], I said to myself, Chicago-style, 'This has got to be a con'"). The truth is Sartre's earnest *Les Chemins de la liberté* trilogy, though not without its stirring passages, suffers when compared with Evelyn Waugh's ostensibly comic, but indubitably great, *Men at Arms* trilogy.

In his introduction, Bellow, acknowledging gaffes of the past, expresses the hope that he has entered into an era of improved errors.

An iffy case is his 1993 pronouncement that "Russia is perhaps done with tyranny and privation. If it develops a free market and becomes a union of commercial republics, it will have to do as we have been doing all along." For the rest, I can only clap hands for his complaints. He mourns America's urban devastation: ". . . the disappearance of a genial street life from American cities; the dank and oppressing odors of cultural mildew rising from the giant suburbs . . . the shift of bohemia from the slums to the universities." He is against subsidized day care, which entitles toddlers to be brought up in pens, like piglets, so that their parents may be free to pursue their careers. Contemporary jargon—say, the prevalence of such words as consensus, role model, entitlement, quality time, or marginalized—appalls him; and to this list I would add the cutting edge. Although, like the rest of us, he still needs his daily news fix, he finds the world of "telegrams and anger" too much with us. "Increasingly, I find myself agreeing with Vladimir Nabokov. A work of art, Nabokov argued, detaches you from the world of common travail and leads you into another world altogether. It carries you into a realm of aesthetic bliss. Can there be anything more desirable than aesthetic bliss?"

Sexual

Harassment

I N RECENT YEARS, Montreal's one surviving English-language daily, the *Gazette,* has raised its consciousness by acquiring a gaggle of knee-jerk liberal columnists, among them one Eve McBride. One day, the alert Ms. McBride complained, in her page-two column, about unwanted touching by slavering males. Clearly Ms. McBride, who had read (not once, but twice) Helen Fisher's *The Anatomy of Love: The Natural History of Monogamy, Adultery, and Divorce,* had in mind men in suits who were actually descended from "the scout, tracker, explorer, scavenger, hunter, and protector," and were possessed by a sexual "restlessness driven by currents buried deep in our human psyche." Put in plain English, she was scribbling about horny guys.

"Consider," she wrote, "the husband of a close friend. At dinner parties, with his wife seated nearby, he has a habit of *secretly* sliding his hand high up the thigh *or on to the breast* of the woman seated next to him—usually one of his wife's friends" (italics mine).

Always eager to learn new dinner party tricks, I sneaked out one day, while my unsuspecting wife was busy elsewhere, to our vegetable garden to retrieve our scarecrow, and seated it next to me at our dining-room table. And then, imagining my wife and two other couples at the table, I attempted, slyly moving this way and that, to *secretly* fondle the scarecrow's breasts. Couldn't get the hang of it.

However, I wasn't raised on Talmudic nuances for nothing, and I decided that maybe Ms. McBride had withheld vital information from her column. Possibly, Eve and her crowd nosh at dinner-party tables that are chin-high. This, it's true, would create difficulties with the soup course, but it would certainly facilitate secret breast fondling, under the tablecloth, as it were, which would be a nice diversion in dim company. Or maybe the husband of Ms. McBride's close friend carries golf balls with him to dinner parties, surreptitiously drops one down the décolletage of the lady seated next to him, leaps up, and says, "Don't you disturb yourself, dear, I'll get it." No, that would be bound to attract attention. A third possibility is that everybody at those dinner parties is visually disadvantaged, that is to say, blind, enabling that devilish fellow to fondle breasts with impunity, passing up and down the table and back again.

"Whatever are you doing?" his wife's friend might ask.

"Wiping the gravy off your blouse."

"Don't you go away until you've removed every spec."

The very next afternoon, while I was drinking with a buddy of mine, the sorry problem of sexual harassment by the descendants of trackers and hunters surfaced again. My friend, a law partner in a large firm, told me that a notice had just been circulated through his offices warning that "leering" now also constituted sexual harassment.

"Leering," according to my *Oxford English Dictionary*, means, "that leers, or looks with side glances," and "leer" is defined as "looking askance; oblique, indirect; sly, underhand." Dr. Johnson, in his dictionary, defines "leer" as "a laboured cast of countenance," and quotes Alexander Pope's usage, "Damn with faint praise, concede with a civil *leer*."

In any event, my friend assured me that being caught out leering during office hours could be grounds for legal action:

Your Honour, my client was leaning innocently over a filing cabinet, her miniskirt unavoidably riding over her bum, when she was horrified to see, reflected in the cabinet, the image of Irving Tannenbaum looking askance at her, his cast of counte-

nance laboured. This uninvited leer, freighted with sexual menace, brought on nightmares. With the help of an analyst, it
retrieved my client's long-buried memories of childhood abuse.
When she was a mere three years old her grandfather used to
bounce her on his lap and tickle her under her jumper. These
vile memories of an old pervert have surfaced only because of
Irving Tannenbaum's leer, and now my client can no longer
achieve orgasm or shop. We demand ten million dollars for loss
of enjoyment of life.

Many years ago the late Irwin Shaw wrote a famous short story
about girl-watching—"The Girls in Their Summer Dresses." In
those innocent days, Shaw's story could be taken as an appreciation
of passing grace and beauty; a celebration of life for those of us who
have been ticketed for only one trip, unlike Shirley Maclaine. But if
Shaw had published his story in these politically correct times, he
would undoubtedly have been condemned by the politically correct
women.

This is not to say that I approve of men who persist in making
unwanted advances: dinner party breast-gropers or subway arse-
pinchers. They are a blight. So are those who whistle, leer, or, assert-
ing office rank, make suggestions that could only lead to what Helen
Fisher has dubbed "clandestine-bonds," or, good heavens, "genetic
payoffs" from guys programmed since prehistory to seek sexual variety. So I am pleased to report that sweetly scented women who
frequent singles bars, in search of a discourse on the politics of meaning, or well-brought-up college girls who repair to a young man's
room at 2 a.m., hoping to exchange ideas on Kierkegaard only to
find themselves jumped on the sofa, need no longer be victimized.
They can, like Cybill Shepherd, Betty Thomas (from "Hill Street
Blues"), Susan Howard (of "Dallas"), Nancy Reagan, and Joan
Rivers, apply for a licence to pack musketry, preferably a pistol filled
with live ammo. In *Armed and Female* (St. Martin's Paperpacks),
Paxton Quigley, an award-winning shootist herself and a former
bodyguard to Yoko Ono, highly recommends either a Glock 17

or a Heckler & Koch P7M8, both of which boast an excellent
INTIMIDATION VALUE:

"The two guns I have chosen as favorites are unique and more
user-friendly than all the 9mm autoloaders I have had the opportunity to test. The Glock . . . pulls double-action every shot. It is much
like a revolver, except that it shoots straighter and faster. . . . The
Heckler & Koch P7 is the Rolls-Royce of 9mm pistols. It . . . has a
special trigger mechanism. This is called a squeeze-cocker, because
the front of the grip must be squeezed and depressed into the grip in
order to arm the trigger. . . ."

Ms. Quigley's book, full of practical information on gun etiquette, benefited from the sage advice of G. Gordon Liddy and
combat gun master Massed Ayoob, director of Lethal Force Insti-
tute. She claims that if a woman is thirty years old now, there's a
fifty-fifty chance of her being raped, robbed, or attacked . . .
or maybe even getting married, I suppose. So it should come as no
surprise that, according to Dr. Paul H. Blackman, a National Rifle
Association lobbyist, some twenty-two million American women
now own their own guns. One of them, Judy Miller, a professor at a
Chicago university, whom I would advise younger readers not to
quarrel with over grades, keeps a loaded pistol by her bedside and
also packs a rod in her briefcase. "The basic issue goes back to self-
worth," this pedagogue told Paxton Quigley, "and whether or not
you are totally committed to leading a good strong life and taking
charge of your own destiny."

In matters of female self-defence, Ms. Quigley eschews javelins,
harpoons, machetes, scimitars, bazookas, or flame-throwers. But before she became such an expert gunperson, she used to carry a steak
knife with her for protection, which could be awkward.

"Madame, you will have to check that knife with your wrap. At
the Four Seasons we provide our own cutlery."

She discarded the steak knife after she learned that "basically a
knife is an assassination weapon: lethal but without stopping power.
To stop someone by stabbing, you would need to stab twenty to
thirty times," which could ruin a woman's clothes.

More information about confounding attackers is available in a fascinating new magazine, *Women's Self-Defense*, edited by Kathy Bentley, and published by Creative Arts, Inc., 4901 N.W. 17th Way, Suite 600, Ft. Lauderdale, Florida 33309. Paxton Quigley is on its advisory board, which I find reassuring. Readers of this magazine are encouraged to acquire bumper stickers saying FIGHT CRIME—SHOOT BACK or INSURED BY SMITH & WESSON. Guns aside, its editors recommend BODYGUARD PEPPER DEFENSE SPRAY—its primary active ingredient an inflammatory agent that is guaranteed to control drunks, drug addicts, and psychotics. "The mucous membrane cells swell to prevent all but life-support breathing. Eye capillaries are dilated so that temporary blindness results." It also comes out strongly in favour of Bianchi's Model D4500 Ranger Black Shadow, a nifty holster of attractive design that fits snugly over the concealed top of a lady's stocking, its "low friction nylon lining allows for quick delivery." This, I must say, would be just the thing for the lady unfortunate enough to be seated next to the horny husband of Eve McBride's friend. As his hand slides secretly up her thigh, he suddenly finds himself fondling a Beretta Model 21 or a Sig Sauer Model 230, and oh boy has he ever learned a lesson.

I am indebted to Morris Wolfe, who writes an entertaining column about magazines in the Toronto *Globe and Mail*, for my information about *Women's Self-Defense*. Unfortunately, I missed the premiere issue, which advertised a most original self-defence device for women. "SAFE-T-MAN," wrote Wolfe, "is a dummy that gives others the impression that you can have a six-foot, 180-pound black man sitting in the car beside you. There are various models. You can choose a clean-cut or tough SAFE-T-MAN," and the ad ventures, "He's a great travelling companion who doesn't give you any lip."

Yes, but SAFE-T-MAN can create social problems. Say, your boyfriend's mother, out for a late-evening stroll, catches a glimpse of you driving into your underground apartment garage with SAFE-T-MAN seated snugly beside you. Back comes the engagement ring the very next morning.

The

Innocents

Abroad

or the New Pilgrim's Progress

M ARK TWAIN, born Samuel Langhorne Clemens in 1835, set out on an "excursion to the Holy Land, Egypt, the Crimea, and intermediate points of interest" on *Quaker City*, a paddle-steamer, sailing out of New York on June 8, 1867. "The proprietors of the *Daily Alta Californian*," wrote Twain in his autobiography, "engaged me to write an account of the trip for that paper—fifty letters of a column and a half each, which would be about two thousand words per letter, and the pay to be twenty dollars per letter."

Thirty-two years old at the time, Twain set sail as just another freelance hack, and he returned as the first true master of the American idiom. This he accomplished at a time when, as Stephen Leacock wrote in his biography of Twain, "of American literature there was much doubt in Europe; of American honesty, much more, of American manners more still." But I knew nothing of this when I first came across the writings of Mark Twain, introduced to them, like most boys of my generation, through *The Adventures of Tom Sawyer*, a gift from an uncle.

I would like to claim that reading Twain for the first time made for an epiphany, but it wasn't the case. I was far more taken with *Scaramouche*, *The Three Musketeers*, *The Count of Monte Cristo*, and *Robin Hood*. Settling into bed for the night, I dreamed of humiliating the dastardly Sheriff of Nottingham with my dazzling swordplay, or galloping off with d'Artagnan and his chums, all for one, one for all. Titled ladies were my heart's desire. My problem was that I knew kids like Tom Sawyer, who might try to con me into painting their fence. It was familiar and, therefore, couldn't count as literature, like, say, Shelley's "Ode to the West Wind," which I had to copy out ten times after my class master caught me ogling a copy of *Sunbathing* in his Highroads to Reading class.

I was a slow learner. And so only later, after I had read *Huckleberry Finn* for a second time, did I grasp that I was in the presence of a great writer, somebody who could convey more about the white American's prejudice against blacks in one seemingly effortless colloquial exchange than many a polemicist could manage in ten fulminating, fact-bound pages.

Huck tells Aunt Sally, "It was the grounding of the steamer that kept us back. We blowed out a cylinder head."

"Good gracious. Anybody hurt?"

"No'm. Killed a nigger."

"Well, it's lucky; because sometimes people do get hurt."

The advertisement announcing the sailing of *Quaker City* claimed there would be cabins sufficient to accommodate "a select company" of one hundred and fifty on a "first-class steamer," which was provided "with every necessary comfort, including a library and musical instruments," as well as "an experienced physician on board." The price per passage, on what was actually America's first venture into mass tourism, a harbinger of the heavy traffic to come, was

$1,250 for adult passengers, who were advised that five dollars per day, in gold, would be sufficient to handle their needs on shore.

Anticipating what would be the case in many an over-promoted tour in years to come, the promised shipload celebrities were notable for their absence. Urgent duties, a bemused Twain noted, obliged the Reverend Henry Ward Beecher to give up the idea, and the Indian wars compelled Lt. Gen. Sherman's presence on the plains.

> A popular actress had entered her name on the ship's books, but something interfered, and *she* couldn't go. The "Drummer Boy of the Potomac" deserted, and lo, we had never a celebrity left!

As with so many of today's so-called love boats, advertised by photographs of decks adorned with sexy, bikini-clad young women, what *Quaker City* did in fact deliver was a plethora of what my daughter calls cotton-tops, or as Twain had it, venerable people, among them, three ministers of the gospel, eight doctors, sixteen or eighteen ladies, "several military and naval chieftains with sounding titles, an ample crop of 'Professors' of various kinds, and a gentleman who had 'Commissioner of the United States of America to Europe, Asia, and Africa' thundering under his name in one awful blast!" And none of them, I'm sure, suspected that they would be the victims of a rollicking satire that still reads freshly more than a century after its first publication.

In Twain's below-decks cabin, which he was to share with a young gentleman, there was room to turn around, but not to swing a cat. Happily, however, the saloon bar, which the unregenerate dubbed the "Synagogue," was a good fifty or sixty feet long, and the ship's company boasted not one, not two, but five captains.

Having crossed the Atlantic several times myself on modern liners equipped with stabilizers—still a sick-making ordeal in heavy seas—I can only marvel at what Twain and his companions must have endured on their little paddle-steamer. But Twain makes reference to only one Atlantic gale, wherein *Quaker City* "climbed aloft as if she would climb to heaven—then paused an instant that seemed like a century, and plunged headlong down again, as from a precipice."

First port of call was in the Azores, and it becomes instantly clear that the free-wheeling Twain, bless him, is not going to be shackled by political correctness. Given today's touchy political climate, I suspect there's sufficient kindling in *The Innocents Abroad* to light a fire of protest under Portuguese, Italians, Moslems, Catholics, Turks, Greeks, feminists, Arabs, American Indians, and other sensitive types. I have no doubt that *The Innocents Abroad*, released today, would be banned in schools, the author condemned as a racist, and possibly, just possibly, finding himself the subject of a *fatwa*.

The Portuguese people of the Azores, wrote Twain, lie, cheat the stranger, and are "slow, shiftless, sleepy, and lazy." He didn't fancy the women of Tangier:

> I have caught a glimpse of the faces of several Moorish women (for they are only human, and will expose their faces for the admiration of a Christian dog when no male Moor is by), and I am full of veneration for the wisdom that leads them to cover up such atrocious ugliness.

Unaware of what would become modish everywhere today, he added, "They carry their children on their backs, in a sack, like other savages the world over." But Twain did allow that "weak, stupid, ignorant" Abdul-Aziz, Sultan of Turkey, Lord of the Ottoman Empire, was a true representative of his people, which is to say he was "by nature and training filthy, brutish, unprogressive, superstitious."

He was not enchanted by Civitavecchia, which he adjudged "the finest nest of dirt, vermin, and ignorance we have found yet, except that African perdition they call Tangier, which is just like it."

Poor Twain was born too soon to appreciate that a "dwarf" is actually a "vertically challenged" person and that "cripple" has been displaced by "physically disadvantaged."

If you want dwarfs—I mean just a few dwarfs for a curiosity—go to Genoa. If you wish to buy them by the gross, for retail, go to Milan. . . . But if you want to see the very heart and home of cripples and human monsters, go straight to Constantinople.

A writer who usually got his priorities right, he was perturbed by the scarcity of whisky in Constantinople, and didn't much care for the Greeks, Turks, or Armenians in town:

[Their] morals consist only in attending church regularly on the appointed Sabbaths, and in breaking the ten commandments all the balance of the week. It comes natural to them to lie and cheat in the first place, and then go on and improve on nature until they arrive at perfection.

Twain was appalled by "the usual assemblage of squalid humanity" that waited outside the pilgrims' camp on the outskirts of Damascus:

They sat in silence, and with tireless patience watching our every motion with that vile, uncomplaining impoliteness which is so truly Indian, and which makes a white man so nervous and uncomfortable and savage that he wants to exterminate the whole tribe.
These people about us had other peculiarities, which I have noticed in the noble red man, too: they were infested with vermin, and the dirt caked on them until it amounted to bark.

He pronounced Magdala thoroughly Syrian, that is to say, "thoroughly ugly, and cramped, squalid, uncomfortable, and filthy." In Jerusalem, a city of a mere fourteen thousand souls when Twain visited, he inveighed against Moslem rule:

Rags, wretchedness, poverty, and dirt, those signs and symbols that indicate the presence of Moslem rule more surely than the crescent-flag itself, abound. Lepers, cripples, the blind, and the

idiotic, assail you on every hand, and they know but one word
of but one language apparently—the eternal "backsheesh."

Twain couldn't know that something like 135 years later the then
right-wing editor of the *Jerusalem Post*, David Bar-Illan, would bran-
dish Twain's condemnation of Moslem rule as a licence for Israel's
sole possession of the city.

The majesty of the Sphinx impressed Twain, but not the "corrugated, unsightly mountain of stone" that formed the great pyramid
of Cheops. In Cairo, of course, he was immediately surrounded
by the usual rabble, demanding backsheesh. But Twain wasn't
nearly as naughty about Cairo as an earlier distinguished visitor, the
twenty-seven-year-old Gustave Flaubert, who was there in 1849,
and wrote in *Flaubert in Egypt: A Sensibility on Tour* that on his first
day in Cairo he was immediately surrounded: "The girls were
making imitation fart sounds with their hands. The boy was excellent—short, ugly, stocky: 'If you will give me five paras I'll bring
you my mother to fuck. I wish you all kinds of prosperity, especially
a long prick.'"

One hundred and twenty-six years after it was first published, *The
Innocents Abroad* can be read not only for its literary delights, and the
pleasures of reading a major writer when he was young and just beginning to flex his muscles, but also as an enduring, no-nonsense
guide for the first-time traveller to Europe and the Holy Land.

The grandchildren of the mendacious guides Twain suffered
here, there, and everywhere will still inveigle travellers "into shirt
stores, boot stores, tailor shops," where they are entitled to a commission on sales. Perdition catch all guides, wrote Twain, after an
experience in Italy with a guide who claimed to be "the most gifted
linguist in Genoa, as far as English was concerned, and that only two
persons in the city beside himself could talk the language at all." In a

memorable exchange, Twain and his chum, the doctor, do manage to get the better of this particular guide, whom they had dubbed Ferguson:

"Come wis me, genteelmen!—come! I show you ze letter writing by Christopher Columbo!—write it himself!—write it wis his own hand! come!"

He led us to the municipal palace. After much impressive fumbling of keys and opening of locks, the stained and aged document was spread before us.

"What I tell you, genteelmen! Is it not so? See! handwriting Christopher Columbo!—write it himself!"

We looked indifferent—unconcerned. The doctor examined the document deliberately, during a painful pause.—Then he said, without any show of interest:

"Ah—Ferguson—what—what—did you say was the name of the party who wrote this?"

"Christopher Columbo! ze great Christopher Columbo!"

Another deliberate examination.

"Ah—did he write it himself, or—or how?"

"He write it himself!—Christopher Columbo! he's own handwriting, write by himself!"

"Why, I have seen boys in America only fourteen years old that could write better than that."

"But zis is ze great Christo—"

"I don't care who it is! It's the worst writing I ever saw. Now you mustn't think you can impose on us because we are strangers. We are not fools, by a good deal. If you have got any specimens of penmanship of real merit, trot them out!—and if you haven't, drive on!"

Shocks of recognition abound in *The Innocents Abroad*. I'm willing to swear, for instance, that the Fergusons Twain suffered in Milan, and elsewhere, were the progenitors of that babbler of statistics who drove my wife and me to Masada, on our extended tour of

Israel in 1992. "Their tongues are never still," wrote Twain. "They talk forever and forever . . . they interrupt every dream, every pleasant train of thought, with their tiresome cackling."

Only last year, arriving at a hotel in Paris, I stood by, a helpless victim, as the doorman removed our bags from a taxi, and extended his hand for a tip. Then another man carried our bags as far as the registration desk, and extended his hand. Finally, a third man lugged the bags to our room, and held out his hand for the obligatory *pourboire*. So I clapped hands at Twain's description of the avarice he witnessed at Vesuvius:

> They seize a lady's shawl from a chair and hand it to her and charge a penny; they open a carriage door and charge for it— shut it when you get out, and charge for it; brush your clothes and make them worse than they were before—two cents; smile upon you—two cents; bow, with lick-spittle smirk, hat in hand—two cents.

Like Twain, I have visited the Haram al-Sharif (the Noble Sanctuary) in the Old City of Jerusalem, and descended the steps of the Dome of the Rock to gawk at the fabled Stone of Foundation, where, it is claimed, Adam was moulded from dust. This is amply proven, wrote Twain, "by the fact that in six thousand years no man has been able to prove that the dirt was *not* procured here whereof he was made."

It was on this busiest of rocks, according to legend, that Cain killed Abel, and Abraham, put to the test by Jehovah, prepared to sacrifice Isaac. Jesus is said to have preached here. And this is exactly where Mohammed stopped on his *isra*, his celebrated nocturnal journey to heaven, in which he travelled from Mecca to Jerusalem and ascended to heaven on his horse. "Where Mohammed stood," wrote Twain, "he left his footprints in solid stone. I should judge he wore about eighteens."

In his autobiography, Twain wrote that he "did not lean heavily on the *Alta* letters" in composing *The Innocents Abroad*. "I found they were newspaper matter, not book matter." He used several of the letters, ten or twelve perhaps, and claims to have churned out the rest, some two hundred thousand words, in sixty days. On one level, surely, *The Innocents Abroad* was meant as an antidote to the insufferably romantic, cliché-ridden travel books of the period, written by intimidated colonials genuflecting to European culture and exaggerating the charms of the Holy Land. Giving them the raspberry, Twain wrote:

> If any man has a right to feel proud of himself, and satisfied, surely it is I. For I have written about the Coliseum, and the gladiators, the martyrs, and the lions, and yet have never once used the phrase, "butchered to make a Roman holyday." I am the only free white man of a mature age, who has accomplished this since Byron originated the expression.

Twain was especially scornful of one Wm. C. Grimes, a hack much given to florid descriptions, and another writer, identified only as C. W. E., author of *Life in the Holy Land*, who easily outdid today's most gushing travel brochure in his celebration of the Sea of Galilee, pronouncing it a "terrestrial paradise." The truth of the matter, wrote Twain, is that the Sea of Galilee, stripped for inspection, "proves to be only an unobtrusive basin of water, some mountainous desolation, and one tree."

Familiar as he was with the grandeur, and incredible variety, of the yet untamed American continent, Twain was far from enchanted with Palestine, venturing that it was a hopeless, dreary, heartbroken land. "The hills are barren," he wrote, "they are dull of color, they are unpicturesque in shape." But Twain could also respond to beauty when he stumbled on it, as he did once in Smyrna, where he observed a passing camel train:

They stride along these streets, in single file, a dozen in a train, with heavy loads on their backs, and a fancy-looking negro in Turkish costume, or an Arab, preceding them on a little donkey completely overshadowed and rendered insignificant by the huge beasts. To see a camel train laden with the spices of Arabia and the rare fabrics of Persia come marching through the narrow alleys of the bazaar, among porters with their burdens, money-changers, lamp-merchants, Alnaschars in the glassware business, portly cross-legged Turks smoking the famous narghili, and the crowds drifting to and fro in fanciful costumes of the East, is a genuine revelation of the Orient. The picture lacks nothing.

Mark Twain, then a largely unknown journalist enjoying a free-bie passage, set sail on *Quaker City* at a time when America's best-known humorists were Petroleum Vesuvius Nasby and Orpheus C. Kerr, long since forgotten, as well as Artemus Ward. Possibly trying too hard for knee-slappers, the early pages of *The Innocents Abroad* suffer from being a tad broad, proffering more burlesque than in-spired satire. But as the voyage proceeds, Twain's voice starts to emerge, gathering assurance and force. The book begins to soar. The comic genius who will go on to write *Huckleberry Finn* and *Life on the Mississippi* declares himself, staking out a territory.

One of the joys of reading *The Innocents Abroad* is the opportunity it affords us of watching the young Twain liberate himself, and Amer-ican writing, from the yoke of the European tradition, doing a nec-essary demolition job on it, and on the pilgrims who revere often second-rate pictures, proclaiming them masterpieces.

"O, wonderful!"

"Such faultless drawing!"

"Such feeling!"

The painting of *The Last Supper* was flawed for Twain, because he couldn't tell whether the disciples were Hebrews or Italians.

The Italian artists painted Italian Virgins, the Dutch painted Dutch Virgins, the Virgins of the French painters were French-women—none of them ever put into the face of the Madonna that indescribable something which proclaims the Jewess, whether you find her in New York, in Constantinople, in Paris, Jerusalem, or in the Empire of Morocco.

With the best of intentions, Jean-Paul Sartre once wrote a foolish polemic denying that there was any such thing as a "Jewish face," but Twain, poor man, didn't realize that identifying "that indescribable something" that proclaimed it could one day be adjudged politically incorrect. Mind you, even the most exacting prejudice-sniffer employed by B'nai B'rith's Anti-Defamation League would have his work cut out trying to label Twain an anti-Semite. If anything he was a Judeophile. In *The Innocents Abroad*, he contrasts the plight of the Jews confined to European and Near Eastern ghettos with their fulfilment in America, where, he wrote, they were treated just like human beings, instead of dogs:

They can work at any business they please; they can sell brand new goods if they want to . . . they can practice medicine among Christians. They can associate with them, just the same as one human being does with another human being; they don't have to stay shut up in one corner of the town; they can live in any part of the town they like best . . . they never have to run races naked through the public streets, against jackasses, to please the people in carnival time; [in America] they never have been driven by soldiers into a church every Sunday for hundreds of years to hear themselves and their religion especially and particularly cursed; at this very day, in that curious country, a Jew is allowed to vote, hold office, yea, get up on a rostrum in the public street and express his opinion of the government if the government doesn't suit him! Ah, it is wonderful.

Trading on his satirist's licence, overstating his case, Twain extols the pristine quality of Lake Tahoe over one as inconsequential as

Lake Como, and the grandeur of his cherished Mississippi opposed to such piddling bodies of water as the Tiber or the Arno, failing to acknowledge the splendour of the bridges over the latter river, or the incomparable beauty of the city it divides. The dull waters of Lake Como, he wrote, would not compare with the wonderful transparence of Lake Tahoe, "where one can count the scales of the trout at a depth of a hundred and eighty feet." Those dark and bloody Florentines, he ventured, call the Arno a river, and they help out the delusion by building bridges over it. "I do not see why they are too good to wade." And the Tiber, he complained, "is not so long, nor yet so wide, as the American Mississippi—nor yet the Ohio, nor even the Hudson."

I must also grudgingly acknowledge that those cultural ruffians who have now taken so vociferously against what they denounce as Eurocentrism do, alas, sometimes make a valid point. Celebrating Columbus, in the Pinta's shrouds, Twain wrote, "he swung his hat above a fabled sea and gazed upon *an unknown world*" (italics mine). A world unknown to Europeans, whose pretensions Twain punctures with abandon in *The Innocents Abroad*, but not to the Indians who were there since time immemorial.

Twain, a writer with an enduring affection for chicanery, and for those who can get away with it, takes obvious delight in the Church of Rome's holiest of Christian relics in the Azores:

> We visited a Jesuit cathedral nearly two hundred years old and found in it a piece of the veritable cross upon which our Savior was crucified. It was polished and hard, and in an excellent state of preservation as if the dread tragedy of Calvary had occurred yesterday instead of eighteen centuries ago.

Then, lo and behold, in the Cathedral of Notre Dame, he is shown "some nails of the true cross, a fragment of the cross itself, a part of the crown of thorns." And, in the chapel of St. John the Baptist, in Genoa, there are the relics again:

We find a piece of the true cross in every old church we go into, and some of the nails that held it together. I would not like to be positive, but I think we have seen as much as a keg of those nails.

But when he finally gets to the Church of the Holy Sepulchre, in Jerusalem, he discovers that the piece of the true cross no longer rests in the niche where they used to preserve it.

The Latin priests say it was stolen away, long ago, by priests of another sect. That seems like a hard statement to make, but we know very well that it *was* stolen, because we have seen it ourselves in several of the Cathedrals of Italy and France.

The vandalism of the *Quaker City*'s pilgrims, a harbinger of offences to come, was a recurring embarrassment to Twain. They break off fragments of Noah's tomb; and, in Damascus, from the tomb of Nimrod the Hunter. Servicing their insatiable appetite for souvenirs, they are at it again in Jerusalem, "hacking and chipping away at those arches that Jesus looked upon in the flesh." In Nazareth, coming upon a chapel rising out of a huge boulder, Twain mused, "Our pilgrims would have liked very well to get out their lampblack and stencil-plates and paint their names together with the names of the villages they hail from in America, but the priests permit nothing of the kind." In Egypt, however, the indefatigable pilgrims are at it once more, actually hacking away at the Sphinx.

Were Twain alive today, I imagine he would be relieved to know that the Japanese have displaced Americans as Europe's most acquisitive and objectionable tourists. Only last week in the Louvre my wife was unable even to glimpse the Mona Lisa in passing, surrounded as it was by hordes of Japanese, none of them the least bit interested in looking at the painting, all of them posing to have their pictures taken in turn before it. They were, however, unable to chip away at it: the Mona Lisa is now sheltered by a glass guard.

A major innovator's work is never done. As I write in London, on March 24, 1995, I learned from this morning's *Times* that Prince Charles, speaking at the British Council's English 2000 project, has warned against the threat to "proper English" from the spread of the American vernacular, which he pronounced very corrupting. Because of American influence, he said, "People tend to invent all sorts of nouns and verbs, and make words that shouldn't be. I think we have to be a bit careful, otherwise the whole thing can get rather a mess."

Obviously Prince Charles has never read Mark Twain, or Mencken on the American language, or Twain's successors (say, Hemingway, Bellow, Toni Morrison, and Raymond Carver, among others) and is unaware of how they have enriched a living language that is constantly evolving. He should be sent, immediately, a copy of *The Innocents Abroad*, the American coming-of-cultural-age book, the first major offering of a great writer, which belongs on a small shelf of Twain classics, alongside *Life on the Mississippi*, *Huckleberry Finn*, and *Connecticut Yankee*.

Going

Places

———————

Germany
1978

THE MAN FROM EXTERNAL AFFAIRS in Ottawa phoned to say, yes, somebody would meet my plane in Frankfurt. "Good," I said.

"How will he recognize you?"

"Well," I ventured, "I could always wear the obligatory yellow armband."

He was not amused.

November 1978 that was, and I was bound for Germany on behalf of external affairs. Flying over to peddle Canadian culture, scheduled to lecture at seven universities, six in West Germany, one in Austria. Grateful for the opportunity, I was also more than somewhat apprehensive. I had been to Germany twice before. Once in 1955 for a stay of six months in Munich, my best friend there a young German herky-jerky jazz musician who played with a band in Schwabbing: the Oakum Street *Fusswarmers*. I was there again in 1959, driving down from London, bound for a winter in Rome with Florence and three-year-old Daniel.

In 1955 the German cities that had been devastated by Allied bombers were still being rebuilt. Munich reverberated day and night to the sound of pneumatic drills. Unnervingly, the determined German workers, unlike their British counterparts, never seemed to take a tea break. Or strike. A young German girl I took to dinner told me

how she and her older brother had been forced to join the Hitler
Youth. "I can't tell you how terrible those years were," she said.

"I'm Jewish, you know."

"But you don't look it," she said, startled.

Four years later Florence and I had to allow that the Rhine, castles soaring out of the mists, was enchanting, and that the country
inns we stopped at served splendid soups, the innkeepers unfailingly
kind to Daniel. Our hearts began to melt. Then, one night as we
were taking our dinner in a truly *gemütlich Gasthaus*, we were surprised by an outbreak of singing from the next room. The waiter
opened the double doors to a private dining room and revealed was a
reunion of old soldiers. Rotund, good-natured fellows they seemed,
solid country folk, but they were singing the "Horst Wessel" song:

> Raise high the flags! Stand rank on rank together.
> Storm troopers march with steady, quiet tread. . . .

Art Rayner, the Canadian official who met me at Frankfurt airport,
was a rumpled, middle-aged man from North Winnipeg. I immediately took to him. We repaired to the bar, as I had two hours to kill
before my train to Trier, where I was to deliver my first lecture.
"Were you in the war?" I asked.

"I was taken at Dieppe."

"My God, weren't you guys handcuffed?"

"Yeah, we were handcuffed and shackled for a while. I was a
prisoner of war for two years."

"What in the hell are you doing here, then?"

"It's like anyplace else. There are some good types and some bad
ones."

Glancing at our bar bill, I whistled, amazed.

"You're going to find it very expensive here. It's the Germans
and the Japanese now, they've got all the money. Funny."

Bound for Trier, the birthplace of Karl Marx, I had to change
trains at Koblenz where, in December 1944, Hitler's Panzers mus-

tered for what was to be celebrated as the Battle of the Bulge. A counter-attack into the Ardennes, calculated to split the U.S. Third Army and push back the Canadians and the British along the Belgian-Dutch border. Among the leaders of this last, desperate lunge was ss General Sepp Dietrich, who was to be sentenced to twenty-five years in jail for the subsequent massacre of American prisoners. My friend Joe Dughi had fought in that battle. Marching to the front, he said, they passed too many dead GIs sprawled on the roadside, some legless, others with burst bellies, even as columns of German prisoners passed alongside, being led to a stockade behind the lines. An enraged GI smashed one in the face with his rifle butt. "Until then," said Joe, "we didn't hate them. But we figured the war was already won. And it seemed such a waste. Those dead GIs. And suddenly we all went berserk, lashing out at the Germans with our rifles."

Trier, in the Mosel Valley, is Germany's finest Roman relic. To this day, when the river is running low in summer, professors and students sift the mud for Roman coins, jugs, and other artifacts. Late at night I checked in to the Hotel Weinhof Petrisberg, high on a hill commanding the town and the river. Grimy after a long day's travelling, I was surprised to discover there was no soap in my bathroom. "Ah, but you are a foreigner," said the innkeeper. "We do not offer soap in German hotels." All the same, he fetched me a bar, the size of a bookmatch. There's a shortage of soap, I thought, because they no longer have recourse to what was once the primary source— Jewish body fat.

Unable to sleep, I turned to the *International Herald Tribune*, which offered proof, if it was still required, that the Germans weren't the only ones culpable in the murder of the six million. In The Hague on November 7, Wim Aantjes, floor leader of Holland's ruling Christian Democratic party, resigned, following the publication of a report accusing him of working for the ss during the occupation of the Netherlands.

In Madrid, a reporter had unearthed Louis Darquier de Pellepoix living in a luxury apartment. The eighty-year-old Darquier, sentenced to death *in absentia* by a French court in 1944, had been commissioner for Jewish Affairs in the wartime Vichy government. The deportation of French Jews had been necessary, he told the reporter "to get rid of those foreigners, these half-breeds, these millions of stateless people who were the origin of all our woes. They wanted the war, they led us into it. It was necessary to get them out as soon as possible, as far as possible." Asked about the million Jews who had been gassed at Auschwitz, he replied, "The Jews are always ready to do anything to make themselves interesting. Yes, they [the Germans] gassed, but they gassed lice. When the Jews arrived at the camp they were told to undress, as is normal, before going to the shower. During that time their clothes were disinfected. After the war the Jews circulated everywhere photographs showing clothes piled up . . . and they whined, 'Look, it's the underwear of our brothers who were exterminated.'"

I was not the first Québécois who had lectured at Trier. I had been preceded by the then Quebec minister of cultural development and retribution, Camille Laurin, who had told the students that in all of North America only the Québécois maintained a European cultural link. I noted that the library of Québécois literature Laurin had provided for the university included no work by Hugh MacLennan, Irving Layton, Mavis Gallant, Leonard Cohen, or me. In the new Quebec, as visualized by Laurin, there would obviously be only *ein Volk, eine Kultur.*

After my lecture my amiable host, Professor Zirker, took me to the museum, where we were shown the town's enviable collection of medieval manuscripts. Then we were led into another room, where the curator had laid out his Jewish artifacts on a long table especially for my perusal. As we browsed through early documents, I cynically concluded that they would come to an abrupt stop in 1933. But I had underestimated the curator. He led me to a poster proclaiming the Nürnberg laws of September 15, 1935, which deprived Jews of German citizenship and forbade marriages between Jews and Aryans. Next he showed me a folio of Jewish identity cards. Photographs, fingerprints, basic information. "Please note," he said, "that this poor man is wearing his First World War medals, as if that was going to help him."

Finally we came to a stack of exercise book pages, lined sheets on which the names and addresses of Trier's Jewish population had been typed. A ruled line had been drawn in red ink through each name, followed by a policeman's notation. To begin with, "DESTINATION LODZ," a euphemism for Auschwitz, and then, simply, "DESTINATION UNKNOWN."

Noticing how flushed I had become, the curator said, "Some, you know, escaped to France."

"Some?"

"A few."

But for most of Trier's Jews there had been no gravestones, just a red line drawn through their names in a policeman's exercise book. That, and a final shower. Zyklon-B.

"Welcome to Ottawa-on-the-Rhine," said Canadian embassy official Paul Adams as I alighted from the train at Bonn. The students I lectured to were lively and intelligent, many of them effortlessly fluent in three languages. Afterwards, an appealing young man approached me. He had travelled to both America and Russia. "Wherever I go," he said, "I am hated by so many people. I didn't make the past. I wish to be proud of being German. What am I to do?"

I certainly didn't hate him, I said, but the Trier exercise book of names still burned bright in my mind, and I had to tell him about that, too.

November 9 that was, the anniversary of *Kristallnacht*, the Night of the Broken Glass. Forty years earlier, on November 7, a seventeen-year-old German-Jewish refugee shot and killed the third secretary of the German embassy in Paris. Two nights later, Germany's synagogues were set on fire. The plate-glass windows of more than seventy-five hundred Jewish-owned shops were smashed, then the shops were looted. Jews were beaten up; they were raped, they were murdered. As sexual intercourse with Jews was forbidden, those who had raped were expelled from the party, but those who had merely murdered were not charged. Insurance money due to the Jews was confiscated, and they were obliged to pay for the destruction of their own property. They were also fined, collectively, one billion marks for, as Goering put it, "abominable crimes."

In 1938 there were 700,000 Jews in Germany. Forty years later the Jewish population was estimated to be 27,000, but *Kristallnacht* was being publicly acknowledged. November 9, 1978, was ordained a day of remembrance throughout Germany. Chancellor Helmut Schmidt, speaking in a synagogue that had been built on the site of the one that had been burnt down in 1938, said there were still no words to express the shame and bitterness or to explain the catastrophe. The chancellor called *Kristallnacht* "a station on the road to hell."

Florence joined me in Bonn, and the next day we drove to Cologne. The bomb damage in Cologne had been enormous, and, as in other pulverized German cities, destroyed buildings had been hastily replaced by grey concrete slabs: apartment buildings that were functional, but grim. Fortunately the old cathedral quarter of the city was largely intact. After my lecture our host, Dr. Pache, took us to a beer hall in the old quarter for dinner. Immediately I recognized a familiar smell and, suddenly, there it was. A stout, blue-aproned waiter sailing past, balancing a trayful of what was unmistakably the grated potato pancakes of my childhood. "Look," I said to Florence with appetite, "latkes."

"Oh, you mean *Reibenkuchen*," said Dr. Pache.

"Do I?"

"It's a traditional Cologne dish."

Traditional in Cologne and in my grandmother's kitchen as well. Jewish and German history is entwined in more than the Holocaust. If I could understand some German, it was because of the Yiddish I could dimly remember from my childhood. Germans call their dumplings *Knödel*; we know them as *knaydl*.

Dr. Pache told us that there were a million unemployed in Germany, and that the new generation of students tended to be resolutely conservative. Though there was a plethora of scholarships available to them to study in America, it was increasingly difficult to find candidates willing to take them up. What concerned the young were jobs with a favourable pension scheme, and they feared being absent for even a year lest they be overlooked.

Having delivered my lecture three times in four days, I escaped with Florence to fabled Baden-Baden for the weekend. The spa of Baden-Baden, in the valley of the River Oos where the Black Forest slopes down to the Rhine, is justifiably famous for its hot springs and elegant casino. Following Dostoevsky, Nietzsche, Bismarck, Napoleon III, and Queen Victoria, who used to summer here, we strolled down the celebrated Lichtentaler Allee, an avenue of oak trees planted as early as 1655, leading us through the English garden with its magnolias, gingkos, tulip trees, and silver maples. Emerging from the tranquil park, however, we were once again caught up in the ever-intrusive more recent past. Posted on a fence outside a church was a sign proclaiming a sermon in commemoration of *Kristallnacht*. Alongside there was a display of photographs that had been taken in Baden-Baden on the night of November 9, 1938, and after. They showed ss officers in the synagogue, smashing religious artifacts, flames curling out of the windows. Jews, their arms raised overhead, being paraded down the town's main street.

In the morning we sought out 2 Baderstrasse, the boarding house where Dostoevsky had lodged with his pregnant wife during the summer of 1867. We found it, but there was no plaque, which seemed rank ingratitude considering how much money he had squandered at the tables.

Monday I lectured in Mainz. The rest of the week we seemed to be constantly rushing to or from railway stations, as I performed three more times in Erlangen, Augsburg, and Vienna. Impressions, images, were caught on the fly. No nook, no cranny between the rocks in the hills overlooking the Mosel was too small or inaccessible to be cultivated with vines. As we travelled up and down the Rhine it was evident, looking at recent construction, that Second World War bomb damage had been almost total. Germany had been flattened. But even as I found myself moved to sympathy, freight trains intruded. Again and again we passed slower freight trains or watched boxcars being shunted in the rail yards. Many of the boxcars seemed ancient and had quite possibly been used in the forties. Scrubbed down, no doubt, since carrying Jews to the ovens of Auschwitz. Watching the boxcars pass renewed my rage.

And yet—and yet—we were treated with enormous courtesy everywhere. Professors couldn't have been more hospitable. The students I met were a most likeable bunch. I vacillated between being upset by the bomb damage that was evidently wanton in some places and feeling that it was not enough.

Striding through the magnificent Volksgarten in Vienna, remnants of imperial grandeur on all sides, the Canadian official who accompanied me pointed out the balcony of the Hofburg from which Hitler spoke after *Anschluss*, the annexation of Austria. "There were hundreds of thousands of Viennese here for the occasion," he said. "No room to move. Everybody cheering wildly. But today, miraculously, you can find nobody, absolutely nobody, in Vienna who will admit to having been there."

I had my difficulties in Germany with anybody fifty years of age or over. Even as we chatted about politics over sherry, or compared cultures at immensely civilized dinner parties, I found myself retreating to wonder, Where were you, my good man, on *Kristallnacht*? Where were you when your Jewish neighbours were being marched down the streets, DESTINATION UNKNOWN? Probably you were too cultivated to be directly involved. Maybe you didn't even approve. But how did you shut out their screams? Did your father draw the shutters? Your mother turn up the gramophone? Where were you, you bastards?

One cold foggy night, standing on a station platform, waiting for yet another train, we became aware of a group of drunken young rowdies. They wore funny hats, red jackets, and staggered about singing in bold voices. I reached for one of my suitcases, ready to swing it if provoked. Then, just as our train pulled in, I finally made out what they were singing. It wasn't the "Horst Wessel" song. It was "We All Live in a Yellow Submarine."

Speaking in that new synagogue in Cologne, on the anniversary of *Kristallnacht*, Chancellor Helmut Schmidt said, "Today's Germans are mostly innocent—more than two-thirds of them born after the war or children during the war. Yet we have to carry the political inheritance of the guilty and draw the consequences. That is our responsibility." The German people, he concluded, could only ask for forgiveness.

Safari

A WEEK BEFORE our scheduled departure for Kenya in 1982, excitement ruled our home. After all, we were soon to abandon wintry Montreal for the fabled Aberdare Salient, Lake Baringo in the Great Rift Valley, and the Masai Mara Game Reserve. Lions, leopards, elephants, zebras, antelopes, and gazelles. Florence and I took to studying Ker and Downey Tented Safari brochures in bed. Our insect-proof tents, we were assured, would include bedside lamps, washbasins, and adjoining shower and toilet tents. African crew would do our laundry overnight, except for women's lingerie, a task they took to be humiliating. Our group was to consist of three couples. All old friends, all new to Africa. Remember, a thrilling covering letter enjoined us, to bring two pair of sunglasses. "It's one thing to drop them from a Land Rover; another, in murky, crocodile infested waters."

A week before we left, my arm rendered leaden by a cholera shot, I repaired to my favourite downtown bar. How about one for the road, a crony asked. "Certainly," I replied. "*But first,*" I added in a voice calculated to boom across the bar, "*I must take my malaria pill.*"

We landed in Nairobi (5,500 feet above sea level, population 835,000) early in the morning, flying overnight from London. A testing time, this, for at the Jomo Kenyatta Airport we were to meet the two guides with whom we would trek through the reserves for the next eleven days. If the chemistry weren't right, we all agreed, the trip could be a washout. Happily, our apprehensions were for nothing. David Mead, forty-three, and Alan Binks, thirty-eight, turned out to be affable, cultured fellows, both of them fluent in Swahili. Truly good companions.

Mead, a Sandhurst graduate, had been in Africa since 1968, a professional white hunter until it was ruled illegal in 1977. Binks, a naturalist and photographer, emigrated to Africa in 1967, and was now a Kenyan citizen. "In England," he said, "the horizon meant the next garden hedge. Here, the space is immense." But, he allowed, there were problems in Kenya. "We have no oil, no natural resources. Just coffee, tea, and tourism."

The Norfolk, where we were to stay overnight, is possibly the most legendary hotel in East Africa. Built in 1904 by Major C. G. R. Ringer, its guest list since then would seem to include just about everybody accounted for in *Burke's Peerage*, as well as Teddy Roosevelt and his son Kermit, Isak Dinesen (Karen Blixen), author of the classic *Out of Africa*, Winston Churchill, and, of course, Mr. Hemingway. Abraham Brock, who arrived from South Africa in 1903, when the lands of the Great Rift Valley were proposed as a projected colony for Jewish settlement—a new Canaan that was just not to be—bought the hotel in 1927. It was now part of the Brock chain, which included Treetops, the Lake Baringo Club, and seven other hotels and lodges. Brock was reported to have played a crucial role in the celebrated Israeli raid on Entebbe, in 1976, which liberated Israeli captives hijacked by the PLO. It was said that he was the one who negotiated refuelling rights in Kenya for the Israeli special forces, en route to Uganda.

There was no need, incidentally, to fret about safari suits. Once installed at the Norfolk, we hurried over to Colpro, a shop on Kimathi Street run by enterprising Indians, where we were equipped with the appropriate cotton safari suits, very reasonably priced, and altered within a couple of hours.

The churning streets of downtown Nairobi teem with persistent hawkers of ugly, factory-made souvenirs. Shoeshine boys lie in wait everywhere. Possibly the only place where you can safely buy authentic indigenous jewellery and artifacts is at the government-run African Heritage, a handsome shop. We paused there so that Florence could select some things for our children. Her modest purchases in hand, she was boorishly thrust aside from the cash-register counter by burly American secret servicemen, as then vice-president George Bush laid out his collection of spears and shields and masks. The elegant black woman clerk toted up the items and handed Bush a considerable bill. "I'm the vice-president of the United States," said Bush. "Don't I get a discount?"

"No, you don't," she replied.

From African Heritage, it was only a short stroll to the famous Thorn Tree Bar at the New Stanley Hotel, an obligatory stop, even if you pass on the impala stew. Ensconced on the terrace, I asked a settler at a neighbouring table about the abortive air force–led coup of last August 1. "What, in fact, happened to the air force?"

"They were, um, disbanded."

"Do you mean . . . liquidated?"

"Quite."

Kenya, independent since 1963, is a one-party state with a population of some fifteen million, maybe fifty thousand of them white. The autocratic successor to the great Jomo Kenyatta, President Daniel arap Moi was staunchly supported by the local press in 1982. On November 13, the page-one headline in the *Daily Nation* proclaimed, "THUGS IN POLLS RACE, SAYS MOI":

Some political *majambazi* [thugs] have joined the race for the Nakuru North parliamentary seat," President Moi said yesterday.

The President said this when he conducted a harambee funds drive at Ol Kalou, Nyandarua District, Central Province. A total of about Sh. 3.5 million was collected.

President Moi, who spoke in Kiswahili, said he did not mind

anybody being elected. But he urged the electorate to vote in a Nyayo man.

He said he did not take pleasure in detaining anybody and added that some political *majambazi* had rushed to enter the race in Nakuru North street.

He also asked the electorate not to elect *wakora* [hooligans]. He said he was not interested in any group and warned people not to blame him if things went wrong.

A story on page four noted that bargain-hunter George Bush might cut short his African tour to fly to Moscow for the funeral of President Leonid Brezhnev, whose death had been announced the day before. And, on page seven, there was an interesting letter to the editor from George Wanyoike of Nairobi:

During the recent Commonwealth Games in Brisbane, Australia, I noticed that while all countries fielded national teams the United Kingdom fielded hers on tribal lines.

There were tribal teams from England, Scotland, Wales and Northern Ireland. What should we expect next time: Eskimos and Quebecan Canadians being fielded as separate teams or Luos, Kikiyus and Kalenjins being fielded as separate teams? This should be discouraged.

A Moi supporter, Raphael Obwori Khalumba, surfaced in the letters column of Nairobi's *True Love with Trust* magazine:

I congratulate President Moi, the government and the Kenya Army, GSU and Police for suppressing the insurgence by the KAF rebels on August 1, 1982. The episode shall remain a dark and unforgettable mark in the Kenya history. The perpetrators of the attempted coup should be hunted down and punished severely. If it were not for our loyal forces, we don't know what shape Kenya would have assumed by now.

God is with the government of Kenya. There is no leadership as dedicated as that of our beloved President Daniel arap
Moi in the whole of Africa. God bless Moi, our country Kenya,
the armed forces, and all the people of Kenya.

Back at the Norfolk my telephone rang and rang, but each time I
picked it up the line was dead. I finally took my problem to the clerk
at the front desk.

"You go back to your room," he said, "and the operator will ring
you."

"But it's no use, don't you see? The line is dead. I can't get a dial
tone."

"You go back. Operator will ring you."

I did. She did. The line was dead. I returned to the front desk.

"Your telephone doesn't work," said the desk clerk. "It will be
fixed."

"Thank you. When?"

"We must get an engineer from the post office."

"When will that be?"

"Unfortunately, he just left. He will return, if he has a car."

A couple of hours later I confronted the front-desk clerk yet
again.

"If the engineer comes," he said, "your phone will certainly be
fixed."

"What if he doesn't come?"

"We like to think he will."

We all went to dinner at Alan Bobbé's Bistro, reputedly the best
restaurant in East Africa. I didn't try the parrot's eye, a specialty, but
I can certainly vouch for the smoked sailfish, the truly giant shrimp
from the Indian Ocean, and the king crab.

Early the next morning, we set out with our guides in two Toyota
Land Cruisers. The eight Africans who would lay out our luxurious

camp in the Aberdare Salient, some one hundred miles north of Nairobi, had moved on ahead of us. In theory you are supposed to keep to the left-hand side of the road in Kenya, but in practice you drive on either side, wherever the potholes are fewest. Again and again we passed *mantatus*, astonishingly overcrowded little makeshift buses run by private entrepreneurs. There were pathetic shanty towns, slapped together out of waste tin and battered crates. Pineapple and coffee plantations. Long, lean, languid Africans tending to papyrus stands by the dusty roadside. Men cutting building bricks out of rock in a roadside quarry, women stooping over tiny vegetable plots, more men ambling along the road, carrying pangas. Indeed, wherever we drove there were people out walking, infinitely patient, the women sometimes carrying black parasols, more often knitting, as they passed, the men in tribal attire, stopping to wave, the children reaching out for candies. And then there were the magnificent flame trees in flower. Fever trees looming over muddy streams. The small whistling thorn, umbrella trees, and the spectacular euphorbia, or candelabra, trees. Finally, at 1 p.m., we arrived at the gates of Aberdare National Park, some sixty-five hundred feet above sea level:

> Visitors enter this national park entirely at their own risk. Please exercise care and keep a safe distance from any dangerous animals. They have the right of way.

Immediately beyond the gates was our first wild beast, a warthog, seemingly bemused, willing to pose for pictures. It was a hefty specimen, say two hundred pounds, with an enormous wart-filled face and two sets of menacing tusks, the lower with a razor-sharp cutting edge. Soon we would discover these hogs are ubiquitous in the Aberdare as well as the Masai Mara, constantly on the trot, followed by their mates and troops of piglets. If animals drank booze, the barrel-chested warthog would be a beer-belter. A hard hat. Ugly yet somehow endearing. The giraffes, on the other hand, which Isak Dinesen described as "rare, long-stemmed, speckled, gigantic flowers," would certainly affect pince-nez and sip Dom Perignon.

We were hardly into the forested salient when David Mead said, "There were elephants through here, maybe in the last hour." And round a bend in the track there they were, seven of them, munching punishingly prickly thorn-tree branches. Elephants, wrote Isak Dinesen, "travelling through the dense native forest . . . pacing along as if they had an appointment at the end of the world." Later we would come upon a herd of them, frolicking in a muddy waterhole. Sometimes, however, they were not so sweet-tempered, alertly extending their huge floppy ears, raising their trunks to trumpet at us. "They are perfectly capable," Binks informed us jauntily, "of stomping on a car, flattening everybody in it." Then he told us about the time a hippo, grazing in the evening, had espied a foolish woman with a camera poised between him and his waterhole, cutting off his retreat. He promptly chomped her to bits. "Of course, I think at least one tourist should be scarfed a year. It adds a certain spice to the safari, don't you think?"

We reached camp, exhilarated, and settled into a delicious lunch. Actually, the best food we would eat in Kenya would be prepared right in camp, our miracle-making chef baking bread and cooking roasts, equipped with nothing more than two metal ammunition cases laid out on a carefully tended bed of hot charcoal.

In the afternoon we caught sight of our first bunch of black-and-white colobus monkeys, squealing as they squirted from tree to tree. Wherever the baboons gathered, two or maybe three of them stood on the high ground to guard against predators. Herds of large black Cape buffalo, their curled horns massive, scowled at us from every open glade. These weighty buffalo, dripping animosity, seemed already cast in bronze.

Here and there in the salient there were large, peculiar craters. "Oh, those," said Mead. "This was once Mau Mau country. They hid out here, living off the land, their only protection against the cold the animal skins that were glued to their backs. The British scatter-bombed the area, hoping to flush them out. All they did was to create havoc for the wildlife."

The densely forested, hilly, dark green Aberdare was filled with breathtaking surprises. Round one rising bend in the road at twilight we came upon our first leopard—liquid, muscular grace—fondly nuzzling the head of a long-dead antelope. Probably not his own kill, Mead explained, because a leopard promptly removes his kill to a high fork in a convenient tree, where he can ravage it at ease, proof against thieving lions and hyenas. Reacting to our presence, the leopard sprung free of the dead antelope, glared at us, and then, even more disturbed by a sudden burst of thunder, retreated into the bush. Not quickly, but with considerable grace.

In the evening, less than twenty-four hours on the land but already old Africa hands, our safari suits gratifyingly mud-caked, we gathered round a fire, prompting Mead to tell us tales of his hunting exploits. A reticent man, he made light of a serious injury he had suffered when a wounded Cape buffalo got his horns into him, "tossing me like I was a piece of paper." There are no stuffed animal heads or horns or tusks mounted in Mead's home on the outskirts of Nairobi. In fact, he made it abundantly clear that he had never gone in for wanton destruction, only very selective killing. If animals were to survive on the reserves for another generation, he felt, sentiment wouldn't do it; it had to be made plain to Kenyans that the animals were a natural resource, a rare economic asset. They brought in tourists. Foreign currency. "The truth is," he said, "I much prefer this kind of safari to hunting."

The next morning we came across a dead buffalo lying in a shallow stream. Probably a lion kill. And then, tracking vultures circling high over a distant hill, we set off in pursuit and discovered an even more malodorous buffalo corpse being devoured by those fierce, ugly birds, a blight of them squabbling over their putrescent spoils.

In the afternoon, en route to Jonathan Leakey's Island Camp, on Lake Baringo, we made a pit stop at the Aberdare Country Club, a grand old colonial mansion, commanding an achingly beautiful view of what had once been a white settler's coffee plantation. Mead told us, "Most of them had to sell. The estates, some of which ran to forty thousand acres, were broken up. But, really, they had little to complain about. They came here worth nothing and sold their farms for half a million quid or better in '63. I think they were jolly lucky."

Bumping over dusty roads through an ever-changing, always-spectacular landscape, we had soon crossed into the Rift Valley country, hot and humid, the dung-coloured hills, seemingly moth-eaten, yielding to soaring purplish walls on both sides. Hard by the Menenga Crater, we drove past President Moi's enormous estate. Here, in the president's very own tribal district, the road, not surprisingly, was actually paved. Finally we took a motorboat across the crocodile-infested waters of Lake Baringo to Leakey's Island Camp, remembering not to drop our sunglasses. The camp, over-looking the lake, is hewn right out of the cliffside, embedded with cacti and desert roses and acacias. Something of a South Seas oasis in the middle of the Rift country. Our double tents, tucked into the cliffside with integrated flush toilets and showers, were certainly commodious, but the food was mediocre. In a land where the fresh pineapple is truly succulent, we were served tinned pineapple juice for breakfast. But never mind; birdwatching the next morning was simply marvellous. I had never seen such a gaudy, splendiferous display. Suffice it to say that there are around fifteen hundred different species of birds in Kenya, almost as many as in all of North America.

In the morning we quit the Island Camp for nearby Lake Bogoria, pausing en route to marvel over the termite heaps that loomed everywhere, some of them twenty feet high, representing fifty years of labour. And then there were the gorgeous elands, the largest antelopes on earth, with their splendid corkscrew horns. Dr. Chris

Hillman, of Nairobi University, writes: "The eland is the most common animal in bushman rock paintings. Louis Leakey reckoned it was second only to the giraffes, over the whole of Africa, for the frequency of depiction in prehistoric paintings and rock engravings." And as we approached the shores of Lake Bogoria itself, there was an endless swirling slash of pink, soon to be revealed as flocks of flamingos, thousands of them.

From Lake Bogoria, we scooted across the country to the Masai Mara, where we would camp for five days. Giraffes. Waterbuck. Herds of roaming elephants. Wildebeests. Prides of lions. Cheetahs. Leopards. Hippos. Crocodiles. Hyenas. Jackals. Baboons. But, above all, herds of exquisite antelope and gazelles: impala, topi, Thomson's gazelle, and Grant's gazelle. Gazelles, gazelles, breaking into a trot and, if alarmed, literally flying across the flat open country.

At first sight, the Masai Mara, its horizon endless, seems the most enchanting of pastoral scenes. All those grazing animals. This, you might think, is how things were in the Garden of Eden. But, on closer examination, it is most certainly not a peaceable kingdom. Put plainly, it's a meat rack—those exquisitely frolicking antelope and gazelles being coolly eyed by the predators on the plain, none more obscene than the loping, slope-shouldered hyena, constantly on the prowl. In the morning, these vile creatures are everywhere, their pelts greasy and bellies bloated.

One evening—a scene right out of hell, this—we came upon a pack of thirty-three hyenas, hooting and cackling as they fed on a freshly dead hippo. Finding the hippo hide impenetrable—although hyenas have the strongest jaws of any animal on the plain—they had eaten their way in through the softer anus, emerging again and again with dripping chunks of meat or gut, thrusting the scavenging jackals aside. The lion may be king of the animals, but, Mead assured me, he had seen a swift pack of hyenas move a lion off its kill more than once. Still, the lions are feared. One morning we caught two cheetahs gorging themselves on a wildebeest, eating hastily, constantly alert for lions who could rob them of their feast. But the lions are not invincible. Another time we came upon two lions on the hunt, attacking a herd of Cape buffalo. Eight of the buffalo formed a line, lowering their heads and charging, driving off the lions.

At twilight we watched the gazelles and antelope cavort, a sight I never tired of, but, come morning, their skulls and ribcages would be strewn across the plain, being picked clean by vultures.

Our camp, neatly tucked into a stand of shade trees, was actually a corner that a bunch of baboons called home. Perched high and quarrelsome in the trees, they did not take kindly to our intrusion, pissing on our tents and pelting them with sticks at night. This, however, was not the only thing to disturb our sleep. After dark there came the shrieking of birds. Hooting hyenas on the prowl. Lions coughing. Once we wakened to find an elephant feeding on a thorn tree only six feet behind our tent.

After we turned in, zipping up our tents, a guard patrolled the camp all night, panga at the ready. He was there to protect not so much us, but rather the kitchen tent from hungering hyenas, capable of biting right through a frying pan.

Weeks after our safari was done, I continued at home to awaken at 3 a.m. to after-images of Africa. A Masai tribesman, his robes brilliantly coloured, his spear in hand, strolling casually towards us across the open plain. A leopard springing out of its cave and darting into the night. Adolescent topis at play, locking horns, testing themselves. Lions lazing in the sun or padding in a slow line through the tall grass. Elephants gathering their vulnerable young into the centre of their circle. And the giraffes, elegant beyond compare, always out there on the far horizon, looming over the trees.

Go, go, before it's gone. Before the rough tracks of the Masai Mara are paved and hamburger havens and pizza parlours spring up and the Masai herdsman who approaches across the plain has his ears plugged into a Walkman. Or is talking into a cellular phone.

Marrakech

CHARGED with anticipation, Florence and I boarded Royal Air Maroc's weekly Montreal-to-Casablanca flight on the evening of Feb. 1, 1985. "Fascinate your seat belts," the stewardess enjoined us. Sound advice, that, as little on board our jumbo jet seemed to work properly. As we took off, overhead baggage compartments whacked open, the locks broken. Reading lights failed to function. The old Arab in the row immediately in front of us curled up to sleep, his bare feet dangling in the aisle. But, what the hell, we were bound—*Insha'Allah*—for Marrakech. The Koutoubia. The souk. The Saayin's tombs. The fabled Djemaa el F'na. Hotel La Mamounia.

Landing in Casablanca the next morning, I resisted an impulse to bark, "Round up the usual suspects." Instead, we joined the scrum for the connecting flight making the short hop to Marrakech. Once settled into my seat, I opened the handsomely produced booklet provided by the tourist office of the Kingdom of Morocco, which began: "Everything in Marrakech entices the authenticity of a secular town, prime in the tradition of the refined and the fairy."

GQ magazine, my ever-obliging employer, had arranged for a man known to them, a trustworthy guide with a rented car, to meet us at the airport. Abdeslam Aarab was to be at our service all week. But he failed to turn up at the airport and after a twenty-minute wait we elected to proceed to Hotel La Mamounia.

"In the shade of the proud Koutoubia minaret," writes Dr. M. Mohamed Sijelmassi in his book, *La Mamounia*, "a few steps from the famed Djemaa el F'na, stands hotel LA MAMOUNIA, serene in its majesty." Palatial, its exterior coloured ochre like the walls of the city. Happily, once inside, there was no mistaking it for a Hilton or Sheraton. This was truly elsewhere. There is a pillared lobby with high carved ceilings, wooden beams, graceful arches and arabesques, sumptuous leather sofas and intimate alcoves, eight-pointed Moroccan star pools, fine chandeliers and carpets. La Mamounia takes its name from the surrounding two-centuries-old park, once called "Arset El Mamoun." Running to some twenty acres, it was originally given to Prince Moulay Mamoun, the fourth son of Sultan Sidi Mohamed Ben Abdellah, as a wedding gift, and here he once entertained his cronies with orchestras and sinuous belly dancers. The walled park is enriched by a splendid display of bougainvillea, acacias, jacarandas, jasmine, palms, and rose bushes, and Florence and I repaired there for a stroll before lunch. Soon enough we ran into other vacationing couples: German, French, and British.

Americans, it's true, may be overfamiliar on holidays. "Hi, my name is Billy. I'm in software." But Europeans are something else again. To begin with, spilling over with good feeling, I greeted other strolling couples with a cheerful good morning, only to be rebuffed. So I adapted to the proper European mode. When I next encountered a couple in that perfumed park I glared at the husband and he glared right back, establishing that we were both not only well bred, but also men of substance.

After lunch, there was a phone call from Abdeslam Aarab. He had met the wrong flight. I told him we were suffering from jet lag and asked if he could meet us outside the hotel at 10 a.m. the next morning. Certainly, he said.

February 3. Sunday. Instead of awakening to the depressing roar of snowploughs churning up the streets below our apartment in Montreal, we rose to the muezzin's call to prayer over a loudspeaker and the swooping of birds in the park. We took breakfast on our balcony, which overlooked the orange grove, and there I got my first insight into the division of labour between the sexes in Morocco.

A man, carrying a long staff, lazily jiggled a tree, sending oranges bouncing everywhere. The three women squatting below hurried to gather them up, carrying them off in baskets balanced on their heads. When they returned the man would nonchalantly jiggle the tree branches again, sending the women scrambling once more.

At precisely 10 a.m. we stepped outside the hotel, where an obviously streetwise young man gave me a cheerful wave. "Are you Abdeslam Aarab?" I asked.

"Yes."

"Good. Have you a rented car with you?"

"We rent car later. Now we take taxi to souk."

"I don't like the look of him," said Florence.

"Oh, come on now. They vouched for him at *GQ*."

Off we went to Djemaa el F'na, where a police car slowed down to scrutinize our guide. He slid swiftly away from us. "I be right back," he said.

"Why are the police interested in him?" asked Florence.

"Relax. He's okay."

Any *berraniyim*—or foreigners—foolish enough to be caught standing still in the swirling Djemaa el F'na, perhaps the most famous square in all of Morocco, are as vulnerable as ducks in season. We were immediately besieged by beggars, cripples, amputees, and Chleuhs—boys clinking tiny finger-cymbals at us. I had run out of coins by the time our grinning guide had returned, sending beggars off with curses. Men streamed past in hooded djellabas, veiled women in haiks: Moors, Berbers, Arabs. Snake charmers and storytellers and dancers and orange vendors were all working the square, which reputedly dates back to the twelfth century, old as the Koutoubia itself. Dodging supplicants, we made for the narrow, winding, rush-covered streets of the souk, where everything imaginable was being sold out of holes in the ochre walls. Spices, kaftans, hammered copper trays, gold, carpets, meat, bread, pots and pans, Spanish fly and hashish. "I will take you to best places to buy," said our guide. "Where no tourists go."

"You see," I said to Florence, "he knows his stuff."

"You never accept first price," our guide said. "You bargain."

Elbowing our way through narrow teeming passages, bargaining as instructed, we bought spices and slippers, a kaftan, and eventually an expensive carpet. In each carpet vendor's shop we were served mint tea by an ingratiating proprietor even as his minions rolled out rug after rug for our perusal: "This one is from the Berber Picasso."

Following every purchase our guide would ask us to wait outside while he darted back into the shop.

"He's collecting his commission," said Florence.

He took us to rent a car and then I told him we were tired, we would return to our hotel for lunch, and wouldn't need him again until five o'clock. "As you say," he sang out, treating us to a cheerful salute before he sped off in my rented car.

"Did you leave him with the registration?" asked Florence.

"Oh, he probably just wants to take his girlfriend out for a spin. Why deny him?"

No sooner did we enter La Mamounia than the desk clerk called me over. "Mr. Richler?"

"Yes."

"Abdeslam Aarab would like you to phone him. He apologizes for being late. He arrived just five minutes after you left. I hope you had an enjoyable morning."

Florence, to her credit, did not say a word, but, in appreciation of my need, led me directly to the Churchill Bar. The real Abdeslam Aarab, who appeared an hour later, turned out to be knowledgeable, unassuming, a good companion. He also had a rented car. "I hope," he said, obviously concerned, "that you didn't buy anything in the souk while you were with that other man."

"Of course not," I said.

Abdeslam commiserated with me as I sweated it out until five o'clock, wondering if our obliging guide would ever show up. Me, I figured he was now on the road to Rabat. In my mind's eye, I added an intriguing item to my *GQ* expense account: "One rented car, still missing, $18,000." But the imposter did turn up at five o'clock, accompanied me to return the rented car, and was promptly dismissed.

Monday morning we set out with Abdeslam for the Koutoubia minaret, built in the twelfth century, its pink stone soaring more than two hundred feet over the city. We visited the El-Mansour mosque and the ruins of the El-Badi Palace, a stork nesting in the reaches of the highest remaining turret. Negotiating our way through the narrow winding alleys of the medina, we turned a corner and stumbled on a funeral procession. Solemn, chanting djellaba-clad men trotting past, rushing a body held aloft on a bamboo stretcher to the cemetery. Making our way between donkey carts and bicycles, we passed wizened old men in burnouses, squatting patiently behind their modest wares set out in the dirt: six pounds of carrots or a pyramid of chicken eggs. Women sifted through mounds of garbage. Every gap in the wall was a shop offering a variety of beans or grain in sacks, or ancient rust-eaten fridges, or automobile tires so worn you couldn't give them away at home. TV aerials sprouted incongruously here and there and in an alley of seemingly abject poverty we came upon a video-cassette shop, displaying films in French and Arabic. Later I was to learn that some of the doors on those narrow smelly streets actually opened into magnificent homes set round cool spacious courtyards. But, on balance, the medina seemed desperately poor. Then, winding around yet another sharp corner, we were surprised by a fashion shoot in progress. Lovely willowy models, their shoes wiped clean of dung, posturing against a background of something like medieval misery.

Marrakech, a city of some 450,000 souls, is set against a backdrop of the Atlas Mountains, their jagged, snow-capped peaks jutting into all but perennially blue skies. Winston Churchill, ensconced in La Mamounia's opulence, loved to paint the surrounding countryside. "We have had very many famous people stay here," said the hotel manager. "Churchill, the Aga Kahn, Nixon, Orson Welles, General de Gaulle, Jimi Hendrix, and what's-his-name, the Kissinger."

Marrakech, an oasis, was first settled in the eleventh century by a Bedouin tribe, the Almoravids, whose power once extended north as far as Andalusia. The original city consisted of a tented encampment, a stone-built casbah, and a stockade surrounded by jujube trees.

Back at La Mamounia, I ate lunch with the hotel's assistant manager. The hotel, often strike-bound, he said, employed 403 workers. "Four hundred and three workers equals 202 Communists," he added.

"I watched some of them harvest oranges the other morning," I said.

The assistant manager sighed. "If 403 workers eat two oranges a day," he said, "that makes 806 oranges."

That night we dined with Abdeslam at Stylia, a restaurant in the medina. We entered through a dimly lit passage redolent of incense, its carpets strewn with rose petals, into what had once been the immense inner courtyard of a private residence. We washed our hands with perfumed towels and then broke off chunks of an excellent pigeon pie followed by an equally succulent tagine of lamb with olives and lemon. The dessert, called M'hanncha, or "the snake," made with the thinnest almond pastry I have ever eaten, was especially grand. But, to tell the truth, after four days of unrelieved spicy exotic fare, the stuff of my dreams was now poached eggs on toast or maybe a tuna salad.

Tuesday we took to the surrounding mountains. Most of the rivers dry, their beds rock-strewn. Tooling past miles of olive groves we often came across very young shepherd boys, long staffs in hand, tending the family's provenance, five or six scrawny sheep. Thirty miles out of Marrakech, we seemed to have plunged back into biblical times. But as La Mamounia's assistant manager put it to me at the poolside, "They are very happy up there in the mountains and they live to be very old without doctors."

On Wednesday we drove into the higher Atlas Mountains, bound for Asni. A spectacular, white-knuckler of a drive it was, too, with many a hairpin turn, the bumpy one-lane road falling away to steep sheer cliffs. Rounding a high bend, you toot your horn, bless the Messenger of God, and hope for the best. Only the most tenacious of trees rose out of crevices between the rocks, and here and there were settlements composed of ochre mud huts.

Until the establishment of Israel there were many Jews rooted in these mountains, but now few remain. As we bounced along in our car, past sickly old men riding sidesaddle on their emaciated donkeys, their wives following on foot, I offered a silent prayer of thanks to an obviously sagacious distant ancestor of mine. Expelled from Zion thousands of years ago, he turned right, making for Poland, rather than veering left for the Atlas Mountains. I strongly doubt the storyteller I saw working a small crowd in a village souk was paid an advance for a tale-in-progress. Or occasionally knocked ideas around with editors over lunch at the Four Seasons.

Thursday we set out for the sea, Essaouira, a two-hour drive from Marrakech. The charming fishing port of Essaouira, its houses sparkling white and blue, is also still known by its Portuguese name of Mogador. Many Jews once lived here, most of them in the wool trade, and among them was Benjamin Disraeli's father.

We made directly for the port, where the fishing fleet had just come in and the men were still unloading their overnight catch of sardines and anchovies, the scavenging gulls hovering overhead. Settling in at one of the many picnic tables by the waterside, we ate charcoal-grilled sardines washed down with l'Oustalet, a local dry wine. Later, our spirits soaring high, we wandered slowly through the market. It was Florence who spotted something of more than passing interest in a grain merchant's hole-in-the-wall shop. Sacks of grain clearly stamped GIFT OF HOUSTON TEXAS NOT FOR SALE.

On reflection, I suppose, it was good to know that the ancient camel routes out of Ethiopia—then stricken with famine—were obviously still functioning.

On our last night in Marrakech we ate dinner in La Mamounia's opulent Moroccan restaurant, L'Bahja, seated on comfortable pillows on low benches, our table partitioned from the next by an intricately carved wooden screen. Moroccan musicians played as we feasted on b'stilla (puffed pastry stuffed with pigeon and almonds), followed by m'hammer (roasted baby-lamb shoulder). And then out came the belly dancer. A pretty girl she was, too, attired in a gauzy orange-and-black costume. She danced suggestively from table to table, actually lying on the floor and simulating intercourse at one point. As she undulated at our table, I slipped a fistful of dinars into her girdle. This gesture did not escape the middle-aged British couple seated on the other side of our carved wooden screen. "Oh, is that what you're supposed to do," said the husband.

"Don't you dare," said his wife.

Opposite us, there was a table made up of four happy couples, Moroccan obviously, sliding easily from French to Arabic and back again. As the strolling musicians stopped to serenade them, one of their number, a dark vibrant girl, suddenly kicked off her shoes and climbed on to the table to slip into her own sensual dance, her eyes on her man all the time. She was splendid. And no officious maître d' hurried over to protest, "We don't do that sort of thing here," or "We'll have to ask you to leave."

But then Marrakech can overwhelm even the most unsuspecting tourist with lust. Another night at L'Bahja, even as the belly dancer cavorted, I fell into conversation with a middle-aged American couple. They were from St. Louis.

"Have you been to the north yet?" the man asked.

Tangier. Rabat.

"No. Not yet," I said.

"It was so cold in the north last night," he said, "that, in order to keep warm, my wife and I had to get into bed together."

Sol

Kertzner's

Xanadu

LONDON, March 21, 1994. Having endured months of London's wintry damp and lowering, snot-grey skies, I was now bound for Heathrow on South African Airways overnight Flight 239 to Johannesburg, from where I would push on to the fleshpots of Sun City, out there in the land of Bop, as it is known to the cognoscente. Sun was what I was after, not trouble, but, only two weeks earlier, IRA hotheads had dumped eight mortars on Heathrow's runways, and Gerry Adams, president of Sinn Fein, had promised more IRA "spectaculars" in the near future. There had also been problems in Bophuthatswana, one of the "independent" black homelands, or dirt-poor ghettos, created by South African President B. J. Vorster in the seventies. On March 11, a convoy of neo-Nazi white ruffians, members of the Afrikaner Resistance Movement (AWB), had charged into Bop in support of its threatened, separatist dictator, Lucas Mangope. Before they were routed by the South African Defence Force, fifty people were killed in two days of skirmishing, and what was to become a famous photograph was flashed round the world. It showed a stopped car, its doors open, one AWB irregular dead in the dirt, another dying, and a third, Alywn Walfaardt, begging for mercy an instant before he, too, was to be wasted by a black policeman. But the day before I was to fly off to Bop there was a reassuring report in London's *Sunday Times*, running under the headline, "FUN AS USUAL AT SUN CITY":

"Nude dancers were strutting their stuff, roulette wheels were spinning and prostitutes of all nationalities were displaying their wares. . . . South Africa's multi-million-pound pleasure resort was back at its hedonistic best last week after a slight hiccup due to the unforeseen closure of the country it operated in. . . ."

And now, cruising at thirty-five thousand feet on board SAA Flight 239, I had two options. I could either watch "The Beverly Hillbillies" or do some homework, dipping into my copy of *A Short History of Africa*, by Roland Oliver and J. D. Fage:

"Shoshangane took his people, the Shangane, northwards to Gazanland, where they conquered and largely absorbed the native Tonga. Zwangendaba and his warriors broke even further afield, sweeping destructively through the highlands around Lake Malawi. Mzilikazi led his Matabele [more correctly Ndebele] across the Drakensberg. . . ."

Eschewing both movie and book, checking out the London time on my wristwatch, I visualized my wife at home watching the Academy Awards on TV with our daughter. As a rule, Florence accompanies me on these trips, but, considerate husband that I am, I thought she should be spared what promised to be sin city. Ordering another cognac to assuage my guilt, I saw myself as a latter day H. Rider Haggard hero, standing tall at the bar of the Sun City Palace in my sweat-stained safari hat, besieged by ivory and diamond smugglers, scantily clad hookers of all nationalities, rhino-horn pedlars, neo-Nazi conspirators, Greek arms dealers, superannuated white hunters, drug kings, and other unsavoury types. "What brings you here, old chap?" one of them would ask.

"A quest for King Solomon's mines," I would respond *sotto voce*, "using a map originally drawn by the Queen of Sheba on the back of a bill of lading, and passed on through the generations in my family.

My grandmother, may she rest in peace, handed it to me on her deathbed."

March 22, Jo'burg. Waiting for my luggage, I fell into conversation with a Californian real-estate operator on a grand tour. "I could buy a house here for four hundred thou that would set me back a million plus in California. Where are you coming from?"

"London."

"They've now got foreigners everywhere, I hear, ruining it. Just like the Mexicans in California."

Graham, the driver who was to take me to Sun City, a two-hour spin, was a fortysomething white South African descended from British immigrants. "Change your money here," said Graham. "They'll rip you off in Sun City."

Graham felt South Africa had been unfairly adjudged a pariah nation by uninformed liberals and commsymps. "The blacks have to be brought along slowly."

"Surely the African National Congress [ANC] is going to form the next government."

"Yes, but they could ruin the economy with their communist ideas. Look at what happened in the rest of Africa."

We tooled past a shanty town, its shacks slapped together from old crates and corrugated tin.

"If this is such a bad country," said Graham, "why do so many illegals come here out of Zimbabwe? To improve themselves, that's why. Hardly a day goes by that one of them doesn't come to my door pleading, 'I'll clean your house, I'll attend to your garden,' anything. No job, I have to tell them."

Driving along a plateau, five thousand feet above sea level, we zipped through dry brush country that, for the most part, lay baking under the sun. But there was also an orange grove, an ostrich farm, and, in the distance, a platinum mine. Bougainvillea and wild-flowers in bloom flourished by the roadside, as did squatters' camps and sheds mounted on cinder blocks that advertised themselves as supermarkets. Barefoot African women, balancing baskets of laundry on their heads, trekked from here to there, hardly giving our car a glance. One African lady was accompanied by a shuffling old man who sheltered her from sun with a brightly coloured parasol.

"There used to be a fence running along this road," said Graham, "to keep donkeys from lying down on the asphalt at night, but the natives stole the post for firewood and the barbed wire to fasten down their roofs."

Every time we slowed down for a T-junction, we were surrounded by swarms of black kids who were selling Cokes out of coolers. "I never stop for them," said Graham, "because they overcharge. Sol, you know, employs fifty thousand people at Sun City and, according to economists, there are all of ten people dependent on each job-holder, which means Sol is the benefactor of fifty thousand people."

Closer to Sun City, we came upon an intact fence that ran along one side of the road. We had reached the perimeter of Pilansberg National Park, some sixty thousand hectares of bush rich in elephant, cheetah, leopard, giraffe, rhino, and lions. "That fence is electrified," said Graham, "to keep elephants from wandering out of the park. You will also notice that trees too close to the fence have been cut down. That's to keep leopards from using them to spring on to the road. Sol's a visionary. He's a great guy. If a lion or something does make it over the fence and eats a native, he pays compensation to the family."

Sol, the benefactor, is said to have spent £144 million on the construction of the palace and the Lost City, both contained within the Sun City complex in the land of Bop. But it seems he is not so popular in Transkei, another "independent" homeland. According to a report published in the London *Guardian*, there is an outstanding warrant for Sol Kertzner's arrest in Transkei. It was issued following Sol's alleged admission to a South African commission of inquiry that Sun International had paid a £400,000 bribe to the former Transkei leader, George Matanzima.

The Lost City comes complete with its own legend:

"Centuries before tall ships were ever dreamed about, long before the dawn of Western civilization, a nomadic tribe from northern Africa set out to seek a new world, a land of peace and plenty," and when they found it "from the jungle rose an amazing city with a magnificent palace, a world richer and more splendid than any they had ever known. . . . Then a violent earthquake struck this idyllic valley, the survivors fled, never to return, and left it to be restored" by Sol Kertzner, ebullient son of Russian-Jewish immigrants, who would bring the Miss World contest to the African bushveld.

And suddenly, leaving the real world of black penury behind us, we were there, passing through the tall gates. Forget Angkor Wat and the Taj Mahal. Never mind the pyramids or the Forbidden City. Instead, think Disneyland and consider these stats: number of bricks used in construction of the Lost City, 30 million; total area of marble, 4,650 square metres; total area of carpets, 50,000 square metres.

"The painting on the palace's rotunda ceiling was created by artists in the same way as Michelangelo painted the Sistine Chapel in Rome. The evocative African landscape, alive with animals and birds, took nearly five thousand hours to complete," which is much faster work than the pope got out of his slacker.

The chandelier in the palace's Crystal Court noshery, five metres in diameter, "hangs over the impressive elephant fountain in the centre of the Crystal Court, topped by four three-metre-high elephants in faux green unicaite. From the elephants' trunks curled over their backs, water sprays into a hammered bronze bowl."

Sam Coleridge's lines immediately sprung to mind:

In Xanadu did Kubla Khan
A stately pleasure-dome decree:
Where Alph, the sacred river, ran
Through caverns measureless to man
Down to a sunless sea.

So twice five miles of fertile ground
With walls and towers were girdled round: . . .

Once I had checked in, I was issued with a palace identity card, which I was warned to keep with me at all times. My room in the Leopard Wing, one of 338 available in Sol's fantasy *albergo*, was handsomely appointed. My ablutions done, I made directly for the Tusk Bar, which I assumed would be jam-packed with horny adventurers looking to connect with hookers of all nationalities, but there was only one other person there, a middle-aged man. I ordered a Bloody Mary that came with an elephant tusk in lieu of a swizzle stick, and introduced myself. "Where is everybody?" I asked.

"They're afraid."

"But there was not even a hint of trouble on the road."

"No, not the road. To leave their homes empty. Unguarded."

Johannesburg's inner city, he explained, was now totally black and crime-ridden. Whites had retreated to the suburbs, every house protected by an Immediate Armed Response sign, which means there is at least one alarm button in each room. If you press one, within four minutes a truckload of men will pull up. They are armed with sawn-off shotguns and a computer printout with the names of everybody entitled to be on the premises. Anybody else can be shot with impunity.

"Most of us have gone liquid," said my Tusk Bar companion, "and the smart money is being sheltered offshore. It's wait-and-see time until next month's election. Buthelezi could start a civil war."

At lunch, I was one of twelve diners in the vast Crystal Court restaurant, which can accommodate 185 guests. My gazpacho tasted a bit tomato tinny, but the deep-fried calamari were just fine, and so was the herbal bread. Looking around, it appeared the other guests were all in their late sixties. Having set out for what was promoted as Sodom with room service, a time-out hideaway where advocates of apartheid could indulge in interracial bonking, I seemed to have stumbled on a resort where senior citizens came to celebrate their golden wedding anniversaries.

Following an afternoon snooze, I returned to the Tusk Bar to join two of Sol's PRs for drinks, both of them bright and engaging: Sue Peeperkorn, out of County Limerick, Ireland, and Delwin

Kriel, a South African born and bred. Conventions had been cancelled. Next week's international tennis match, I was told, was poorly booked, but an up-and-coming concert by Canadian rocker Bryan Adams was sold out. Other stars who had already played Sun City included Frank Sinatra, Dolly Parton, Cher, Rod Stewart, Elton John, and Shirley Maclaine. "You have wonderful psychics," said Shirley, "and it's no wonder. Just look at all the minerals you have beneath you." I also learned, much to my chagrin, that I was not the first illustrious novelist to visit. Ivana Trump had already been here, and so had Sidney Sheldon, and *they* had got to judge a Miss World pageant along with Bo Derek.

"Sol has a five-year contract with the Miss World people," said Sue, "but this year could be iffy. We just don't know what's going to happen. It's too bad Sol isn't here. You must meet him. He's great."

"A visionary," I said.

"Yes," said Delwin. "You know, he employs five thousand people in Sun City and that means some fifty thousand are dependent on him for their livelihood."

Traipsing through a man-made grotto, which protected me from an artificial waterfall, I carried on to dine alone in the all but empty Villa del Palazzo, which "seems to float like a jewel box of colour on a cushion of sparkling water" and promised "pizzas by Leonardo worthy of a hanging in the Uffizi Gallery." My first-rate *guazzetto di pesce* was followed by an equally satisfactory *stracci ripieni al funghi di stagione*. But, alas, my cognac snifter was heated, and the waiter who brought over the humidor was under the impression that you clip a cigar by chopping it just short of half.

The Lost City, spread over fifty-five acres, is contained within the Sun City complex, which contains three more, conspicuously less opulent, hotels: the Cascades, the Sun City, and the Cabanas. An efficient shuttle-bus service runs between the hotels and the entertainment centre. The latter is strictly honky-tonk, dark and mirrored, filled with banks of slot machines, attended here and there by grim, solitary ladies. Eschewing both the topless Viva Sun City! floor show and the porn cinema, I made directly for the casino, and promptly dropped two hundred dollars at the roulette tables. Then I went to mourn my losses at the Flamingo Bar, where I had been told there would be a good deal of action, but there was hardly anybody there.

Back in my room, I switched on SkyTV, and there, one night after the event, was the appalling Whoopi Goldberg hosting the Academy Awards. No, thank you.

Not since the late, great Bugsy Siegal invented Las Vegas has there been anything like Sol Kertzner's creation in the bushveld—a licence to print money.

Item: Anybody who was savvy enough to invest in Sun International (which owns twenty-nine other hotels worldwide) in 1985, and hung in there until 1992, enjoyed an average return of 60 per cent per annum, including capital gains and dividends.

Sol, who grew up in a poor Johannesburg suburb, showed early promise, peddling everything from chips to chewing gum as a kid. The former welterweight boxing champion of South African Universities founded Sun International (or SunBop) in 1983 and, since then, has seen it grow into the third-largest casino/resort group in the world, with holdings that include the Ruhl Casino in Nice. And Sol, zipping around the world in his private jet, constantly fingering his worry beads during seventeen-hour work days, now owns elegant homes in Cape Town, the Chiltern Hills near Oxford, and the Côte d'Azur. But the rambunctious hustler, who was voted South Africa's Jewish Businessman of the Year in 1993, now also has his problems.

Sun City was conceived during apartheid, at a time when gambling and interracial sex, never mind nearly nude bimbos bumping and grinding on stage, were *verboten* in Calvinist South Africa; but once the ANC forms the government in April it will lift the ban on gambling, and Sol's thirteen-year monopoly will come to an end. Even when I was in South Africa, weeks before the election, Johannesburg's two English-language daily newspapers, the *Star* and the

Citizen, were advertising strip shows, massage parlours, escort and other life-enhancing services available right in town. Something else. After the election, once the "independent" land of Bop is incorporated into South Africa, Sol is also bound to lose his tax-free status. But I wouldn't worry about him. He is connected. Nelson Mandela's daughter spent her honeymoon as Sol's personal guest at the Sun City hotel in Mauritius. And Sol, a notable aesthete, has magnanimously joined hands with the ANC to set up a South African arts and cultural foundation. "I have little doubt the ANC will see the benefits of private enterprise," he has said. "And they know it is the only system that will survive."

March 23. After breakfast, I set out with Delwin Kriel for a grand tour of the Lost City.

For openers, we stopped at the fabled Valley of the Waves, an eighteen-hectare playground where six-foot-high machine-propelled waves break on an artificial sandy beach, and trippers can drift down the Sacred River, or Thundering Lagoon, in inflated tubes, or dunk in the Royal Baths. Then we risked crossing the Bridge of Time, which vibrates every twenty minutes, puffing steam, simulating a volcano eruption or earthquake, just to make visiting Californians feel at home. Our safe crossing took us into the Temple of Courage, with its near-vertical 250-foot waterslides, the Mamba and the Viper. Opposite the slides, there stood the barred entrance to the Diamond Mine. "But there have never been diamonds here, I'm afraid," said Delwin, who went on to recommend a visit to Pilandsberg National Park. "I want you to know," he said, bursting with pride, "that all the lions in the park have been tested for AIDS."

Startled, I dropped my elephant-tusk pen, pinched from my room. *Gay lions! Or Kings of the Forest who used dirty needles!* "How come lions can test HIV-positive?" I asked.

"Eating infected monkeys," he said.

The Temple of Courage led to the Entertainment Centre, with its Jungle Casino, in which I already considered myself a shareholder.

Under "a roof of twinkling stars, the melodious sound of tinkling coins filling the air," there are 468 slot machines, each one thoughtfully provided with a stool. These include the Double Nutty, the Rhinestone Monkey, the Crazy Crocodile, and the biggie—the Dream Machine—which can pay out a £400,000 jackpot for a £3 bet.

We also dropped in on the Lost City golf course, designed by Gary Player, its clubhouse a simulated ruin, and, on my insistence, took a golf cart to the thirteenth hole, where I could look in on the crocodile pool.

We then proceeded to Sol's 25-hectare instant jungle and rain forest, irrigated by a computer-controlled system that has 30 kilometres of piping, 9,000 overhead misters and 2,500 sprinklers. The jungle boasts 1.2 million imported plants and trees, some 7,000 orchids brought in from Brazil, Borneo, Java, and China, dangling from 36 jacaranda trees. Its pride is a 48-ton baobab tree, uprooted in Transvaal, and listed in the *Guinness Book of World Records* as the largest transplanted tree in the world. Patrick Watson, the jungle's designer, has said, "I was in search of an epic, romantic look for my fantasy forest, like the location for an Indiana Jones adventure."

We crossed a swinging rope-and-board bridge, shivering at the spectacle of a giant toy black spider glued to a rock. And I noted with pleasure that Sol was a conscientious caretaker of the environment he had created. He had had wastepaper baskets nailed to trees here and there, a thoughtful convenience that was surely unknown to Tarzan and Jane in their time.

More guesties for din-dins in the Crystal Court tonight. Chinese out of Hong Kong and Taiwan. Some Japanese toting camcorders and cameras. Others are German or Dutch. Following my solitary dinner, I head for the Viva Sun City! floor show and find the theatre one-third full. Cottontops, mostly. Well now, I enjoy looking at tits, but I am capable of appreciating only one pair at a time. But here, as everywhere in Sun City, excess is the rule, and forty bare bouncing tits strike me as comic, rather than titillating. So I quit after twenty minutes and repair to the Jungle Casino, eschewing the *salle privée*, where the minimum wager is 10,000 rand. Even so, I quickly drop another $200.

Back in my room, channel hopping, I come across another Academy Awards repeat, this time on channel three. Maybe there is justice to be found in this world after all. Possibly those who introduced apartheid have been condemned to watch Whoopi Goldberg, delivering her asinine one-liners with unwarranted confidence, from here to eternity.

March 24. To begin with, I felt strongly that if natural grace rather than new money was the prerequisite for booking into the palace, it is the whites who would be waiting on the blacks here. Bop's blacks are an uncommonly handsome bunch. But in Sol's make-believe Africa, they are humiliated by the outlandish costumes they are obliged to wear. The doormen turbaned and berobed, the waiters in the Tusk Bar sporting leopard-print vests, and the chambermaids tricked out in brightly coloured dashikis. They have also been programmed to be oppressively polite, even obsequious, and after three days they began to get on my nerves. It had become impossible to pass a black in the hall without his asking, "Enjoying yourself, sir?" or to get through a meal without the waiters demanding again and again, "Everything pleasing you, sir?"

Stopped for a single malt in the Tusk Bar at noon, and asked if, this time, I could please, please, please have it without an elephant-tusk swizzle stick.

The bartender, his English shaky, misunderstood, and brought me a handful. "Will this be enough, sir?"

A fat man out of East Texas joined me at the bar. "My ancestors come from Ireland," he said, "and there's more trouble there than here."

"Enjoying yourself here?" the bartender asked.

"Everything's excellent," he said. "Perfect."

"Then I hope you come back again and stay longer," the bartender said.

The Texan told me, "I was in the park yesterday and I saw two rhinos, a baboon, a hippo, and two lions."

"Some of those lions suffer from AIDS," I said.

"No shit."

"They eat infected monkeys. You go home and tell your wife you are now HIV-positive because a lion bit your hand, and I'll bet she doesn't believe you. She'll think you were screwing around here."

"You gay or something?"

"Both."

"Excuse me," he said, gulping down his drink.

Three forty-five p.m. If I hurried down to the thirteenth hole, I could be just in time to watch the crocs being thrown their daily chicken feed. Instead, I caught up with Jerry Inzerillo, CEO of Sun City resorts, in his office. Jerry, an immediately recognizable and engaging type, is a streetwise New Yorker: he's been in the hotel business for twenty-five years, starting out as a busboy when he was a mere thirteen-year-old. He put in five years at the Las Vegas Hilton, three at the Fontainbleau in Miami, and he was co-founder, with Steve Rubell and Ian Schrager, of Morgan's.

"Tell me," I said, "where can I find a historical source book for the origins of the Lost City?"

"Actually, it's conceptual."

"Sorry?"

"Sol thought wouldn't it be wild to come up with a fable about a nomadic tribe that was wiped out by a volcano, and whose lost city he revived. Sol, you know, employs five thousand people here, which is a support system for fifty thousand."

"He's a visionary."

"He's put together some team."

Jerry was an adviser to the ANC, helping them plan the coming presidential inauguration ceremony. "Look, we know how to do it, but it's the first time for them." He also told me that the palace ran a *chemin de fer* game for Chinese high rollers, the minimum bet

100,000 rand. "One night," he said, "we were up two million with only a half-hour or so to go, and ended up a million in the hole before the game was over."

March 25. Put in a morning baking by the poolside and avoided the Tusk Bar until early evening. I'm a regular now, greeted warmly, and offered handfuls of elephant-tusk swizzle sticks even before I sit down.

Fell into conversation with a couple of affable air-conditioning technicians out of Johannesburg who had come to do some repairs, and had been invited to stay the night. Gary and Andy were both Brits. They had come out years ago because of the climate, the better standard of living available to whites, and because there was too much waiting to fill dead men's shoes in England. Gary professed to be reconciled to an ANC government, but was worried about the Communists in their camp, the celebrated Joe Slovo prominent among them. A day earlier, F. W. de Klerk's National party had run a full-page ad in the *Citizen* warning about the Communist wolves hiding within the ANC's sheep's clothing. It claimed that, of the top fifty ANC candidates, twenty-five were Communists and three were former Communists. The South African Communist party, it said, had its own agenda, which stated, "The ultimate aim of the party is the building of a Communist society."

"Look at the rest of Africa," said Gary. "Ruined economies. Civil wars. No industries. Why, those poor bastards from Zimbabwe come over here just to buy plastic pails. Look, I employ blacks. But they're not qualified artisans."

"Do you have live-in black help at home?"

"I couldn't put up with them. They steal you blind. But I'm not prejudiced, you know."

Then he told me a story.

"Mandela goes to see Clinton in Washington to ask for advice. 'What you need,' says Clinton, 'are men around you who are capable of making quick decisions.' Then, to illustrate his point, he calls in a guy called Corbett. 'Tell me,' he says to Corbett, 'your mother has a child and it's not your brother and it's not your sister, who is it?' 'Me,' says Corbett. 'You see,' Clinton says to Mandela. So Mandela goes home and calls in Cyril Ramaphosa. 'Your mother has a child, but it's not your sister and it's not your brother, who is it?' 'I'll get right back to you,' says Ramaphosa. And, out in the hall, Ramaphosa stops Joe Slovo. 'Your mother has a child, and it's not your brother and it's not your sister, who is it?' 'Me,' says Slovo. So Ramaphosa returns to Mandela's office. 'It's Slovo,' says Ramaphosa. 'No, it isn't,' says Mandela. 'It's Corbett.' You're not laughing. Don't you get it?"

"I get it."

"Have you been to the staff bar yet?"

"No."

"Let's go."

The staff bar, the liveliest I'd been to, was crowded with repair and maintenance men, whites mostly, immigrants from England and Ireland, all of them running scared.

"We're isolated in Sun City," one of them said, "but ten miles from here they could now be hacking each other to death with pangas, for all we know."

The only hint of trouble in Sun City was the armoured troop carriers parked discreetly here and there, just in case.

"As things stand," another man said, "our homes here, our meals and electricity, are free. But once we are incorporated into South Africa, all that will be taxed."

"We're at risk here," somebody else said. "Look at the newspaper ads, it's like apartheid in reverse. All the employers are advertising 'affirmative action' jobs."

"It's the Americans who are to blame, you know. They favour the blacks everywhere but at home. They don't give a damn what happens to us and our families."

March 26. Spent my last morning in Sol's glitzy take on Xanadu at the poolside, going through my notes. A TV crew had arrived, representing a local Californian channel, and they began to move among the sunbathers, asking questions and filming. When they reached me, I protested, "Sorry, but you can't interview me. I'm wanted for stock-market fraud in Canada. The RCMP would pay plenty to know where I was." And that much said, I ducked behind my newspaper. Ten minutes later I espied their cameraman surreptitiously filming me from the far side of the pool.

Late that afternoon a driver picked me up for the hundred-mile spin to the airport. Within minutes, we were back in the real Africa of desperate black poverty and disease, no artificial waterfalls anywhere. Bigmouth, I thought, as we got closer to Johannesburg. That TV crew, smelling possible reward money, had probably phoned on ahead, and the cops who had been alerted would prevent me from boarding my flight to London. Happily, that was not the case. But, looking ahead, as we cruised at thirty-five thousand feet over the Kalahari Desert, I imagined the film taken of me by the poolside couriered to Ottawa, baffled RCMP fraud-squad mavens studying it, scratching their heads.

Egypt's
Eleventh
Plague

R EADING THE ENTRAILS was far from reassuring.
On October 13, 1992, a couple of weeks before my wife and I were to check out the pyramids at Giza and then embark on a Nile cruise, realizing a long-cherished dream for her, the front-page headline in the *Jerusalem Post* read, "CAIRO QUAKE KILLS AT LEAST 350. MANY CHILDREN DIE IN STAMPEDE."

The lead story began: "*Cairo*—The most powerful earthquake in Egypt's history, which hit shortly after 3 p.m. yesterday, killed at least 340 people and injured 4,000. Egyptian Prime Minister Atef Sedki said, 'These are the figures we have so far . . . God only knows.'"

At the time, Florence and I were happily ensconced in a comfortable apartment in Mishkenot Sha'ananim, Jerusalem's official artists' guest house, with splendid views of the Old City.

"What do you think?" Florence asked.

"Well now, what we could do, once in Egypt, is slaughter a lamb that is without blemish, a male of the first year, and take the blood and strike it on the doorposts of our hotel room, and if an ill-tempered Jehovah decides to punish Pharaoh's progeny with another earthquake, the rumbles will pass over our quarters, as it is written," I said, opening the Bible to the appropriate passage, "'. . . and when I see the blood, I will pass over you, and the plague shall not be upon you to destroy you, when I smite the land of Egypt. . . .'"

"Then we're still going?"

"Absolutely."

A week later, Egyptian musketeers, members of Gamaa al Islamiya, a Muslim fundamentalist coven, ambushed a tour bus in central Egypt, *where we were heading*, killing a young British nurse and wounding two others. This was the first such incident since October 2, when riflemen hiding on a banana plantation on the banks of the Nile had opened fire on a tour boat filled with 140 Germans, failing to take out even one of them but managing to wound three Egyptian crew members. And then out there in Port Said, on October 25, a Muslim religious crazy stabbed three Russian tourists, two of them women, and fled.

In Asyût, a fundamentalist hotbed on the shores of the Middle Nile, some two hundred miles south of Cairo, every Friday the imam of the Rahman mosque calls for payola for the families of two thousand Gamaa members he claims the government has locked in the slammer. On the wall of one house in Asyût—between a Star of David and a drawing of Jerusalem's Dome of the Rock with a fist brandishing a rifle coming through the roof—somebody has scrawled, "MUSLIMS, BEWARE, THE JEWS ARE COMING."

The Jews, the Catholics, the Protestants. Americans, Germans, Italians, Spaniards. Infidels of all sizes and persuasions. In 1991, something like three million trippers descended on Egypt, raining $3 billion in hard currency on the parched land. Tourism, in fact, is Egypt's largest foreign-currency earner. But once word got out that infidels are in season (and that snipers are taking potshots at them from the banks of the Nile), thirty-eight chartered flights to Egypt were cancelled in the last two weeks of October, and airlines reported many additional cancellations of regularly scheduled flights by still more chicken-shit travellers who probably got mugged in Amsterdam instead. Even so, our El Al flight out of Ben Gurion Airport, on the night of October 29, was full. Middle Americans, mostly. The quacking rather than the silent majority. Tour groups who had already been to Bethlehem, Nazareth, and Jerusalem. Grizzly, beer-bellied old codgers wearing silly hats advertising Medinah Tours, and their unsexed drip-dry wives, favouring nylon windbreakers, stretchy slacks that narrowed at the ankles, and sneakers. The men called their wives "Mummy" and the women responded by calling their husbands "Daddy."

The woman who sat beside me, anxiety-ridden on take-off, snuggled in nicely once the TV monitor lit up and began to play an episode of "The Golden Girls." "Oh, look," she cooed. "And I'll bet we're soon going to get a nice little snack," she added, flashing a menacing smile at our stewardess.

The one-time young socialist firebrand within me clapped hands because these obviously far-from-sophisticated folks could now afford to "do" Egypt, yes, but the snob I had long since become wished that these tiresome old fools had booked another flight. Obviously Jehovah, my grudgy deity, still had it in for Pharaoh's people and had decided to hit them with an eleventh plague, the worst of all: guided tours from America, Germany, and Japan. The camera-laden battalions we would encounter everywhere, busload after busload, lining up before the entry to Cheops's pyramid at Giza, each one sporting a zippered money belt like an abdominal front porch. Trooping through the Temple of Luxor, often on a collision course. Shooting videos of one another at Karnak, their collective sweat a real threat to the incredibly beautiful wall paintings in Ramses' tomb. I found consolation in the book I had brought with me, *Flaubert in Egypt: A Sensibility on Tour*, translated and edited by Francis Steegmuller. In 1849, the randy twenty-seven-year-old Flaubert, a fancier of hookers, toured Egypt with his friend Maxime Du Camp. A year later he would return to France and sit down to begin to write *Madame Bovary*. But meanwhile, on December 4, 1849, only a few days into Cairo, he would write to a friend back home:

> To amuse the crowd, Mohammed Ali's jester took a woman
> in a Cairo bazaar one day, set her on the counter of a shop, and

coupled with her publicly while the shopkeeper calmly smoked his pipe.

On the road from Cairo to Shubra some time ago a young fellow had himself publicly buggered by a large monkey—as in the story above, to create a good opinion of himself and make people laugh.

A marabout died a while ago—an idiot—who had long passed as a saint marked by God: all the Moslem women came to see him and masturbated him—in the end he died of exhaustion—from morning to night it was a perpetual jacking-off. Oh, Bouilhet, why weren't you that marabout?

Quid dicis the following fact: some time ago a *santon* [ascetic priest] used to walk the streets of Cairo completely naked except for a cap on his head and another on his prick. To piss he would doff the prick-cap, and sterile women who wanted children would run up, put themselves under the parabola of his urine and rub themselves with it.

Goodbye—this morning I had a letter from my mother—she is very sad, poor thing. Talk to her about me.

Tooling through the streets of Cairo at 11 p.m., keeping a sharp eye out for gay monkeys and Muslim women pleasuring the intellectually disadvantaged to death, I failed to espy either. However, the streets were vibrant, once we shot past affluent Heliopolis into Cairo proper. Brightly lit hole-in-the-wall shops were still open. Fly-ridden carcasses, suspended on hooks, swayed in the night breeze in a butcher shop not much bigger than a storage cupboard. Alert vendors stood guard over street-corner carts laden with an abundance of tempting-looking produce: apples, tomatoes, melons, bananas. But we had been warned not, on any condition, to eat uncooked food in Egypt and to drink nothing but mineral water. Or cognac. Or Scotch. And so, in the absence of Macallan, I would learn to brush my teeth with Glenlivet, which has it all over Listerine, I must say.

There were donkey carts everywhere. Our driver, negotiating the traffic, was constantly leaning on his horn, as was anyone else who had one. In Egypt, obviously, the credo is, I toot, therefore I am. Pedestrians, inured to the cacophony, ignored the onrushing cars and the battered pick-up trucks that served as buses, bulging with passengers. Men wearing white kaftans passed before us with their black-robed wives, many of whom carried babes in arms. There's a baby born in Egypt every twenty seconds. The population of Cairo, officially twelve million—but more likely much higher— is said to increase by fifteen hundred per diem. The poor are rooted in unbelievable squalor. According to the *Middle East* magazine:

> . . . jerry-built shanties are thrown up overnight to accommo- date Cairo's burgeoning population. Additional storeys are added to existing blocks of mudbrick-built tenement slums without planning regulations. Few people care and in the un- likely event of the planning authorities becoming involved, a bribe to the right official will almost certainly prevent further aggravation. It is not unusual for buildings to come crashing down in Cairo, killing or maiming their occupants . . . traffic clogs the streets and pollutes the air, overburdened sewer and water systems burst and block streets. . . .

Amid such penury, we swallowed our guilt and opted for opu- lence: the legendary Mena House Oberoi at Giza, on the other side of Cairo. Even arriving late at night, we could see that the surround- ing grounds were magnificent. Date palms, sycamores, the scent of jasmine everywhere. Mena House, once a royal lodge, has been a grand hotel for many years now, its public rooms rich in marble floors, vaulted ceilings, enormous chandeliers, beaten-brass tables, carved wood doors, and other exotica.

Awakening early the next morning, I swept the bedroom curtains aside for a look at the desert, only to find my view blocked by a bloody big pile of stones—that is to say, the Great Pyramid, where Cheops was planted. Clearly far from self-effacing, Cheops required a tomb that was made of more than two million blocks of limestone, some of them weighing fifteen tons apiece. According to Herodotus, it took 100,000 workers ten years just to construct a causeway to move the stones, and another twenty years to build the pyramid. The Great Pyramid was ancient long before Abraham's sojourn in Egypt, never mind Moses', so Menachem Begin got it wrong when he said to Sadat, "I've come to see the work of my forefathers."

Cheops's pyramid (along with its two lesser companions, the pyramid of Chephren, Cheops's son, and that of Mycerinus, his grandson) is justifiably considered one of the seven wonders of the ancient world, and that afternoon we hired a guide, licensed to speak English, to escort us around the site. He was contemptuous of the smaller, sometimes crumbling pyramids of Giza: "They was for nobles or womens and womens not equals mens."

The Great Pyramid, no matter how many photographs of it you have seen, is an astonishing sight. But approaching it on foot, we were besieged by vendors and supplicants, old men and boys, offering T-shirts, posters, sunhats, bottles of mineral water, camel or horseback rides, a helping hand to enter the pyramid—everybody after baksheesh, the grease that turns the Egyptian wheel. I began to peel off and distribute £1 notes (worth roughly thirty cents each), until I grasped this was the equivalent of sending out a mating call, and I began to curse, breaking free.

The Pharaohs didn't trust their subjects and usually had false entries cut into their tombs; Cheops, however, had *no* entry—until grave robbers in search of jewels, gold statuettes, and other collectibles made one. We filed through that entrance. A bad mistake. Bent over double, we negotiated a long, narrow passageway reeking of stale sweat. Careful to avoid bat shit, we ascended at a forty-five-degree angle, even as others were clambering back, short of breath. Alas, when we finally got into the burial chamber, we discovered that it was empty—except for barefoot urchins, palms outstretched. Once liberated from the pyramid, I ran smack into an American tour group about to descend. "What's it like down there?" somebody asked.

"Terrific," I said, "but watch out for snakes."

"What's that?"

"Believe me, you're perfectly okay as long as you don't step on one."

It is worth braving the banks of tour buses, the groups on the march, unfailingly led by a woman holding a national flag or a colourful umbrella, and the swarms of pedlars, to visit the museum that holds the solar boat, discovered only in 1954, that was to transport Cheops's *ka*, or soul, into the afterlife. It's a beauty. One hundred and forty-three feet long, made up of more than twelve hundred pieces of timber, mainly cedar of Lebanon. There are perfectly preserved hand-carved oars and a sinuous bow that is tipped with a carved papyrus blossom.

And then, lo and behold, there is the Sphinx.

"Why it is," our guide asked, "the Sphinx has it head mans and body of lions? It is to show intelligence of mens and muskels of beast togethered."

The glorious Sphinx, so ancient nobody knows when it didn't protect the necropolis of Giza against intruders to the sacred precincts, has now been made to speak in nightly *son et lumière* shows: "With each new dawn, I see the sun-god rise from the far bank of the Nile. His first ray is for my face, which is turned toward him, and for five thousand years I have seen all the suns man can remember come up in the sky. I saw the history of Egypt in its first glow, as tomorrow I shall see the east burning with a new flame."

The Sphinx, owing to its splendour, will be forgiven such latter-day Disneyland babble. Its name, derived from the Greek for "compound creature," was bestowed on it by Herodotus. Over the wasting centuries, it has survived the visitations of Alexander the Great, Napoleon, and Dick and Pat Nixon, but it is now seriously endangered by the rumble and exhaust fumes of the fleets of tour buses passing far too close to it.

The perspicacious Flaubert, incidentally, taking a stand against the Eurocentric view of our cultural past more than a century before anybody else challenged it (maybe even anticipating Sheik Anta

Diop's claim that civilization's cradle was black), wrote of the Sphinx: ". . . it exactly faces the rising sun, its head gray, ears very large and protruding like a negro's, its neck is eroded . . . [and] the fact that the nose is missing increases the flat, negroid effect. Besides, it was certainly Ethiopian; the lips are thick."

On Sunday, November 1, we rose before dawn to catch the 6:15 flight to Luxor (Thebes), where we would board the HMS *Salacia*, bound for Karnak Temple, Esna, Edfu, Kôm Ombo, and the Aswan Islands . . . four nights and five days drifting down the Nile, another of my wife's prayers answered . . . while I daydreamed of Nubians obligingly fanning us with palm fronds . . . *and crazed fundamentalists, hunkered down amid the banana trees on shore, using us for target practice.*

"Hey, Mohammed, baby, I'm sure you got a Jew that time."

"*Allah Akbar*, man."

"That's worth ten points, isn't it?"

Approaching the HMS *Salacia*, I inspected the length of its hull twice before boarding, checking it out for bullet holes. It turned out to be a handsome ship, its stylish public rooms finished in mahogany or oak veneer, every one of its staff of sixty unfailingly gracious. The four-decker vessel boasted a swimming pool and a Jacuzzi, fifty-six cabins, and nine suites. Our nifty little suite had two toilets. To be blunt, this proved not so much a luxury as a blessing—no, a necessity—once the dreaded "Gippy Tummy" struck the two of us. But I'm getting ahead of myself.

A couple of hours after boarding, we noticed a program posted opposite the purser's desk that promised us nights of wild abandon. Belly dancers. Snake charmers. A costume ball, where dour German men could dress like Yasir Arafat, sans facial stubble and pistol, and pleasingly plump, giggly Italian women could show up in costumes more appropriate to a pasha's harem. By this time, I should point out, we had been joined by two tour groups. A platoon of disciplined, unsmiling Germans, and the even more numerous Italians, who would turn out to be wonderfully unruly, ignoring sailing schedules, returning from a temple or bazaar tour only when it pleased them.

Tamer El Narsh, vice-president of Trans Egyptian Travel, which is the sole proprietor of the HMS *Salacia* and its two sister ships, the *Neptune* and the *Triton*, told me that when his father first went into the business, in 1958, there were only a few tour boats plying the Nile, but now there are close to two hundred. Tourists come from everywhere these days, including Israel. Israeli intellectuals I met in Jerusalem and Tel Aviv have a soft spot for Egypt. Again and again they told me how cultivated and gentle the Egyptians were, and they were right.

The *Salacia*, we learned, would not actually sail until noon the next day. First we were to visit the Temple of Luxor and then the Temple of Amon-Ra at Karnak. Luxor Temple was built by Amenhotep III (who ruled Egypt in the eighteenth dynasty) in honour of the great god Amon-Ra, his wife, Mut, and their son, Khonsu. One dynasty later, Ramses II decided it was time the temple got a face-lift, as it were. So for openers, he had six colossal statues of himself stationed at the entrance, four standing and two sitting. Ramses was an interesting Pharaoh, a generous commander-in-chief who promised his GIs bounty money for each enemy blown away. Legend has it that, in order to claim his *pourboire*, a foot soldier had to bring back a severed hand of the fallen. Soon the soldiers, given to inflating body counts even back in those days, were arriving with sacks full of hands. Unfortunately, a survey of the battlefields soon established that many a fallen Egyptian comrade was now missing a hand, sometimes both. Ramses II maintained the bounty system but, mindful that Egyptians were circumcised, put in place a new policy. He ordained that as proof of a kill, a trooper had to bring back an uncircumcised cock. This has led me to suspect that in the time of the Exodus from Egypt, it was not God's injunction that led to the circumcision of Jewish males, nor was it a question of personal hygiene. It was the fear of money-crazed Egyptian cavalry falling on them during the night in Sinai, harvesting uncircumcised dicks—a cash crop. In other words, a circumcised prick was bounty-proof.

After tramping about a number of temple sites, each one magnificent, I grasped that no sooner did your average Pharaoh mount the throne than he enlisted thousands of the unwashed to begin constructing a pyramid, temple, or tomb for him that had to be bigger than the one for whoever had preceded him. Some Pharaohs sent workers with chisels to expunge the cartouche (the signature enclosed in a rectangular box) of their predecessor from temple pylons, replacing it with their own moniker; they also had their predecessor's image, and that of any god they did not favour, chiselled out of the temple walls. The wall reliefs a Pharaoh ordered cut into the temples, civilization's first storyboards, usually show him being blessed by, or at least being chummy with, a number of gods and goddesses (say, Amon-Ra, Osiris, Horus, or Isis) and proffer inflated accounts of his victories in the field. Reaching out to touch a relief chiselled into a temple wall something like four thousand years before, buried and preserved under blowing desert sands for centuries, painstakingly unearthed probably less than a hundred years ago, you can't help but feel a certain charge, even a connection. After all, my forefathers used to work here, under conditions less than ideal, and if Jehovah hadn't hit Pharaoh with those ten plagues, I might now be moulding bricks without sufficient straw out there in the punishing heat, as it is written: "Our ancestors were slaves to Pharaoh in Egypt but God brought us out from there 'with a strong hand and an outstretched arm.' If the Holy One, Blessed be He, had not brought our ancestors out of Egypt, we and our children would still be slaves to Pharaoh in Egypt."

One of the most fascinating rooms in the Temple of Luxor is the birth room, whose wall reliefs depict the birth of Amenhotep, as invented by his flacks. Amenhotep, like most other Pharaohs, believed that his daddy was none other than the god Amon-Ra and had pictures cut into the walls to prove it.

The Great Temple of Amon-Ra at Karnak, its entryway guarded by an avenue of Sphinxes, is not merely a temple, it's a temple within a temple where almost all the Pharaohs of the New Kingdom had tall tales about their exploits chiselled into walls and pylons and obelisks and colonnades. On the entrance pylon to the inner temple of Ramses III, that Pharaoh is shown wearing the double crown, ruler of both Upper and Lower Egypt, and holding a group of prisoners by the hair with one hand even as he raises a club to bash them with the other. Amon-Ra is also there, handing him the sword of victory.

Karnak offers proof that the Israelites, who quit Egypt in such haste that there was not even time to bake proper bread, did at least manage to take an idea with them. Entry to Karnak's innermost temple, which once held a statue of Amon-Ra, was forbidden to all but Pharaoh and his high priest, even as at Solomon's temple, in Jerusalem, only the high priest was allowed into the sanctuary where God was said to reside in the holy ark. And there is a monument at Karnak that celebrates the last time the Egyptians were able to defeat the Israeli army. It depicts the victory of Shishak over Rehoboam, son of Solomon, when Solomon's temple was robbed of its riches:

> And it came to pass in the fifth year of King Rehoboam, that Shishak king of Egypt came up against Jerusalem: he took away the treasures of the house of the Lord, and the treasures of the king's house; and he took away all: and he took away all the shields of gold which Solomon had made.

The next morning, still docked at Luxor, we set out to visit the fabled valleys of the Kings and Queens. If the only thing we saw in Egypt was the tomb of Ramses VI, then putting up with the airport hassle, the ubiquitous tour buses, the importuning vendors, the hustlers, the oppressive heat, and even the debilitating "Gippy Tummy" would still have been worth it. The tomb, begun by Ramses V, is made up of five long corridors, two chambers, an antechamber, and a tomb chamber. The bas-reliefs on the walls show the deceased appearing before Ra-Harakhte, Osiris, Nut, and other gods and goddesses. The painted ceiling of the tomb chamber is considered one of the most important in a valley that includes the tombs of Amenhotep II, Thutmose III, Ramses IX, and, of course, Tutankhamen.

After the mummified Pharaohs of the New Kingdom had been entombed in the valley, passages were sealed, ostensibly assuring the monarchs that their burial chambers, unlike those of their ancestors, would be impervious to grave robbers. They were proved wrong, with the notable exception of King Tut's tomb, which yielded such an abundance of riches when it was uncovered by Howard Carter in 1922. The treasures, which took them ten years to catalogue, are on display in the Cairo Museum. They include the coffin of solid gold, weighing 2,961 pounds, that holds King Tut's remains.

Pulling out of the valley in a taxi, pursued by T-shirt vendors, leaving kaftan pedlars behind to bite the dust, swerving to avoid moth-eaten donkeys on the road, our driver naturally tooting his horn at every opportunity, we careered through what struck me as an all-too-typical Egyptian village. Crumbly mud-and-brick huts. The stench of raw sewage. Fly-ridden, hole-in-the-wall shops. Leathery old men squatting in the dirt. But our guide assured us that the villagers wouldn't budge even if they were paid thousands of dollars. They were, she said, grave robbers, every last one of them, their mud huts perched atop the tombs of nobles, rich in jewellery, gold, and artifacts that could be sold abroad, either to museums or to private collectors.

Back on board ship, determined to avoid an embarrassing incident, I made a dash for the loo and then ascended to the deck as we finally set sail for Esna, Edfu, and the Aswan Islands. Leaning against the rail, I watched as we drifted past fields of sugarcane, and date-palm and banana plantations, the Nile's fertile shores incredibly narrow, the desert always encroaching. On the evidence, indigenous farming and fishing methods haven't changed much in the past five hundred years. I saw a bullock pulling a wooden plough, guided by a barefoot man wearing a long white djellaba. Long, narrow skiffs on the river were each manned by two fishermen, the seated one minding the nets and the other standing on the prow and slapping the water again and again with a long paddle, trying to get the somnolent fish to rise from the bottom.

The next day, our merry Italians late but accounted for, our German tour group hanging in by the closed dining-room doors, ready to charge, we left Esna and set sail for Edfu and the Temple of Horus. By this time I was templed out, weary of the heat, the swarms of pedlars, the increasingly monotonous Nile shoreline, and my bruised and burning bowels. I was also ill-tempered because I wouldn't be able to watch the U.S. presidential results on TV that night and would have to go to bed without knowing who had won. The next morning, however, once we had gone ashore at Aswan, I had our guide ask a couple of pedlars who had taken the prize.

"Cleenton, Cleenton," said one, but the other chanted, "Boosh, Boosh."

Egyptian images that will remain with me.

In the courtyard of the Temple of Luxor, a grizzled, barefoot man, wearing a djellaba, pumped his legs up and down, slowly, slowly, kneading mud in a huge container, even as he fed straw into it. This, understandably, made for a certain frisson. But a glance satisfied me that he wasn't an Israelite who hadn't caught up with the good news, and on a closer look, neither was he four thousand years old. Clearly, the manufacture of mud bricks hadn't changed since the days of Moses.

Even as temple reliefs proclaim that Ramses won the battle of Qadesh, routing the Hittites, when actually the results of the conflict were inconclusive, there are signs, which I passed while driving through Heliopolis, advertising an exhibition celebrating the "triumph" of the Egyptian army in what it calls the October 1973 War and the Israelis call the Yom Kippur War. The truth is, although the Egyptians delivered a stunning blow to the cocksure Israelis as they charged across the Suez Canal, that before the UN enforced a halt the Egyptian army was all but encircled and Israeli tanks were within striking distance of Cairo.

And just as some of the Pharaohs were addicted to chiselling out relief images of their predecessors, laying claim to their accomplishments by cutting a fresh cartouche into a temple wall, so too, some four thousand years later, did President Sadat have Nasser's image, coupled with that of Khrushchev, chiselled out of a monument to the construction of the High Dam, supplanting it with his own.

And then there was the day we drove out of Cairo to neighbouring Sakkara, site of some of the oldest pyramids in the land. If one stood on the crest of a windswept dune on the very edge of the Sahara, there were only more dunes as far as the eye could see. But I was convinced that if I set out across that seemingly uninhabited desert, around every dune, waiting to pounce, would be barefoot boys vending Coca-Cola, pedlars armed with necklaces and scarabs and Sphinx paperweights.

Oh, one thing more. A few days after we left Egypt, I read in the *International Herald Tribune*:

Egypt suspended Nile cruises through a region rocked by fundamentalist violence, Cairo tourist industry sources said Monday. Officially, the reason was the low water level but the sources believed the real reason was to protect tourists. The decision to close the Minya-Asyût stretch effectively halted cruises between Cairo and Aswan in the south.

London

Then and Now

OR SOMETHING like fifteen years, Florence and I saw out the long winters rooted in our dacha on the shores of Lake Memphremagog, in Quebec's Eastern Townships, where the season's prime social-cum-cultural event was the Wild Game Dinner at the Owl's Nest, perched out there on the 242. In deference to animal lovers, wild-game dinners are now illegal in Canada, but only if there's a charge, and so our admirable publican, Robert George, Esq., laid on the victuals gratis for this by-invitation-only feast in our down-home version of the Century or Garrick clubs.

The Owl's Nest banquet was calculated to make any committed carnivore salivate. The side tables were laden with wild turkeys, deer livers sizzling in pans and bubbly cauldrons of stewed porcupine, grey squirrel, and black bear—coyote steaks were frowned upon as being too chewy. For those inclined to barf at the very thought of such fare, a barbecued thigh of tame cow was provided, the trusting beast having been plugged between the eyes only a few days earlier by our good man Coz. The delicacies were washed down with quarts of Molson's Ex and a brand of Ontario vino that could, in a pinch, also serve to clear car windshields of frost or refill a cigarette lighter. Smoking, bawdy language, and sexual harassment were encouraged, but "wacky-tobaccy" was not tolerated. We were a respectable bunch.

Dress was informal. However, the men were expected to wash their feet or at least wear shoes. The ladies could be counted on to turn up in stretchy ski pants, which tended to be silver with naughty yellow stripes, Day-Glo orange, or swan's breast white with black polka dots. In the absence of a string quartet, the management provided a fiddler, screechy beyond compare, or somebody who could master the battered piano with the six missing keys. This long, enchanted evening usually culminated in one of the celebrants breaking a chair over the head of a neighbour, his hollered explanation charged with baffling sexual contradictions, as in, "You've been screwing my woman, you fucken little faggot!" The morning after this bacchanal, we were bound to learn that at least one of the guests, shovelled into his pick-up at 4 a.m., had totalled it on the drive home.

Other wintry cultural events included Dart Nite at the Owl's Nest, Band Nite at the Thirsty Boot, various church Bingo Nites, and the Fish Dinner at the Hooter, the lake perch having been caught through the ice by obliging welfare bums. Once the sap had begun to run, following the sugar snowfall of late March, the season concluded with a pancake breakfast featuring freshly boiled maple syrup.

All through the winter, insights into the social ferment and changing mores of the republic to the south were effortlessly acquired by watching Oprah Winfrey and Sally Jessy Raphael, our daily intellectual fare during the Owl's Nest Happy Hour. True, we had to do without the frisson of a daily court circular or a Nigel Dempster column, so we learned to depend on the social page of the Sherbrooke *Record* for tittle-tattle about the local artistos and glitterati. Titillating dispatches were provided by the leading hostess in each Townships settlement. A typical paragraph in the *Record*, the first newspaper to bear the imprimatur of Conrad Black, might inform us that Mrs. Marylou Grant, of South Bolton, entertained her niece, Sally Mae, of Brockville, Ontario, to tea last Tuesday. Or that following an all-night booze-up in the legion hall across the border in North Troy, Vermont, Roger "Sweet Pea" George, of Mansonville, laid on a *petit déjeuner* of lake perch, home fries, and smuggled vodka for his good companions.

My point is that winters in the Townships are convivial, life-enhancing, but undemanding. If you never venture out into the snowdrifts at night, but curl up on the sofa to watch a hockey game on TV instead, you haven't missed a thing, and that's the way I like it.

But in the autumn of 1993, my restless wife and I eschewed the Townships and acquired a flat in London, establishing it as our new winter quarters. Alas, we had been in London for only a month when I realized that we had settled among vulgarians and that I would now have to endure cultural overload that could oblige me, any night of the week, to get into a suit and tie and charge out into the rain to attend one or another of the oppressive cornucopia of plays, concerts, or vernissages available. I came to dread the mailbox thud that announced the arrival of *What's On* and *Time Out,* weekly guides to the action. But first a few words about the inherent vulgarity of the best educated of the natives, most of whom tend, ironically, to be offended by American self-promotion. When you're asked to a dinner party in one of their homes (a half glass of warm, sickening sweet Sainsbury's champers, followed by a tiny quail al dente, bouncing off your fork), the first thing you see is the aggressive display of cards on their mantelpiece. Rows of invitations to country weekends, glamorous dinner parties, book launchings, screenings, auctions of Ming dynasty finger bowls, rave nights at the local steam bath, wine tastings, and fashion shows of lingerie-for-chaps, all of which you were too unimportant to be asked to attend, you count-for-nothing twerp.

A quick perusal of *Time Out* reveals the week's depressing choice of political demonstrations, lectures, gallery openings, museum special events, concerts, and plays. The more raunchy *What's On* also recommends the no doubt incomparable services of Scheherazade, "striking dominant masseuse, extensively equipped," and Andrea's corrective rubdown "for the man's who's [*sic?*] secret ambition is to become the powerless victim of a Beautiful Black Woman." Each according to his need.

In a typical week I could have my couch-potato consciousness raised by joining a demo at the Hackney Town Council to support kooky Jane Brown, a local school headmistress who had refused to take her students to a *Romeo and Juliet* ballet because it celebrated only heterosexual love. That is to say, the teach was unaware of the Bard's subtext, the Freudian meaning of the sword Romeo used to, um, penetrate Tybalt. I could also join a demo, outside the Foreign Office, to complain against sanctions imposed on huggable Saddam Hussein, or another protest, this one at the gates of the Sudanese embassy, to register my discontent at the human-rights offences against the Nuba people, my brothers on the Tree of Man.

Lectures on offer are even more intriguing. I could catch Gideon Kossoff, of the London Anarchist Forum, holding forth on "Anarchism and Ecology" at Conway Hall; or Barry Crawford, at the Edge Gallery, on "After the Red Menace—What Next?"; or Duncan Hallas, at the North Finchley Library, on "Marxism—Ideas That Can Change the World?"

I could also choose from among eighty-five classical music concerts, among them the intriguing *Lavomatique*, at the Launderette in Hackney, "a Concerto for String Orchestra backed by a Demolition Squad." Nine operas are available, but *Rigoletto*, my favourite Verdi, at the Royal Opera, would set me back £236 for a pair of decent seats, never mind taxis or splits of bubbly and damp sausage rolls between the acts. I would rather play my Mozart, Bach, or Dixieland CDs at home, puffing on a Davidoff, than attend another concert where whoever is seated beside me is bound to be a compulsive hummer or teeth-grinder. Nor will I feel deprived if I skip the Independent Art Space's exhibit of Linda Moulton Howe's photographs of "cattle mutilations thought to be carried out by aliens. Ears, genitals, lower jaws, and anuses are commonly removed and the blood syphoned off." I could also do without Ron Haselden's show at the Museum of Installation: "The room is dark, nearly filled with a stretched white 'sheet' anchored at an acute angle. Strange sounds from Peter Cusack's 'Environmental Recordings' emanate from speakers: noises of the building itself—the hubbub of daily sound."

That week there were fifty-three plays running in the West End, and the curtain rose nightly on another twenty-five productions in the burbs. Among the West End's dubious attractions were a batch of Lloyd Webber's derivative, overblown musicals and, of course, *Miss Saigon*, then in its fifth year. But if I get my rocks off watching a helicopter land, I could go to Heathrow.

Years ago I would attend National Theatre productions of Shakespeare and make an annual pilgrimage with Florence to Stratford-on-Avon, but not any more. I absolutely refuse to suffer another production of *Julius Caesar*, its poetry redeemed by some hotshot director who has set it in Berlin, circa 1938, with the latest Royal Academy of Dramatic Arts graduates tricked out in ss uniforms. Nor will I tolerate a daring new production of *Hamlet*, freshly seen, as it were, by another innovator, set in the Kremlin. Or an East Asian Co-prosperity production of *Lear*, everybody wearing costumes left over from the last staging of *The Mikado*. Happily, I did manage to avoid 1992's highly praised *A Midsummer Night's Dream*, directed by fellow Montrealer Robert Lepage, adjudged a theatrical genius by many, which was set in a mudbath. Florence, who did attend, risking the first row, was issued with a plastic raincoat to protect her from the inevitable splashing.

I was nineteen years old when I first came to London in 1950, sailing on the *Franconia*. One night at the bar I sat next to a guy with angry red boils on his neck who was missing two front teeth, which meant that he had to be a hockey player. He was going to join a team in Brighton. "Come to my cabin," he said. "I got something I want to show you."

He fished a half-trunk out from under his bunk, opened it, and revealed two dozen pairs of nylon stockings. "Did you bring any with you?" he asked.

"Well, um, I usually wear wool socks," I stammered, retreating towards the door.

"Hey, I've been told that even the most frigid of those British broads will do anything for a pair. You shoulda brought some."

My intended short stay in London extended to more than two decades. The first of my many chilly bed-sitters was in a basement on Belsize Avenue, Hampstead, at a time when, in Calvin Trillin's phrase, "people of all kinds spoke of central heating as a frivolous and basically unhealthy affectation favoured by Americans." Food rationing was still in place, and that's how I discovered, inadvertently, that there *was*, after all, an international Jewish conspiracy. One day, my ration book in hand, I trotted over to a butcher shop on Haverstock Hill. The butcher, a thick-necked brute, glanced at my ration book, sized me up, and demanded, "You Jewish?"

Ready, but not eager, for a fight, I snarled back, "Yes. I am."

He led me into a back room of his shop, wrapped five lamb chops in a parcel, patted my cheek, and said, "A Jewish boy can't live on these rations. You come in here, you ask for Hymie."

In the early fifties I still believed that a continuing education was more beneficial than a couple of fingers of single malt Scotch or a snooze, so I was a sucker for those political bores who then advertised their sermons in the classified ad pages of the *New Statesman*. I was cured, however, after the night I let Doris Lessing talk me into going to hear Harry Pollitt, then general secretary of the British Communist party, speak about his recent visit to China. "In the last five years," he told enthusiasts, "the Chinese have increased their electrical power by 500 per cent."

I leaned towards Doris and whispered—too loud as it turned out—"That means one billion Chinese can now lay claim to five hundred light bulbs."

"Provocateur," hissed the lady immediately behind me, poking me with one of her knitting needles.

I met Florence in London, and four of our five children were born there. Over the years I graduated from bed-sitters in Hampstead, Highgate, and Brixton to a flat in Swiss Cottage and finally to our own house on Kingston Hill. Colin Wilson published *The Outsider* and for a week was pronounced a genius. Kingsley Amis, John Wain, and John Osborne were tagged Angry Young Men. Harold Pinter, Iris Murdoch, and Arnold Wesker were also heard from.

Joan Littlewood put working-class characters on stage in Stratford East as more than comic relief and, on that jewel set in a silver sea, it was considered daring. Jack Clayton broke new ground in the cinema with his film of John Braine's *Room at the Top* (for which I had rewritten the screenplay without credit, so that nobody knew about it until Clayton spilled the beans years later in a profile of him that appeared in the *Daily Telegraph Magazine*). *Beyond the Fringe* was deservedly a smash. Peter Cook founded *Private Eye* and we all watched David Frost and Co. on Sunday nights in "That Was the Week That Was." One night a bunch of us went to Wembley to see Henry Cooper fight Cassius Clay, as he was still known at the time. A chant went up from the crowd: "Use your 'ammer, 'enry"—and the East End greengrocer dropped an astonished Clay to the canvas with his wonderful left hook. But Cooper was a notorious bleeder. Clay began to work on his head, and won the bout after blood began to spurt from an artery in Cooper's forehead.

Other names to conjure with in London's so-called Swinging Sixties were Jean Shrimpton, The Beatles, Twiggy, Ian Fleming, slumlord Rachman, Albert Finney, instant vacuum cleaner millionaire John Bloom, Mary Quant (who urged Sloane Rangers to "think pink" and trim their pubic hairs in the shape of a valentine), Bernard Levin, Mark Boxer, Kim Philby, and of course John Profumo and those legendary bimbos, Christine Keeler and Mandy Rice-Davies.

In 1972, the party over, I was no wiser but considerably older. Looking around, I found that other expatriate commonwealth writers who had luxuriated too long in London, writers whom I respected, had been driven to composing novels set in the biblical past or on imaginary planets. Alarmed, I decided it was time to go home and pay my dues.

Ensconced in London again, twenty-one years later, if only for the winters, I had to wonder whether I was doing the right thing. The TLS was not reassuring. In a review of Adam Sisman's biography of

A. J. P. Taylor, David Cannadine wrote that a couple of Taylor's closest friends were "social misfits": Sir Lewis Namier because he was Jewish, and Lord Beaverbrook because he was a Canadian. I just happen to be both.

There were surprises. The most unpleasant, in my case, was that the phones now worked. In the sixties, my day's work done, I liked to pour myself a Macallan's and pick up the phone, hoping to luck into a crossed line. One evening I caught a man calling from a pub, judging by the background noises. "Can you get out tonight, luv?" he asked.

"Not tonight," she said. "*It's his birthday.*"

"Oh, just for a quick drink and a cuddle."

"I had to bake him a cake."

"Oh, no."

At which point the best I could come up with was a throat-clearing cough.

"Was that you, luv?"

"I thought it was you."

"*Hang up immediately!*"

One morning my agent called to say a visiting Canadian film producer had asked for my home number, but he hadn't given it to him. However, I knew the man and promptly phoned him at his hotel. The stranger who answered my call said, "I want fried eggs, sausages, and coffee."

"I'm afraid there's been a misunderstanding."

"There's been no misunderstanding. When I wakes up, I wakes up hungry. I want two eggs, sausages, coffee, and don't forget the toast."

"You can't have it."

"What's that?

"You heard me."

"I wish to speak to the manager at once."

"I am the manager."

"Then I'll be coming right down to punch you in the nose."

"I'll be waiting for you, you little prick," I said, hanging up.

Culture shocks. I had to adjust to a reshuffling of the ideological deck. Kingsley Amis, who had once written a pamphlet for the Fabian Society, had been born-again a Thatcherite. Paul Johnson, who had edited the *New Statesman* in my time, had moved even farther to the right. I missed absent friends and acquaintances: the incomparable Tony Godwin, who used to be my editor at Weidenfeld and Nicholson; Georgia Brown, who had died too young; Terry Kilmartin, that most gracious of literary men. Brian Inglis, editor of the *Spectator* in the sixties, was also no longer among the quick. In Inglis's day, I was once told, Evelyn Waugh used to send in a postcard every week to point out grammatical errors in the most recent issue of the magazine.

The Canadian colony had been diminished. Bernard Braden was no longer with us and neither was that ridiculous but endearing bumpkin Roy Thompson. Thompson, riding a fortune acquired in Northern Ontario, had once tried to buy the Toronto *Globe and Mail*, our English-language newspaper of record, but was pronounced too undignified to be its proprietor. Stung, he retreated to Edinburgh and then London, where he eventually purchased the *Sunday Times*, the *Times*, and—his licence to print money—a commercial TV channel. Sent out to interview Thompson, I complimented him on the splendid Sydney Nolan hanging on his office wall.

"It was chosen for me by Lord Snowdon. I hate it," he said, "but it's constantly going up in value."

Things change. Back in the late fifties, during the exciting days of live TV drama, I wrote a play for ITV's "Armchair Theatre." Sydney Newman, the executive producer, sat in on a rehearsal and was shocked to hear one of the characters say, "God damn it!"

"That line will have to go," he said.

So Ted Kotcheff, the director, told the actor to edit out the line whenever Newman was in the neighbourhood, but of course he was to reinsert it in the actual production. Today, however, there is hardly a TV drama produced without its spill of four-letter words, frontal nudes, and bonking scenes. In the dark hours of the night, I fear Kotcheff and I are to blame. God damn it, we made the break-through.

And speaking of breakthroughs, lo and behold, in 1993 ice hockey rated front-page attention in the *Sunday Telegraph* sports section, having attracted 1.2 million fans the previous season. But it was not the game I cherished, scores tending to run 16–4 or 19–8. Furthermore, traditional displays of brotherly love on ice (boarding, cross-checking, hooking, tripping, spearing) were unknown in the decorous British Ice Hockey Association, where even negative thoughts could earn an itinerant Canadian hockey bum two minutes in the sin-bin. Even more disconcerting, the native play-by-play announcers, unlike those in Canada, enjoyed a vocabulary of more than two hundred words.

"The Racers' staunch left-winger, acquiescing to a surreptitious back pass from his line-mate, makes a frightfully devious move on the Devils' defenceman, and just succeeds in hoisting the puck over the Devils' goaltender, who has sprawled prematurely, earning his coach's opprobrium, no doubt."

Its encouraging fan support notwithstanding, our national sport was still suspect in some quarters. On a quick trip to London in the summer of 1992, I picked up a copy of the *Evening Standard* only to discover that a know-nothing sportswriter, Michael Herd, had led off his page with a shocking, unprovoked attack on hockey. He dared to ask, "Do we have to import this legalised violence?" He then went on to say that on September 12–13, Wembley Stadium would be the scene of the first NHL game to be played in deprived Britain since 1959. The Montreal Canadiens, he noted, would be meeting the Chicago Blackhawks, the latter group "renowned as the most physical ice hockey team in the world. Stu Grimson, their left wing, is known as the Grim Reaper." The fastidious Herd concluded, "I will do my damnedest to avoid Wembley that weekend and, instead, have a gentlemanly game of golf."

A good thing that Herd, averse to violence, didn't opt for a soccer match, as I did, on September 2, risking my life at Queen's Park, taking in a contest between Arsenal and the Queens Park Rangers.

It was unlike any hockey game I have ever attended: the streets bordering the Loftus Road stadium were thick with mounted policemen and policewomen, bobbies patrolling with guard dogs, paddy wagons and ambulances at the ready. The neighbourhood reeked of stale cooking oil and anger on a short leash.

The first thing to be said about the stadium, which quickly filled up for the match—with hardly a woman to be seen—was that its proprietors obviously assumed that fans had no knees, the rows were that tight together. It is also true to say that enthusiasts confined to standing throughout the match on either side of the pitch—one side willing to kill for Arsenal, the other equally committed to the Rangers—were more entertaining than the players, their chants and rhythmic handclapping rocking the stadium. Many of the fans, unfortunately—including those in our section—suffered from weak bladders. And as the facilities were limited, even primitive, they were given to pissing against the nearest wall—or down your back, from the row behind, if they couldn't wait. So if you must take in a soccer match on your trip to London, do bring your raincoat, and out of consideration for native customs, don't shed it even if there is hardly a cloud in the sky. Remember, this isn't a hockey game, where the fans are toilet-trained and, at their very worst, in moments of wild abandon, will toss their hats or overshoes on to the ice.

In search of trade news on that same flying visit to London, I picked up a copy of the *Sun*, if only because its literary pages include excerpts from recent books. The September 7, 1992, *Sun*, for instance, reprinted some letters from Radio One deejay Simon Mayo's *Further Confessions*, a collection of disclosures from listeners. One, at least, is worth quoting in full:

> My ex-husband was one of those types who didn't believe marriage meant you were supposed to be faithful.
>
> Fortunately he also liked spicy foods. While chopping chillies, I discovered that if you accidentally touched a scratch the result was unbelievable pain and agony.

So it didn't take much imagination for me to find a way to spice up my husband's illicit sex life. I decided to rub red-hot chilli-pepper juice all over his underpants. It wasn't long before he was complaining of a terrible burning in his wedding tackle. Convinced he had picked up some awful social disease, he stopped his philandering.

I am now happily divorced and my confession is not to ask forgiveness of my horrible ex, but to beg forgiveness of his girl-friends who no doubt suffered as badly as him.

The letter was signed, "Joy, somewhere in England."

In the winter of 1993, I noted that, with the exception of the *Independent*, the quality broadsheets (the *Daily Telegraph*, the *Times*, the *Guardian*) continued to feature endlessly boring articles about the royal follies. Would Princess Di, unequalled as a manipulator of the press, sue for divorce? Should Chuck, the Tampax fetishist, be denied the throne? Can Prince Andrew read and chew gum at the same time? Is Prince Edward "a friend of Dorothy"? Certainly the most intellectually stimulating of the recent spill of books about the Windsors was Dennis Friedman's *Inheritance: Psychological History of the Royal Family*, wherein he speculated about Prince Charles's toilet-seat collection:

"To use a lavatory seat it is necessary to turn one's back on it. When Charles adds to his collection he acts out his own sense of re-jection. The lavatory seat becomes a metaphor for his wish to retali-ate against all those who, at one time or another, have turned their backs on him."

Julie Burchill, writing about the Queen Mum ("I like the old biddy") in the *Modern Review* ("Low Culture for Highbrows"), was less insightful but more saucy, noting, among other things, the matriarch's affection for her "almost exclusively homosexual" household staff:

"We know of a time when, kept waiting for her customary evening cocktail by her squabbling servants, she went below stairs and announced, 'When you old queens have finished fighting, this old queen wants her gin and tonic.' Even more liberally, a courtier caught cottaging and kept overnight in the cells was met the next morning by the QM's car, a bouquet and a card—'Naughty Boy!'"

In a sidebar to Ms. Burchill's tribute to the old biddy, another reporter observed that the death of the Queen Mum will be one of the most extensively prepared for events in British history:

"When she finally pops it, no one will be able to accuse Buckingham Palace or the media of being caught unawares. . . . A Great Funeral cortège now regularly practises its full regalia procession down the Mall at four in the morning."

The *Daily Telegraph* is said to have a twenty-four-page colour supplement ready, and the ever-alert Japanese have also joined the circling buzzards. It has been reported that a Tokyo TV channel has had a prime camera spot on the Mall reserved for the past twenty years at a cost of £1,000 per annum.

Back-scratching is a traditional feature of the London literary life, end-of-the-year best-book lists being provided by individual authors to the quality press, enabling them to shamelessly plug the works of lovers, mistresses, and other scribblers to whom they owe money. Far more amusing was the *Sunday Times*'s 1993 "Beyond the Critical List" round-up, which saluted, among others, the Literary Husband of the Year.

"'He was the ideal husband for a novelist. . . . You could stop him in mid-bonk and ask, "What are you feeling now?" and he would do his best to answer. You see, he understood research,'" said Anne Fine, discussing her first husband with Maureen Cleaver of the *Telegraph Magazine*.

The *Sunday Times* also applauded the Image of the Year, choosing a passage from Armistead Maupin in *Maybe the Moon*: "His groin hovered over me like a dirigible, iridescent as a butterfly's wing in the morning light."

More mischief was available in the December 1993 issue of Auberon Waugh's monthly *Literary Review*, which awarded its first annual Grand Booby Prize for Bad Sex in Fiction. In his report on readers' entries, Waugh ruled out passages from obvious porn novels and made it clear that what he was after was an inept and unnecessary sexual episode in a so-called literary novel. Alas, my favourite entry failed to win. It came from *Defiant Pose*, a novel by Stewart Home: "Terry experienced orgasms as an action replay of the revolutionary uprising in Russia, 1905. Love juice boiled through his prick like workers pouring out of a factory after a mass meeting had decided on a strike."

Florence and I returned to London not only because it was our other home, but also to avoid punishing Canadian winters. So I was delighted, only a week after we had unpacked, to stumble on a double-page ad in the *Telegraph Magazine* advising motorists not to drive in snow unless it was absolutely necessary. This admonition would, of course, be sufficient to clear Canadian roads of traffic for months on end. Out for my late-afternoon stroll it also amused me to watch indigenous, understated old money mixing uneasily, in Harrod's, with visiting, bejewelled Eurotrash and grabby, parcel-laden Japanese tourists making home movies of each other standing up or sitting down, entering or leaving elevators. Pubs, where I had once stopped for a restorative tipple, had become impossible, fruit machines thunking away and unspeakable music throbbing at umpteen decibels. The miniskirt was back, unfortunately indulged in by too many who hadn't been blessed with the legs for it; or by women of a certain age who should have given it up at the same time as they did incense, Rolling Stone concerts, CND marches, and R. D. Laing's goofy decrees. On the King's Road, some women also favoured leggings, which reminded me of my father's long winter underwear, although they tended to be more brightly coloured. Others also fancied nasal earrings, which were not only singularly ugly but also, I imagined, made sneezing a torment. An even worse blight were cellular phones, and those yuppies who wouldn't dream of settling down at a restaurant table without one.

In the months preceding our move to London, I found it worrying to read in the *Spectator* and elsewhere that muggings, car and house break-ins, and even the theft of garden statuary, were now commonplace. But after five months in residence I had yet to be mugged or robbed and, the squalor of Leicester Square notwithstanding, London still struck me as the rarest of cities, a place where the small civilities were still observed.

British ignorance of matters Canadian was something I still found jarring. Take, for instance, an all too typical, egregious error that appeared in Alan Clark's *Diaries*. Having once traversed the Northwest Territories at thirty-five thousand or more feet, qualifying him as an expert, if only of the Westminster standard, he pronounced it "*utterly* lifeless." Actually the tundra's shores are rich in seals, whales, and arctic char, and the tundra itself in edible fowl and caribou in summer, all of which has been sufficient to feed, heat, and clothe the resourceful Inuit since time immemorial. Indigenous delicacies I highly recommend include raw seal's eyes and cubed fat or caribou hump, either dish more yummy than tinned baked beans on white bread toast, traditional fare on Clark's wee offshore island.

Mindless anti-Americanism flourishes in London now, even as it did when I first settled there, among disgruntled Little Englanders of both left and right. Back in the fifties, Kingsley Martin complained in the *New Statesman* that Superman was the quintessential American fascist fantasy figure and, to prove his point, he noted that he was a blond Aryan. But the truth is Supey's hair is black, and he was the creation of a lonely Jewish boy out of Toronto who never married because in real life he was unable to find a girl as pure as the Lois Lane he had invented. I had only been back in London for a couple of months when I came across the thumb-sucker in the *Guardian* that ventured Michael Jackson was being hounded in America only because he was a talented black who had grown too big for his boots. But the sex police had also pursued Gary Hart, Pee Wee Herman, Woody Allen, and, more recently, Senator Robert Packwood and President Bill Clinton for being naughty. Once the new puritans pick up the scent they are indifferent to colour or creed. Then there was the case of Auberon Waugh, who raged weekly in one publication or another against the hamburger and other American delights, largely because, as he has whined again and again, no American publisher had been sagacious enough to publish his best-selling autobiography, *Will This Do?* However, I suspect Waugh has also failed to find a French, Italian, or Egyptian publisher for his book. Surely Waugh, a publican and wine-club pedlar himself, should appreciate that some domestic brews simply do not travel well.

Playing catch-up during our first few weeks back in London, I tried not to look baffled when confronted by new words at dinner parties: say, "quangos" or "whinging." I missed the *Listener,* a sad loss, but caught up with the refreshingly irreverent *Literary Review,* the twee *Oldie,* an increasingly tired *Private Eye,* and even the *Big Issue,* worthy but unreadable. I discovered that the once scathing David Frost had been reduced to every celebrity's panting poodle. To begin with, I took five morning newspapers in a desperate attempt to sort out names new to me: say, Stephen Fry, Will Self, and Jeremy Paxman, among others. Eventually I settled on two morning newspapers, the *Guardian* and the *Daily Telegraph,* and would then wander out at noon to fetch the *International Herald Tribune,* if only to find out what was going on offshore. British broadsheets, undeniably well written, now seemed to favour columns of opinion over reportage. I came to dread stumbling on a loopy little news item on Monday, revealing that a young offender had been sent on safari at the taxpayers' expense, or that a Labour backbencher wished to ban flirting or staying up after ten o'clock, because I knew that these stories would provoke a deluge of opinion. For the rest of the week Waugh, Ingrams, Booker, Chancellor, et al. would feast on these items, taking it as a licence to pontificate. Failing that, these unashamed washers of each other's laundry would proffer opinions of their rivals' opinions, which they could be counted on to find wanting.

Happily, it was still possible to light up a decent cigar in good London restaurants without health fascists protesting, but, by 1993, drinkers who drive were increasingly at risk. The nefarious road minister, one Robert Key, threatened to reduce the permitted booze levels to *zero tolerance.* And, unfortunately, according to a survey undertaken by a motoring company, this Draconian measure was supported by 72 per cent of drivers. However, a spokesman for the Royal Automobile Club did point out that a total ban on alcohol would also mean that drivers could no longer lunch-munch sherry trifles, never mind demolish a coq au vin.

On the other hand, the *Independent* proffered welcome news for those degenerates who fancy an occasional snort of recreational drugs, a habit that renders them vulnerable to a snap urine test when they apply for a job with certain multinational corporations for which they are otherwise eminently qualified. Look here, should your pee printout read OPOA+POS, registering more than one incriminating miligram of morphine per litre of urine, don't despair. Do not crumble before your righteous corporate interviewer. Act outraged. Promptly confess to being a poppy-seed bagel addict. And charge your interviewer with being a racist, prejudiced against traditional Jewish delicacies, and threaten to sic the B'nai B'rith Anti-Defamation League on him.

According to the report in the *Independent*, "The poppy seeds used by bakers carry traces from the opium poppy's seed capsule. These contain morphine, though not so that you would notice. The trace is enough, however, to give rise to a damning entry in your personnel file."

Sprung to adolescence during the Second World War, I was brought up on Great Britain, rather than Little England. Blood, sweat, and tears. The Few. The Empire's finest hour. Dunkirk. Tobruk. Churchill, before I found out he was a drunk, a warmonger, and a racist. But some fifty years on, I'm beginning to wonder who actually won what my generation still calls "the war." The constantly shrinking pound now genuflects to the Almighty Deutschmark and the Greater East Asia Co-prosperity Sphere extends to the Midlands. A regular reader of the *Economist*, I could understand that it was not necessarily a bad thing that BMW had taken over Rover, discomfiting the Japanese who already owned a large chunk of the last British-owned automobile company, but all the same I was appalled to turn on "The News at Ten" one night and catch a parliamentary committee of inquiry grovelling to the CEO of Honda in the U.K. "Do you think the Japanese will be insulted?" a Labour MP asked. "Is it possible they won't want to invest here any more?"

My memories of parliamentarians of size were still vivid: Churchill, Nye Bevan, Gaitskell, Macmillan, and Ian Macleod, among others. So I wondered what sins citizens of the U.K. had committed to be sentenced to 1993's pipsqueak cabinet and Opposition front bench, little more than footnotes to history. Then, come the early spring of 1994, a committee of parliamentary mice were off to Malaysia to plead with their officials to buy British, and this once proud island began to advertise itself abroad as a country with the cheapest EC labour costs, billing itself as a European Taiwan.

London, even more plausibly, could easily have billed itself Sodom-upon-Thames.

On this scandal-ridden, sex-crazed island, this demiparadise, this England, we were not distressed every morning in the early spring of 1994 by the trials of Canada's post-colonial life—the latest pronouncements of Lucien Bouchard, Preston Manning, or Jolly Jock Parizeau. Instead, we were nourished by a daily dose of prurience, our pleasure compounded by the fact that the new guardians of morality were none other than journalists, hacks hitherto justly celebrated for gin-swilling, skirt-chasing, and expense-account fiddling. As a rule, it was one or another of the tabloids that nabbed a sinning actress or politician. Then the quality broadsheets, professing to be shocked by such gutter reportage, would regurgitate the sleaze in detail, albeit disapprovingly.

One of the first to fall was a pretty actress, Gillian Taylforth, star of "Eastenders," a TV soap, who was charged with gross indecency. Driving home from the Ascot races, where she and her fiancé had consumed a good deal of champers, the amorous couple pulled over on a motorway shoulder, only to suffer an alert bobby (or Peeping

Tom) who caught Ms. Taylforth, he said, leaning over to tend to her fiancé, lickety-split as it were. The *Sun* shone on this exploit, giving it lots of play, and an outraged Ms. Taylforth sued for libel. In the ensuing trial, judge and jury were invited to witness re-enactments in the couple's Range Rover. A woman who was a *Sun* feature writer demonstrated, even as she giggled with embarrassment, how she could—if her seat belt were unfastened—bury her head in a driver's lap. Ms. Taylforth, on the other hand, claimed that they had made an emergency stop because her fiancé was suffering from an acute attack of pancreatitis, and she had unzipped him, lowered his trousers, and stroked him with her hand only to ease his pain. But judge and jury wouldn't swallow that. Certainly not after George Carmen, QC, representing the *Sun*, had acquired and played a private party video, which revealed Ms. Taylforth simulating fellatio on a sausage and saying, "I give good head." And pricey head, she might have added, because her indiscretion set her back an estimated £500,000 in legal costs, qualifying her, I daresay, for an entry in the *Guinness Book of World Records* as the most generous known purveyor of oral sex.

Our people's tribunes in Canada, responding to the public's opprobrium, now outdo each other in self-denial. Westminster MPs, otherwise as resoundingly mediocre as our own, have at least proved themselves more raunchy. Tabloid snoops have caught one Tory after another fathering an illegitimate babe, servicing four mistresses simultaneously, or pausing for "a kiss and a cuddle" with a pert, miniskirted research assistant. These sad tales tend to follow the same pattern. A day or two after an MP has been unmasked, his erstwhile inamorata spills the beans to one or another of the tabloids, earning an estimated £25,000 for revealing that the dirty old man who corrupted her innocence also fancied wearing her lingerie, or being made to stand in the corner with his face pressed to the wall, or having his toes sucked. Then, only three days later, the MP, appropriately contrite, meets reporters outside his country home, arm in arm with his wife, sturdy and curvy as an oak tree, wearing a tweed skirt and army boots with steel toes. "Reggie has been a bad boy," she says, "but I am standing by him. We are a happily married couple and we are now going off on a long overdue hol," either in Marrakech, if some understanding lobbyist is picking up the bill, or Blackpool, if that isn't the case.

When Tory MPs are not caught being naughty boys or girls, they will, on occasion, invent their own steamy sex episodes for profit. Take, for instance, the case of Edwina Currie. Her excruciatingly banal potboiler, *A Parliamentary Affair*, was an uneasy mix of Westminster tour guide, retailing at length every hoary old parliamentary anecdote, and soft-core porn. Its tiresome heroine, obviously Ms. Currie's doppelgänger, is the stunning Mrs. Elaine Stalker. She has been an MP for only a couple of months before she repairs to the flat of Roger Dickson, a Tory whip, sinks to her knees uninvited, unzips him, and provides gratis what cost Ms. Taylforth all that money. Then the pair (*Stalker* and *Roger Dick*son, get it?) engage in a bit of sophisticated banter that hasn't been equalled since Noel Coward was in his prime.

"Maybe I should start a new career, as a public heart-throb," says Dickson. "How does the adorable Ms. Stalker think I would get on?"

"Extremely well, if that equipment is anything to go by," she responds. "You should be proud of what you've got. It certainly gives a different meaning to Honourable Member."

To somebody who had been rooted in London through the salacious sixties (the publication of the Duchess of Argyll's diaries, rating the sexual prowess of her lovers; and the Profumo affair) the latest sex follies all begin to smack of *déjà vu*, if only the new sinners would troop off to Toynbee Hall, seeking redemption by doing good works among the poor. My feeling that I had been there before was certified when it was revealed that the foolish old Lord Buck and his trophy bride of dubious origins, Bienvenida, had actually spent their honeymoon night in the bridal suite at Cliveden, country seat of the Astors, where Profumo had first espied Christine Keeler prancing nude by the poolside. Bienvenida's indiscreet lover, Sir Peter Harding, chief of the defence staff, did at least salvage some dignity by resigning once he was caught out, rather than attempting to ride out the embarrassment like so many Tory MPs before him. Even so, this business was far richer in comedy than tragedy. It was the stuff of a P. G. Wodehouse novel, or a Feydeau farce. Consider some of the details.

Lord Buck met his Spanish sex-bomb at a dinner party for a pro-nuclear pressure group called Families for Defence and, to this day, seems most put out because he lost custody of the couple's King Charles spaniels, Pebbles and Cocoa, and doesn't even appear to have been granted visiting privileges.

Sir Peter Harding was accused of being especially culpable because he had been responsible for a Ministry of Defence Discipline and Standards Paper:

"Thirty-two. *Adultery Outside the Military Community.* Married or single officers who enter into adulterous affairs outside the military community jeopardise their status as an officer should the circumstances of the affair become public, and if it brings either the officer or the Army into disrepute." Put plainly, this seems to rule, on Sir Peter's standard, that it's acceptable to bonk another man's wife so long as the cuckold in question is another officer and a gentleman.

The pin-ups of the deplorable Bienvenida plastered throughout *News of the World*, her paymaster, also struck me as more comic than titillating. My favourite, which showed her in a sheer, brief black outfit, was enhanced by cutlines which read:

"THE LADY PACKS A POUCH! Garter a load of this! Glamorous Lady Buck keeps a tiny bottle of something warm and sensual in a black pouch strapped to her thigh." Nonsense. On the evidence of the story so far, it's probably a tape recorder.

Years ago Philip Roth observed that the satirist's lot had become impossible, his wildest inventions rendered anodyne by daily news reports. And, back in the sixties, Peter Cook ventured that the Emerald Isle was bound to sink giggling into the sea. They were both right.

Pedlar's Diary

VAUDEVILLE ISN'T DEAD. But the traditional song-and-dance men, jugglers, animal acts, and stand-up comics have been displaced by jet-lagged authors, a far less entertaining bunch, who will read from their works in bookshops on the circuit, wherever at least eight potential customers can be found. On a typical week in Los Angeles, the *Los Angeles Times Book Review* (October 29, 1997) lists no less than eighty pedlars reading in various locations. These include Peter J. Harris, author of *The Vampire Who Drinks Gospel Music*; Mollie Katzen, who has written *Mollie Katzen's Vegetable Heaven*; Terry Berland, who will discuss his very own *Breaking into Commercials*; Jared Diamond, author of *Why Sex Is Fun*; and a highly suspect "writers' workshop for teenage girls" in Beyond Baroque, out there on Venice Boulevard. To be fair, the same week there are also some better-known scribblers working the territory; John Berger, James Ellroy, Judith Rossner, Arundhati Roy, and Will Self.

September 16, 1997. Montreal. A day before starting out on a cross-Canada book promotion tour, the omens are bad. Striding down Crescent Street, late in the afternoon, bound for my favoured watering hole, I am stopped by a gentleman from Vancouver. "Aren't you Mordecai Richler?"

"Yes."

"Let me shake your hand. I've read everything you've written. I think you're wonderful."

"Well, thank you."

"Now let me ask you a question. What do you do for a living?"

Then there is a letter from a college in Hamilton, Ontario, inviting me to speak: "Your book, *The Apprenticeship of Duddy Kravitz*, has long been a fixture in our English classes. Students are amazed to discover that you are still alive."

September 17. Toronto. In town to deliver the Donner Foundation lecture, I first submit to lunch with Ms. Jan Wong, a *Globe and Mail* columnist. "How tall are you?" she asks.

Five feet eight, I say, startled.

"And how tall is your wife?"

"Why do you want to know?"

"I need to describe you."

Pursuing her literary inquiries, she asks if our children are getting a Jewish education. Married to a Jew herself, she allows, with a self-satisfied smile, "We have a seder every Friday night."

"That must be a Jewish-Chinese custom. We manage it only once a year. On Passover."

Finally, she is annoyed with me. "You're not living up to your reputation. You didn't have much to drink. I think it's because you're trying to impress me."

There's a six-page fax waiting for me back in my hotel room. It's from Knopf Canada. A list of interviews, readings, and book signings I'm to do cross-Canada. I've been wary of morning-show TV interviewers ever since one of those relentlessly cheerful young women squeezed me in for a couple of minutes between a cooking demonstration and a chat with a spiritual healer. Brandishing my novel, she demanded, "Is this a true story or did you just make it up out of your head?"

Publication wasn't always such an ordeal. When I was a young writer, living in London, I would deliver my manuscript to my publisher, who would immediately remind me of the unearned advance on my previous effort. When my novel came out nine months later

I would sit at home waiting for cherished friends to phone and read aloud my worst review, just in case I had missed it. Those, those were the days when novelists could be condescending about travelling salesmen, men who lugged their sample cases from town to town, but we have long since joined the club. Last time out in New York, I was driven in a limo from bookshop to bookshop, popping in to sign copies of my novel, preceded and followed by other writers in other limos signing theirs. Bookshops can return unsold copies of a book to the publisher, but they can't refund those that are autographed. So the publisher's flack who accompanies authors on these excursions usually says something like, "I'll chat up the sales staff and while they aren't looking, you sign as many goddamn copies as possible."

Bruce Jay Friedman once told me that he had gone to do a signing in a Boston bookshop only a day after his new novel had earned a rave review in the *Boston Globe*. Nobody turned up. "What would have happened," he asked the bookseller, "if my novel had been panned yesterday?"

I have had a somewhat similar experience. Maybe ten years ago I was invited to Montreal's annual Salon du Livre to sit with the translator of a new French-language edition of *The Apprenticeship of Duddy Kravitz*, our table stacked high with books. Our moment arrived after a voice booming out of a loudspeaker announced to the milling crowd that we were now available for signings at booth number twelve. Ten minutes passed and nobody came. Finally a man stopped at our table. He pulled out a cigarette and asked, "Got a light?"

September 18. Toronto. My marching orders from Knopf Canada read: "Twelve-thirty p.m. The *Globe and Mail* (national) with Liz Renzetti. At Avalon Restaurant (private booth where you can smoke, etc. . . .)" *Private booth? Etc?* What's expected of me, I wonder?

"Three p.m. One hour. *Eye Weekly* magazine (local) with Robyn Gillam (woman)."

Now that I am an aging pro (man), somebody who has been around the block (national) possibly once too often, I don't make rookie mistakes. I will, for instance, no longer do radio or TV call-in shows. Once, at a late-night call-in show in Chicago, I sat round a table with two other writers. We watched, astonished, as the technician in the control booth rapped on his glass window and held up a message for our host. "Remember, Dave," it read, "this is a night of the full moon."

When my turn to sell came, I went on, as required, about the torments of my difficult craft. How hell is a blank sheet of paper, and so forth and so on. Then a listener addressed a question to me: "All that's well and good, Mort, but I live on the North Side, and I want to know how come there was no garbage collection this week?"

And now I've been out there peddling for only a few days and I am already weary of the most frequently asked questions:

"Why did you write your novel in the first person?"

"Why not?"

"Do you use a computer, Mr. Richler?"

"No, every morning I slip into my Armani silk dressing gown and monogrammed velvet slippers by Dior, and begin to write with my goose-quill pen."

September 25. Fly to London with my wife for British publication of *Barney's Version*. Good news and bad news. Splendid reviews in both the *Daily Telegraph* and *Sunday Times*, but Melvyn Bragg has cancelled my appearance on BBC-Radio's "Start the Week" and John Walsh of the *Independent* no longer wants to take me to lunch at The Ivy, as I have already been interviewed by Mark Steyn, in Montreal, for the *Daily Telegraph*.

London is still in mourning for Princess Diana, whose death proved a bonanza for British newspapers, which increased their press run by twenty per cent, and for florists as well. A friend of mine, stopping at a kiosk to buy flowers for his wife a few days after Diana's death, was told, "Sorry, sir, but there's a fifty per cent surcharge this week."

The tabloids, pledged to good behaviour after the demise of the troubled princess, have already thrown in the sponge. Tit and bum photographs are back, including, after a brief absence, the *Sun*'s topless page-three girl: "Hello, campers! Say hi-de-hi to Leah, 17, making her page 3 debut today. The Manchester maid used to work in a holiday camp. But she packed her bags so we could check out her chalet nice curves instead. We certainly think she deserves a break in the Sun."

Happily, I discover British intellectuals have more serious concerns, namely, was Robin Hood gay? Cambridge historian Barrie Dobson feels Robin was a regular sort of guy. "The relationship between Little John and Robin is interesting," he says, "but with no suggestion of homoeroticism." However, it ain't necessarily so, according to Stephen Knight, professor of English at the University of Wales in Cardiff. In a coming conference, he promises to look into Robin's taste for cross-dressing: "There will be a discussion about Robin's sexuality—what were they doing in the woods, why were they wearing tights, and that kind of thing."

Meanwhile, TV Channel Four has taken a hard look at bisexuals, also known as "greedies," who are disdainful of straights, whom they have dubbed "monosexuals." Professional masseuse and cook Felicity Diamond, a proud switch-hitter, says, "It's not about greed for a number of partners. I want the best, not the most. I have lots of friendships and good relationships and sometimes they become sexual. When I like people I don't care what genitals they have."

October 1. Manchester. My British publisher, Chatto and Windus, has arranged for me to do a reading at Waterstone's bookshop, but this also happens to be Rosh Hashanah, so many of my people have cancelled. Militant feminist Andrea Dworkin is reading in another room at Waterstone's. An incurable romantic, Ms. Dworkin has written: "Intercourse remains a means, or the means, of physiologically making a woman inferior: communicating to her, cell by cell, her own inferior status . . . pushing and thrusting until she gives in." On the other hand, she doesn't believe that all men are rapists, which is awfully decent of her.

The *Sunday Independent* has launched a campaign to decriminalize pot, its initiative backed by more than one hundred heavy-hitters in business, the arts, science, and politics. They include authors Harold

Pinter, Martin Amis, Auberon Waugh, and Fay Weldon, film directors Mike Leigh and Peter Greenaway, numerous doctors and psy-
chiatrists with the most impressive credentials, as well as the Marquess
of Bath and the Marchioness of Worcester. But it strikes me that at
least one supporter of the initiative is vulnerable to a charge of special
pleading. He is the Rev. R. H. A. Scott, M.A. Oxon, who is currently
serving four years in the slammer for growing cannabis.

My own feelings are mixed. I also favour decriminalizing pot,
but I fear if this campaign were successful in North America it could
ruin the economy of Florida, and could oblige many an underpaid
Montreal gendarme to live off his salary.

London, in early October, is still balmy, sidewalk cafés flourish-
ing, but I do notice one change. Strolling down the King's Road, I
see an increasing number of bald-headed women. I'm not sure
whether this is the new fashion, however ill-advised, or if the women
have been treated for head-lice. In either case, I am not impressed.

October 5. Back in Montreal. Time to check out a week's mail.
A professor at an Ontario university is writing a paper on minor novelists and wants me to answer twenty-six questions. An eyeglass
museum in Tennessee would like a pair of my old spectacles. An
invitation to lecture, beginning, "We are a non-profit society. . . ." I
read no further. A query from Knopf Canada's publicist in Calgary
inviting me to appear on a CBC-Radio show called "Mountain Top
Music":

"This interview is a personal profile of Mr. Richler. They have
requested the following information:

1. His five favourite pieces of music
2. The title and author of his favourite book
3. Where he would like to spend his last days on earth (This can
   be anywhere, a mountain top, an island, at home, etc.)

October 6. Toronto again. More TV, radio, and press interviews,
followed by an evening reading at the University of Toronto's Con-
vocation Hall. Afterwards, at the book-signing, I am confronted by

a hostile young woman: "I read your last novel, *Solomon Gursky Was Here*. It took me two years. WHAT A STRUGGLE!"

October 7. Toronto. I pick up a copy of the Montreal *Gazette*. Bad news from home, as Quebec's loopy language wars continue.

Although Florence and I spend the winter months in London, for the rest of the year we are installed in our cottage on the shores of Lake Memphremagog in Quebec's Eastern Townships. The nearest hospital, La Providence, is in the neighbouring town of Magog, and our family has always been treated with courtesy there. But now there is a scandal. No, perfidy. The alert Rodrigue Larose, of the Mouvement Estrien Pour le Français, has discovered handwritten signs *in English* on the premises, loose-leaf sheets bearing the words "emergency admissions." This is illegal, of course, because the Townships' 44,563 anglophones make up only 9 per cent of the population. "Make no mistake," said a horrified Larose, "loose-leaf scribbling is one sure step on the road to full-fledged signs made by professional sign-makers."

Larose is also concerned because the Quebec government intends to introduce English lessons in francophone schools in grade three, instead of grade four. Impressionable eight-year-olds, he fears, will be exposed to "contamination." And Jacques Poisson, president of the MEF, feels his crusade against "creeping anglicization" is a thankless job. "We're accused of being fanatics and narrow-minded bigots."

Obviously not the case, Larose told the *Gazette*, because the MEF allows that if an English-speaking crash victim turns up at the hospital with two broken legs, the victim should be addressed in English. "We're perfectly willing to accept that."

October 8. Ottawa. Reading and signing at the National Public Library. A man asks me to inscribe a copy of my novel "To Judith," and requests that I add a personal message. "Think of something witty," he says.

I protest that I don't know Judith, so I can't add a personal message.

"I doubt that she'll have time to finish it anyway," he says, grabbing the book. "She's suffering from terminal cancer."

October 18. Victoria, Vancouver Island. Midway through my reading, at the Open Space Gallery, the microphone begins to leak music from a local rock station. First time I perform with a back-up group. Among those waiting to have a book signed, there is a pretty young girl. "My mother enjoys your work," she says. Somebody else tells me, "My husband was in your class at Baron Byng High. He couldn't come tonight. Heart attack. One minute he was reading the *Globe and Mail* at the breakfast table, and the next he keeled over." I don't recognize the name, but I say I remember him well.

October 19. Vancouver. Last time I was here, locals were complaining about the influx of Chinese from Hong Kong, and how they had inflated real-estate prices. Now the same people are fulminating because so many of the Chinese are leaving, worried that they could soon be taxed on their overseas earnings. Real-estate prices are collapsing. My minder says, "The parents return to Hong Kong, and leave their teenage kids behind in those big houses, just in case. They're usually left with a clothes allowance of forty thousand dollars. White kids hit them for protection money during school lunch hours."

Interview with a woman from the *Western Jewish Bulletin*. She wants to know, speaking frankly, is it true that I'm an anti-Semite?

Item: A story, possibly apocryphal, told to me by a Hollywood film director. Years ago, Daniel Fuchs, a gifted novelist and short-story writer, was hired to work on a screenplay in Hollywood with his idol, William Faulkner. Faulkner, a sensible man, did not suffer Hollywood easily. He was drunk most of the time. Following a difficult couple of weeks, the sensitive Fuchs said, "Mr. Faulkner, this collaboration is not working."

Faulkner agreed that was the case.

"It's not working," said Fuchs, "because you're an anti-Semite."

"Yes," said Faulkner, "but I don't like Gentiles either."

October 21. Florence has to fly home and my flight takes me to Calgary on a cloudless day. The mountains, as always, are spectacular. Last time I was in Calgary, I stopped somebody and asked him if he could direct me to the main street. "We haven't got one," he said.

October 22. At Calgary airport, bound for Winnipeg, I cannot find a copy of my novel in the bookshop. I ask the teenager behind the counter, "Have you got a copy of *Barney's Version*?"

"Jeez. They went so fast, we haven't got any left. But I could order you one from our other shop."

"I don't need one. I wrote it. Now why don't you reorder?"

"Not a bad idea."

At my book-signing at the McNally Robinson Bookstore, in Winnipeg, a young woman says, "My father used to live just upstairs from you on Jeanne Mance Street."

"I remember him well," I say, but I never lived on Jeanne Mance Street.

October 23. Montreal. Home at last. But, late in January, I will have to set out again, this time on my American book-peddling tour. Last time out, I remember staggering off a plane in Seattle, having already been overnight in six other cities. The minder who met me eyed me suspiciously. "Have you been drinking?" she asked.

"*Certainly not.* But I wouldn't mind if we stopped somewhere before my first interview."

"We can't do that. Your first interviewer is a Mormon."

"They all are."

"I said Mormon, not moron."

"Whoops. Sorry about that."

Back in the early fifties, in London, I used to drink occasionally with Louis MacNeice in a pub round the corner from the BBC. He told me that he had once been to lecture in Montreal. Two nice club ladies met him at the airport. "I'd like to stop for a drink first," said MacNeice.

"Oh, you mustn't worry, Mr. MacNeice. We'll be serving tea at the hall."

"I mean a drink drink," he said.

So they stopped at the Ritz-Carlton Hotel, he told me, and waited for him in the car outside: "You'll find what you want in there."

So it goes.

Sports

Eddie
Quinn

ON JULY 28, 1939, the following item appeared in the Montreal *Gazette*:

FORUM WRESTLING
TO RESUME AUGUST 8

At a meeting of the Montreal Athletic Commission, yesterday morning, Eddie Quinn, of Boston, was granted a matchmaker's licence as representative of the Forum in succession to Jack Ganson. . . . [Quinn] was given permission to go ahead with the arrangements for his first big show on August 8. . . . Yvon Robert, formerly recognized locally as heavyweight champion, will appear in the inaugural program. . . .

Apparently Quinn intends to have no traffic with the "noble experiment" which was Ganson's swan song locally; that of a return to straight, scientific wrestling. Quinn stands solidly behind rip-roaring rassling with all the frills. He is not even daunted by the plethora of "champions" that infest the mat landscape. . . . Referring to Ganson's attempt to take the fun out of wrestling, Quinn said, "The public will not fall for that pink-tea stuff."

Quinn, who used to drive a taxi in Brookline, Massachussetts, never looked back. In 1960 he not only promoted all the wrestling matches at the Montreal Forum, but, as he said, "I got most of Canada, Boston, thirty per cent of St. Louis, and fifty per cent of Chicago. Things have gone pretty fast in the last twenty years."

So fast, in fact, that Quinn was netting as much as a quarter of a million dollars a year for his activities. He had made wrestling the number-two spectator sport in Quebec.

Quinn, who necessarily travelled a good deal, was a difficult man to catch up with. His offices, Canadian Athletic Promotions, were in the Forum. The first time I dropped in there were two men seated in the outer office: Larry Moquin and somebody called Benny. Moquin, who books the wrestlers for Quinn, used to be a famous performer himself. He was a semi-pro football player when Quinn discovered him. Benny, a greying, curly-haired man-of-all-jobs, reminded me of the horseplayers I used to know as a kid round the roaring Main.

Moquin and Benny were playing gin rummy, ten-dollar bills changing hands often. The phone rang a couple of times and Moquin, his tone belligerent, said, "He's gone fishing. Yeah." Once Benny answered the phone, held it, and looked quizzically at Moquin. "For God's sake," Moquin said, "he's gone fishing."

Actually, I was waiting for one of Quinn's publicity men, Norman Olson, to show up. The first thing Olson said to me after he came in was, "Are you here to knock us?"

I told him no.

Olson, in his early thirties, was a fat, swarthy man with a little black moustache. "Eddie isn't here," he said.

"He's gone fishing," I said.

Olson laughed. "Aw, Eddie's in the pool. He's in the pool all day. On the phone. His phone bills come to two thousand dollars a month."

Quinn lived in the town of Mount Royal, one of Montreal's more affluent suburbs. His swimming pool, he would later tell me, held 38,500 gallons of water and cost him $12,000. Olson got him on the line and all at once the office jumped to life. Everybody wanted to talk to Eddie, who had just flown in from Chicago. "How's the

Irishman?" Olson asked with a nervous little laugh. There was a pause. "Sure," Olson said, intimidated. "I'll fix it."

Dan Parker, then the *New York Daily Mirror*'s sports editor, had made a sarcastic remark in his column about Quinn having one world champion wrestler in Montreal, another in St. Louis, and a third in Chicago.

"Parker doesn't like Eddie," Olson said. "There's more to wrestling than meets the eye. We've got all kinds of people coming here. I know one psychiatrist who never misses a match. All day people tell him nutty things. At night he comes here. It relaxes him." Olson believed that wrestling, like golf, had great therapeutic value. "The immigrants come here," he said, "because it makes them feel good inside to see the Anglo-Saxon, the blond guy, get it. The French like it too, you know. It's a release for them." He felt that TV had given the sport a big boost. One-hour shows in Detroit and Chicago, he said, outdrew other sports. Before TV, Killer Kowalski and Yukon Eric drew only $1,500 at the gate in Chicago, but after three months of appearing on studio shows with a small invited audience, the same two performers drew $56,000.

Quinn, Olson predicted, would begin to run studio shows out of Montreal as soon as his contract with the CBC ended. "These days," he said, giving the TV set an affectionate slap, "you've just got to come to terms with the one-eyed monster. But it's killed the nightclubs, you know. Today only the walkers will bring them in." Walkers, he explained, were girls who took their clothes off on stage, slipped into them again, and then drank with the customers on commission. "I could tell you a lot about this town," he said.

Olson gave me a couple of wrestling magazines, tickets for the next show, and promised to arrange meetings for me with Killer Kowalski and Eddie Quinn. "Eddie's a wonderful guy," he said. "He's got a wonderful sense of humour."

In the outer office Benny and Moquin were still playing gin rummy. Moquin was losing.

"You'll like Kowalski," Olson said. "A lovable guy."

Before going to the match the next night I read up on the sport in *Wrestling Revue* and *Wrestling News*. The former, a most spirited quarterly, featured biographies of top performers, action pictures, and an especially informative department called Rumours versus Facts, wherein I learned that 640-pound Haystack Calhoun does *not* suffer from a glandular disorder (he's a big boy, that's all), and that Skull Murphy does *not* rub a special kind of animal grease over his hairless head so that opponents cannot hold him in a headlock (in Skull's own words, "I use ordinary Johnson's baby oil on my head. I find it helps to prevent irritation from rubbing on the dirty canvas"). However, Princess Zelina, slave girl of the hated Sheik, *does* come from a royal family in Lebanon (her old man, living in penurious exile in London, hopes to regain his throne before long). In *Wrestling News*, which is actually a section of *Boxing Illustrated*, I was taken with a defence of girl midget wrestlers by Buddy Lee. In a truculent piece titled "Don't Sell These Girls Short," Lee assured his readers that those "pint-sized pachyderms, Baby Cheryl, a real toughie for one so tiny, and Little Darling Dagmar, 'the Marilyn Monroe of the Maulin' Midgets,' are a couple of sweet kids, happy with their work."

Both magazines rated Killer Kowalski as number three among the world's wrestlers. This was especially gratifying to me as the following night I was to see the Killer battle "Nature Boy" Buddy Rogers for the world championship and an $18,000 winner-take-all purse.

There were, I'd say, only about four thousand fans at the Forum for the occasion. Many of the older men still wore their working clothes. The teenagers, however, favoured black leather jackets, their names implanted with steel studs on the back. The most engaging of the preliminary performers was Tiger Tomasso, an uncouth villain who not only eye-gouged and kicked below the belt but also bit into his opponent's shoulder when aroused.

Before the main bout a precautionary net was tied around the ring. This was necessary because Kowalski, a strapping six feet seven, is, all the same, a most bashful performer, given to fleeing the ring when the going gets rough. Not only that. Struck the slightest blow, he tends to whine and even plead for mercy from his opponent. Even so, the wily Pole made short work of the golden-haired Nature Boy and won the coveted championship belt. This was a popular win with all us non-Anglo-Saxons.

The next afternoon, back in the modest offices of Canadian Athletic Promotions, Kowalski told me, "I indulge in lots of histrionics in the ring. I shout, I snarl, I jump up and down like a madman. Am I mad? I earn more than fifty thousand dollars a year."

Kowalski told me that he used to work on the Ford assembly line in Windsor for fifty dollars a week. He was paid more than that for his first wrestling match in Detroit, and quickly realized that he was in the wrong business. A top performer in 1960, Kowalski wrestled three times a week, usually for a percentage of the gate, and lived with his brother and sister-in-law in a house he had recently bought in Montreal. He was thirty-three years old, and expected to be able to go on wrestling until he reached his mid-forties. Meanwhile, against that retirement day, Kowalski had been investing his money in securities.

"I've built up a personality," he said, "a product, and that's what I sell. Ted Williams is no different. Why do you think he spit at the crowd that day? It's showmanship. Everything is showmanship today. Richard Nixon has his act and I have mine." Kowalski bent over and showed me a scar on his head. "Last week in Chicago," he said, "after I'd won a match, my opponent hit me over the head with a chair. You think he wanted to hurt me? He wanted to make an impression, that's all."

Norman Olson, who had joined us earlier, now began to stir anxiously. "You're forgetting that wrestling takes a lot of natural ability," he said.

"Sure," Kowalski said.

"You've got to keep in shape."

"The most dangerous thing," Kowalski said, "are those crazy kids. They come to the matches with clothespin guns and sometimes they shoot rusty nails at us. Once one got embedded in my side." Kowalski also pointed out that young performers, taking part in their first big match, are also a threat. "They're so nervous," he said, "they might do something wrong."

I asked Kowalski if there was any animosity among wrestlers.

"No," he said.

"Tell him about the night here when you ripped off Yukon Eric's ear," Olson said gleefully.

"Well," Kowalski said, "one of my specialties is to climb up on the ropes and jump up and down on my opponent. One night Eric slipped aside, trying to avoid me, and I landed on his ear, ripping it off. He was very upset and he fled to his dressing room. Before long the dressing room was full of reporters and relatives and fans. Finally Eric looked up and asked for his ear. He'd forgotten it in the ring. The referee had picked it up, put it in his pocket, and by this time was showing it to all his friends at the other end of the Forum. When they got it back from him it was too late to sew it on again."

A few days later Olson arranged for me to have lunch with Eddie Quinn in the Kon-Tiki Room in the Mount Royal Hotel. Quinn was already there when I arrived, seated with one of his referees and Olson. He wore rings on both hands—one was an enormous signet and the other was diamond-encrusted. A chunky man with an expressive if hardbitten face, he spoke out of the corner of his mouth, just like promoters did in the movies. "There's nothing left," he said, "but death and taxes. They belt you here, they belt you there. I just go on to keep people working. The government takes all the money, you know." He turned to the referee. "I dropped ten thousand this morning," he said.

"You're used to it."

"That doesn't mean I like it."

"Eddie's got a wonderful sense of humour," Olson said.

"You're too fat, Norman. Hey, where's your broad?" Quinn asked the referee. Then, turning to me, he added, "We're waiting for a French chantoosie."

"She's at the hairdresser's upstairs."

"Well, go get her. We want to eat."

The referee hurried off. "Hey, what's your name?" Quinn asked me. "Norman here says to call you Moe for short but not for long."

"Norman's too fat."

Quinn laughed and slapped my knee. The referee returned with the girl. "Meet the Freedom Fighter," Quinn said. "She was Miss Europe. She worked with Chevalier. She can't sing, either."

The referee shook with laughter.

"Say hello to Mr. Richler," Quinn said to the girl. "Hey, waiter. Another round of the same." The waiter handed Quinn a menu. "How do you order this stuff?" Quinn asked, and then he made some loud, unintelligible noises that were supposed to sound like Chinese. The Chinese waiter smiled thinly. "Just bring us lots of everything," Quinn said, and then he turned to me. "You like this food? Looks like it's been through a sawmill. Hey, waiter, if you don't know what to get us, just call the health board and ask them to recommend something."

"Eddie's a natural-born kibitzer," Olson said.

I asked Quinn about Yvon Robert, the most popular performer ever to wrestle in Quebec. "Around here," Quinn said, "it used to be the pope, Robert, and Maurice Richard. In that order."

"Robert was great great," Olson said.

Quinn, who had a phenomenal memory for facts, told me the exact date, place, and take of his most successful bouts. In 1959, he drew ten thousand people to the Forum with a novel attraction, boxer versus wrestler. Former world heavyweight champion "Jersey" Joe Walcott took on Buddy Rogers, the Nature Boy. Rogers dived for the canvas immediately and seldom rose higher than a low crouch. In the first round Walcott nailed the wrestler with a hard right and seemed to have him nearly out, but in the third Rogers got Walcott's legs and Walcott quit.

Quinn's biggest gates came from the three Yvon Robert matches against the incomparable Gorgeous George. George's gimmicks included long curly hair that he had dyed blond and a female valet who used to spray the ring with perfume before the wrestler himself deigned to appear. Religious leaders objected to the gorgeous one's effeminate antics and brought pressure to bear on the Montreal police. As a consequence, George never wrestled in the Forum again.

I asked Quinn about midget wrestlers. "The crowd loves 'em," he said.

The girl who had sung with Chevalier produced some photos of herself and handed them around. She explained that she had to take the photos to a theatrical agency round the corner and asked Quinn if he would accompany her.

"Delivering pictures is Benny's department," Quinn said. He seized a linen napkin, wrote a phone number on it with a ballpoint pen, and handed it to the girl. "Call Benny," he said. "Hey, waiter"— Quinn made some more Chinese-like sounds—"the bill." He didn't look at the amount. Turning to me, he said, "Shall I sign it Eddie Quinn, the Men's Room?"

I smiled.

"We must meet again and talk," he said. "Come to my pool one day. Norman will fix it."

"Sure thing," Norman said.

On the way out we ran into the French chantoosie. She told Quinn she owed the bellboy a dime for the phone call. "Here, kid," Quinn said, and he handed the boy a dollar.

"Couldn't we walk there?" the girl asked Quinn once more.

"Walking is Benny's department. I only walk as far as elevators."

A couple of nights later I went to another wrestling match, this time at the small Mont St. Louis Gym. There wasn't much of a crowd, but those who did turn up were fierce. There were several fist fights. A fan attempted to break a folding chair over Killer Kowalski's back. On the whole, though, this was an evening of in-different performances. Obviously, wrestlers, like actors, need a big, responsive audience. Only Tiger Tomasso, a dedicated performer, put on a good exhibition: spitting, eye-gouging, biting.

I was lucky enough to meet the Tiger a week later.

I had asked Olson if, once the wrestlers started to travel on the summer circuit, I could drive with one of them to Three Rivers. Olson arranged for Ovile Asselin, a former Mr. Canada, to take me out. Asselin picked me up at four in the afternoon and we drove to a road junction, outside of town, where we were to meet another wrestler, Don Lewin. While we were waiting, two other cars, both Cadillacs, pulled up and out stepped Tiger Tomasso, Eddie Auger, Maurice Lapointe, and three other wrestlers who were on the card that night. I immediately went up to chat with the Tiger.

Tomasso told me he used to be a deskman in a hotel in Hamilton. All the wrestlers used to stay there, and he began to work out with them. Finally, he went into the game. "What are you doing here?" he asked.

I was writing an article, I explained, as two pretty girls in shorts strolled past.

"That's the only kind of article I'm interested in," Tomasso said.

Eventually Lewin, a surly ex-marine, arrived, and he, Asselin, and I drove off together. Lewin, a suspicious type, wouldn't talk much in my presence. He had performed in Buffalo the previous night and had been driving all day to make the date in Three Rivers. He was, understandably, extremely tired. And unfriendly. On arrival in Three Rivers, he made it clear that I would have to find another lift back to Montreal.

There was only a thin crowd at the seedy little arena in Three Rivers, and Lewin, excusably, pulled his opponent out of the ring after five minutes of lacklustre wrestling and held him there long enough to be disqualified. Larry Moquin arranged for me to be driven home by a young French Canadian who had taken part in a tag-team match earlier in the evening. His side, the villainous one, had lost.

The wrestler had taken a bad fall and on the drive back to Montreal he kept rubbing his back. "Tomorrow," he said wearily, "I have to go to Hull. I'm working there."

"Don't you guys ever take time off?" I asked.

He explained that you had to be available when a promoter wanted you; otherwise you were considered unreliable. "It's a dangerous profession," he said. "My insides are all shaken up. You take your life in your hands each time you step in the ring." He had wrestled for a long time in Florida, where a Puerto Rican fan had once knifed him. "But that's a good territory. They liked me there. The worst was the West." Once, he said, he had driven 450 miles each way to make matches in two western cities. Four wrestlers, taking turns at the wheel, had managed the trip there and back within a day. "The worst things are canvas burns. They're extremely painful and we all get them. Sometimes they last a week, other times a month." Suppressing a yawn, he added, "I used to sell cars. I could always go back to that. I like meeting the public."

Gordie

C LEARLY, he came from good stock.

Interviewed on television in 1979, his eighty-seven-year-old father was asked, "How do you feel?"

"I feel fine."

"At what time in life does a man lose his sexual desires?"

"You'll have to ask somebody older than I am."

His son was only five when he acquired his first pair of skates. He repeated the third grade, more intent on his wrist shot than reading, developing it out there in the sub-zero wheat fields, shooting frozen horse buns against the barn door. When he was a mere fourteen-year-old, working in summer on a Saskatoon construction site with his father's crew, both his strength and determination were already celebrated. He could pick up ninety-pound cement bags in either hand, heaving them easily. Preparing for what he knew lay ahead, he sat at the kitchen table night after night, practising his autograph.

Gordie Howe was born in Floral, Saskatchewan, in 1928, a child of prairie penury, and his hockey career spanned thirty-two seasons in five decades. The stuff of legend.

Gordie.

For as long as I have been a hockey fan, Mr. Elbows has been out there, skating, his stride seemingly effortless. The big guy with the ginger-ale bottle shoulders. I didn't always admire him. But as he grew older and hockey players apparently younger, many of them younger than my oldest son, he became an especial pleasure. My God, only three years older than me, and still out there chasing pucks. For middle-aged Canadians, there was hope. In a world of constant and often bewildering change, there was one shining certitude. Come October, the man for whom time had stopped would be out there, not taking dirt from anybody. Gordie, Gordie, the old fart's champion.

Gordie Howe's amazing career is festooned with records, illuminated by anecdote. Looked at properly, within the third-grade repeater there was a hockey pedagogue longing to leap out.

Item: In 1963, when the traditionally stylish but corner-shy Montreal Canadiens brought up a young behemoth from the minors to police the traffic, he had the audacity, his first time over the boards, to go into a corner with Mr. Elbows. He yanked off his gloves, foolishly threatening to mix it up with Howe.

"In this league, son," Howe cautioned him, "we don't really fight. All we do is tug each other's sweaters."

"Certainly, Mr. Howe," the rookie said.

But no sooner did he drop his fists than the old educator creamed him.

Toe Blake, another Canadien who played against Howe, once said, "He was primarily a defensive player when he started, and he'd take your ankles off if you stood in front of their net."

That was in 1946, when eighteen-year-old Gordie, in his first season with the Detroit Red Wings, scored all of seven goals and fifteen assists. Thirty-four years later Steve Shutt, who wasn't even born in 1946, reported a different problem in playing against the now silvery-haired legend. "Sure we give him room out there. If you take him into the boards, the crowd boos, but they also boo if you let him get around you."

Which is to say, there were the glory years (more of them than any other athlete in a major sport can count) and the last sad ceremonial season, when even the fifty-two-year-old grandfather allowed that

he had become poetry in slow motion. But still a fierce advocate for
his two hockey-playing sons, Marty and Mark.

"Playing on the same line as your sons," Maurice Richard once
observed, "that's really something."

When I finally caught up with Howe, I asked him if, considering
his own abilities, it might have been kinder to encourage his sons to
do anything but play hockey.

"Well, once somebody said to Marty, 'Hey, kid, you're not as
good as your father.' 'Who is?' he replied."

Consider the records, familiar but formidable. Until Wayne Gretzky came along, Gordie Howe had scored the most assists (1,383)
and, of course, played in the most games (2,186). He won the National Hockey League (NHL) scoring title six times and was named
the most valuable player (MVP) six times in the NHL and once in the
World Hockey Association (WHA). He had scored more goals than
anybody (975—801 of them in the NHL). His hundredth goal, incidentally, was scored on February 17, 1951, against Gerry McNeil of
Montreal as the Red Wings beat the Canadiens 2–1 on Maurice
Richard Night. Obloquy. And a feat charged with significance for
those of us who cut our hockey teeth debating who was really
numero uno, Gordie Howe or the other No. 9, Maurice "Rocket"
Richard of the Montreal Canadiens.

Out West, where the clapboard main street, adrift in snow, often
consisted of no more than a legion hall, a curling club, a Chinese
restaurant, and a beer parlour, the men in their peak caps and lum-
berjack shirts—deprived of an NHL team themselves, dependent on
CBC-Radio's "Hockey Night in Canada" for the big Saturday night
game—rooted for Gordie. One of their own, shoving it to the condescending East. Gordie, educating the fancy-pants frogs with his
elbows. Giving them pause, making them throw up snow in the corners. But in Montreal, elegant Montreal, we valued élan (that is to
say, Richard) above all. For durable Gordie, it appeared the game was
a job in which he had undoubtedly learned to excel, but the exploding Rocket, whether he appreciated it or not, was an artist. Moving
in over the blue line, he was incomparable. "What I remember most

about the Rocket were his eyes," goalie Glenn Hall once said.
"When he came flying toward you with the puck on his stick, his
eyes were all lit up, flashing and gleaming like a pinball machine. It
was terrifying."

Seven years older than Howe, Richard played eighteen seasons,
retiring in 1960. Astonishingly, he never won a scoring championship, coming second to Howe twice and failing two more times
by a maddening point. He was voted MVP only once. But Maurice
Richard was the first player to score fifty goals in fifty games. That
was in the 1944–45 season, in the old six-team league, when anybody netting twenty goals was considered a star. Toe Blake, once
a linemate of the Rocket and a partisan to this day, maintains,
"There's only one thing that counts in this game and that's the Stanley Cup. How many did Jack Adams win with Gordie and how
many did we take with the Rocket?"

The answer to that one is that Detroit took four cups with Gordie
and the Canadiens won eight propelled by the Rocket. However,
Richard's supporting cast included, at one time or another, Elmer
Lach, Blake, Richard's brother Henri, Jean Beliveau, Boom Boom
Geoffrion, Dickie Moore, Doug Harvey, Butch Bouchard, and
Jacques Plante. Howe had Sid Abel and Terrible Ted Lindsay playing
alongside him and there was also Alex Delvecchio. He was backed
up by Red Kelly on defence, either Glenn Hall or Terry Sawchuk in
the nets, and, for the rest, mostly a number of journeymen. Even so,
the Red Wings, led by Gordie Howe, finished first in regular season
play seven times in a row, from 1949 to 1955. They beat the Canadiens in the 1954 Stanley Cup final and again in 1955, although that
year the issue was clouded, a seething Richard having been suspended for the series.

"Gordie Howe is the best hockey player I have ever seen," Beliveau has said. Even Maurice Richard allows, "He was a far better all-
round player than I was."

Yes, certainly, but there's a kicker. A big one.

The Rocket's younger brother, former Canadiens centre Henri
Richard, has said, "There is no doubt that Gordie was better than

Maurice. But build two rinks across from one another. Then put
Gordie in one and Maurice in the other, and see which one would
be filled."

Unlike the Rocket, Bobby Hull, Bobby Orr, and Guy Lafleur, Howe
always lacked one dimension. He couldn't lift fans out of their seats,
hearts thumping, charged with expectation, merely by taking a pass
and streaking down the ice. The most capable all-round player the
game may have known was possibly deficient in only one thing—
star quality. But my oh my, he certainly could get things done. In the
one-time rivalry between Detroit and Montreal, two games linger in
the mind—but first a few words from Mr. Elbows himself on just
how bright that rivalry burned during those halcyon years.

  "Hockey's different today, isn't it? The animosity is gone. *I mean
we didn't play golf with referees and linesmen.* Why, in the old days with
the Red Wings, I remember once we and the Canadiens were travelling to a game in Detroit on the same train. We were starving, but
their car was between ours and the diner, and there was no way we
were going to walk through there. We waited until the train stopped
in London and we walked around the Canadiens car to eat."

  Going into a game in Detroit, against the Canadiens, on October
27, 1963, Howe had 543 goals, one short of the retired Rocket's then
record of 544. The aroused Canadiens, determined not to allow
Howe to score a landmark goal against them, designated Henri
Richard his brother's record keeper, setting his line against Howe's
again and again. But in the third period Howe, who had failed to
score in three previous games, made his second shot of the night a
good one. He deflected a goalmouth pass past Gump Worsley to tie
the record. Howe, then thirty-five, did not score again for two
weeks, until the Canadiens came to town once more. Again they put
everything into stopping Howe. But, in the second period, *with
Montreal on the power play*, Detroit's Billy McNeill sailed down the ice
with the puck, Howe trailing. As they swept in on the Canadiens
net, Howe took the puck and flipped a fifteen-foot shot past Charlie

Hodge, breaking the Rocket's record, one he would later improve on by 127 NHL goals.

Item: In 1960, there was a reporter sufficiently brash to ask Howe when he planned to retire. Blinking, as is his habit, he replied, "I don't want to retire, because you stay retired for an awfully long time."

Twenty years later, on June 4, 1980, Howe stepped up to the podium at the Hartford Hilton and reluctantly announced his retirement. "I think I have another half-year in me, but it's always nice to keep something in reserve." The one record he was terribly proud of, he added, "is the longevity record."

Thirty-two years.

And just possibly we were unfair to him for most of those years. True, he eventually became an institution. Certainly he won all the glittering prizes. But true veneration always eluded Howe. Even in his glory days he generated more respect, sometimes even grudging at that, than real excitement. Outside of the west, where he ruled supreme, he was generally regarded as the ultimate pro (say, like his good friend of the Detroit years, Tiger outfielder Al Kaline), but not a player possessed. Like the Rocket.

In good writing, Hemingway once ventured, only the tip of the iceberg shows. Put another way, authentic art doesn't advertise. Possibly, that was the trouble with Gordie on ice. During his vintage years, you seldom noticed the flash of elbows, only the debris they left behind. He never seemed *that* fast, but somehow he got there first. He didn't wind up to shoot, like so many of today's golfers, but next time the goalie dared to peek, the puck was behind him.

With hindsight, I'm prepared to allow that Gordie may not only have been a better all-round player than the Rocket, but maybe the more complete artist as well. The problem could have been the fans, myself included, who not only wanted art to be done, but wanted to see it being done. We also required it to look hard, not all just in a day's work.

A career of such magnitude as Gordie Howe's has certain natural perimeters, obligatory tales that demand to be repeated here. The signing. The injury that all but killed him in his fourth season. The rivalry with the Rocket, already dealt with. The disenchantment with Detroit. Born-again Gordie, playing the WHA with his two sons. The return to the NHL with the Hartford Whalers. The last ceremonial season, culminating in his final goal.

History is riddled with might-have-beens. Caesar, anticipating unfavourable winds, could have remained in bed on March 15. That most disgruntled of stringers, Karl Marx, might have gone from contributor to editor of the *New York Tribune*. Bobby Thomson could have struck out. Similarly, Gordie Howe might have been a New York Ranger. When he was fifteen, he was invited to the Rangers' try-out camp in Winnipeg, but they intended to ship him to Regina, and he didn't sign because he knew nobody from Saskatoon who would be playing there. The Red Wings wanted him to join their team in Windsor, Ontario. "They told me there would be carloads of kids I knew, so I signed. I didn't want to be alone."

The following season, the Red Wings handed Gordie a $500 bonus and a $1,700 salary to play with their Omaha farm club. ("Twenty-two hundred dollars," Gordie said. "I earn that much per diem now.") A year later he was with the Red Wings, signed for a starting salary of $6,000. "After we signed him," coach Jack Adams said, "he left the office. Later, when I went into the hall, he was still there, looking glum. 'All right, Gordie, what's bothering you?'"

"'Well, you promised me a Red Wing jacket, but I don't have it yet.'"

He got the jacket, he scored a goal in his first game with the Red Wings, and he was soon playing three- even four-minute shifts on right wing. A fast, effortless skater with a wrist shot said to travel at 110 miles per hour. Then, in a 1950 playoff game against the Toronto Maple Leafs, Howe collided with Leaf captain Teeder Kennedy and fell unconscious to the ice. Howe was rushed to a hospital for emergency surgery. "In the hospital," Sid Abel recalled, "they opened up Gordie's skull to relieve the pressure on his brain and the blood shot to the ceiling like a geyser."

The injury left Howe with a permanent facial tic, and on his return the following season, his teammates dubbed him "Blinky," a nickname that stuck. Other injuries, over the years, have called for some four hundred stitches, mostly in his face. Howe can no longer count how many times his nose has been broken. There also have been broken ribs, a broken wrist, a detached retina, and operations on both knees. He retires with seven fewer teeth than he started with.

The glory years with Detroit came to an end in 1971, Howe hanging up his skates after twenty-five seasons. Once a contender, the team had gone sour. Howe's arthritic wrist meant that he was playing with constant pain. Hockey, he allowed, was no longer fun. But, alas, the position he took in the Red Wings' front office ("A pasture job," his wife, Colleen, said) proved frustrating, even though it was his first $100,000 job. "They paid me to sit in that office, but they didn't give me anything to do."

After two years of retirement, the then forty-five-year-old Howe bounced back. In 1973, he found true happiness, realizing what he said was a lifelong dream, a chance to play with two of his sons for the Houston Aeros of the WHA. The dream was sweetened by a $1-million contract, which called for Howe to play for one season followed by three in management. Furthermore, nineteen-year-old Marty and eighteen-year-old Mark were signed for a reputed $400,000 each for four years. A package put together by the formidable Colleen, business manager of the Howe family enterprises.

Howe led the Aeros to the WHA championship; he scored one hundred points and was named the league's most valuable player. Mark was voted rookie of the year. A third son, Murray, later shunned hockey to enter pre-med school at the University of Michigan. Murray, who was twenty years old in 1980, also wrote poetry:

So you eat, and you sleep.
So you walk, and you run.
So you touch, and you hear.

You lead, and you follow.
You mate with the chosen.
But do you live?

Gordie went on to play three more seasons with the Aeros and two with the Whalers, finishing his WHA career with 174 goals and 334 assists. With the demise of that league and the acceptance of the Whalers by the NHL in 1979, Howe decided to play one more year so that the father-and-sons combination could make it into the NHL record books.

It almost didn't happen, what with Marty being sent down to Springfield. But they finally did play together on March 9 in Boston. And then, three nights later, out there in Detroit, *his* Detroit, Gordie finally got to take a shift in the NHL on a line with his two sons, Marty moving up from his natural position on defence. "After that game, Gordie could have just walked off," Colleen said. "'I've done all I've ever wanted,' he told me."

I caught up with Gordie towards the end of the 1980 season, on March 22, when the Whalers came to the Montreal Forum for their last regular-season appearance. Before the game, Gordie Howe jokes abounded among the younger writers in the press box. Scanning the Hartford line-up, noting the presence of Bobby Hull and Dave Keon, both then in their forties, one wag ventured, "If only they'd put them together on the ice with Howe, we could call it the Geritol Line."

Another said, "When is he going to stop embarrassing himself out there and announce his retirement?"

"If he's that bad," a Hartford writer cut in, "why do they allow him so much room out there?"

"Because nobody wants to go into the record books as the kid who crippled old Gordie."

Going into the game, Hartford's seventy-second of the season, Howe had fourteen goals and twenty-three assists, and there he sat

on the bench, one of only six Whalers without a helmet. The only
player on the team old enough to remember an NHL wherein salaries
were so meagre that the goys of winter had to drive beer trucks or
work on road construction in the summer.

There were lots of empty seats in the Forum. It was not the usual
Saturday night crowd. Many a season ticket holder had yielded his
coveted seat in the reds to a country cousin, a secretary, or an unlucky nephew. Kids were everywhere. Howe, who had scored his
eight hundredth goal a long twenty-three days earlier, jumped over
the boards for his first shift at 1:27 of the first period, the Forum
erupting in sentimental cheers. He did not come on again for another five minutes, this time joining a Hartford power play. Howe
took to the ice again with four and a half minutes left in the period,
kicking the puck to Jordy Douglas from behind the Montreal net,
earning an assist on Douglas's goal. Not the only listless forward out
there, often trailing the play, pacing himself, but his passing still notably crisp, right on target each time, Howe came out six more times
in the second period. On his very first shift in the first period, he
threw a check at Réjean Houle, sending him flying. Hello, hello,
I'm still here. But his second time out, Howe drew a tripping
penalty, and the Canadiens scored on their power play. The game, a
clinker, ended in a 5–5 tie.

In the locker room, microphones were thrust at a weary Gordie.
He was confronted by notebooks. Somebody asked, "Do you plan
to retire at the end of the season, Gordie?"

"Not that fucking question again," Gordie replied.

So somebody else said, "No, certainly not. But could you tell me
what your plans are for next year?"

Gordie grinned, appreciative.

A little more than two weeks later, on April 8, the Whalers were
back, it having been ordained that these upstarts would be fed to
the Canadiens in their first NHL playoff series. This time the Canadiens, in no mood to fiddle, beat the Whalers 6–1. Howe, who didn't

play until the first period was seven minutes old, took his first shift alongside his son Mark. He only appeared twice more in the first period, but in the second he came on again, filling in for the injured Blaine Stoughton on the Whalers' big line. He was ineffectual, on for two goals against and hardly touching the puck during a Hartford power play. Consequently, in the third period, he was allowed but four brief shifts. There must have been some satisfaction for him, however, in the fact that Mark Howe was easily the best Whaler on ice, scoring the goal that cost Dennis Herron his shutout.

The next night, with Montreal leading 8–3 midway in the third period, the only thing the crowd was still waiting for finally happened. Gordie Howe flipped in a backhander. It was his sixty-eighth NHL playoff goal—but his first in a decade. It wasn't a pretty goal. Nor did it matter much. It was slipped in there by a fifty-two-year-old grandfather who had scored his first NHL goal in Toronto thirty-four years earlier when Carl Yastrzemski was only seven years old, pot was something you cooked the stew in, and Ronald Reagan was just another actor. "Hartford goal by Gordie Howe," Michel Lacroix announced over the P.A. system. "Assist, Mark Howe." The crowd gave Gordie a standing ovation.

Later, in the Whalers' dressing room, coach Don Blackburn was asked what his team might do differently in Hartford for the third game. "Show up," he said.

Though the Whalers played their best hockey of the series in the next game, they lost in overtime. In the dressing room, everybody wanted to know if this had been Gordie's last game. "I haven't made up my mind about when I'm going to retire yet," he said.

But earlier, in the press box, a Hartford reporter had assured everybody that this was a night in hockey history: April 11, 1980, Gordie Howe's last game. He said Whaler director of hockey operations Jack Kelley had told him as much. "They've got a kid they want to bring up. Gordie's holding him back. The problem is they don't know what to do with him. I mean, shit, you can't have Gordie Howe running the god damn gift shop."

The triumphant Canadiens stayed overnight in Hartford, and I joined their poker game: Claude Mouton, Claude Ruel, the trainers, the team doctor, Floyd "Busher" Currie, Toe Blake. "Jack Adams always used him too much during the regular season," Toe said, "so he had nothing left when the playoffs came round."

"Do you think he was really a dirtier player than most?" I asked.

"Well, you saw the big guy yesterday. What did he tell you?"

"He said his elbows never put anybody in the hospital, but he was there five times."

Suddenly everybody was laughing at me. Speak to Donnie Marshall, they said. Or John Ferguson. Or, still better, ask Lou Fontinato.

When Donnie Marshall was with the Rangers, he was asked what it was like to play against Howe. In reply, he lifted his shirt to reveal a foot-long angry welt across his ribcage. "Second period," he said.

One night, when then Winnipeg general manager John Ferguson was still playing with the Canadiens, a frustrated Howe stuck the blade of his stick into his mouth and hooked his tongue for nine stitches.

But Howe's most notorious altercation was with Ranger defenceman Lou Fontinato in Madison Square Garden in 1959. Frank Udvari, who was the referee, recalled, "The puck had gone into the corner. Howe had collided with Eddie Shack behind the net and lost his balance. He was just getting to his feet when here's Fontinato at my elbow, trying to get at him.

"'I want him,' he said.

"'Leave him alone, use your head,' I said.

"'I want him.'

"'Be my guest.'"

Fontinato charged. Shedding his gloves, Howe seized Fontinato's jersey at the neck and drove his right fist into his face. "Never in my life had I heard anything like it, except maybe the sound of somebody chopping wood," Udvari said. "*Thwack!* And all of a sudden Louie's breathing out of his cheekbone."

Howe broke Fontinato's nose, he fractured his cheekbone, and knocked out several teeth. Plastic surgeons had to reconstruct his face.

The afternoon before what was to be Howe's last game, I had taken a taxi to his house in the suburbs of Hartford. "You can't be a pauper living out here," the driver said. "I'll bet he's got racehorses and everything. There's only money out here."

Appropriately enough, the venerable Howe, hockey's very own King Arthur, lived down a secluded side road in a town called Gastonbury. Outside the large house, set on fifteen acres of land, a sign read HOWE'S CORNER. Inside, a secretary ushered me through the office of Howe Enterprises, a burgeoning concern that held personal-service contracts with Anheuser-Busch, Chrysler, and Colonial Bank. A bespectacled, wary Howe was waiting for me in the sun-filled living room. Prominently displayed on the coffee table was an enormous volume of Ben Shahn reproductions.

"I had no idea," I said, impressed, "that you were an admirer of Ben Shahn."

"Oh, that. The book. I spoke at a dinner. They presented it to me."

After all his years in the United States, Howe remained a Canadian citizen. "I can pay my taxes here and all the other good things, but I can't vote." One of nine children, he added, the family was now spread out like manure. "It would be nice to get together again without having to go to another funeral."

Sitting with Howe, our dialogue stilted, not really getting anywhere, I remembered how A. J. Liebling was once sent a batch of how-to-write books for review by a literary editor, and promptly bounced them back with a curt note: "The only way to write is well and how you do it is your own damn business." Without being able to put it so succinctly, Howe, possibly, felt the same way about hockey. Furthermore, over the years, he had also heard all the questions before and now greeted them with a flick of the conversational elbow. But, for the record, Howe adjudged today's hockey talent bigger and better than ever. Wayne Gretzky reminded him of Sid Abel. "He's sneaky clever, the puck always seems to be coming back to him. Lafleur is something else. He stays on for two shifts. I don't mind that, but he doesn't even breathe heavy." Sawchuk was the best goalie he ever saw and he never knew a line to compare with Boston's Kraut Line: Milt Schmidt, Woody Dumart, Bobby Bauer. Howe was still bitter about how his years in Detroit came to an end with that meaningless front-office job. "Hell, you've been on the ice for twenty-five years, there's little else you learn. I was a pro at seventeen. Colleen used to answer my fan mail for me, I didn't have the words. Now it's better for the kids. They get their basic twelve years of school and then pick a college."

Determined to surface with fresh questions, I asked when he planned to retire.

"I can't say just yet exactly when I'm going to retire, but I'm the one who will make that decision."

The next morning, in the Whalers' offices, Jack Kelley asked me, "Did he say that?"

"Yes."

"He's retiring at the end of the season."

Almost two months later, on June 4, Howe made it official. "It's not easy to retire," he told reporters. "No one teaches you how. I found that out when I tried it the first time. I'm not a quitter. But I will now quit the game of hockey."

Howe had kept everybody waiting for half an hour after the scheduled start of his 10 a.m. press conference. "As it got close to 10:30 I had the funny suspicion that he had changed his mind again," Kelley said.

But this time Howe left no doubt in anybody's mind. "My last retirement was an unhappy one, because I knew I still had some years in me. This is a happy one, because I know it's time."

An ice age had come to an end.

"They ought to bottle Gordie Howe's sweat," King Clancy of the Maple Leafs once said. "It would make a great lineament to rub on hockey players."

Yes, certainly. But I remember my afternoon at Howe's Corner with a certain sadness. He knew what was coming, and before I left he insisted that I scan the awards mounted on a hall wall. The Victors Award. The American Academy of Achievement Golden Plate Award. The American Captain of Achievement Award. "I played in all eighty games this year and I got my fifteenth goal in the last game of the season. Last year I suffered from dizzy spells. My doctor wanted me to quit. But I was determined to play with my boys in the NHL. I don't think I have the temperament for coaching. I tried it a couple of times and I got so excited, watching the play, I forgot all about the line changes."

That afternoon only one thing seemed to animate him. The large Amway flow chart that hung from a stand, dominating the living room. Gordie Howe—one of the greatest players the game had ever known, a Canadian institution at last—Blinky, the third-grade repeater who had become a millionaire—now distributed health-care items, cosmetics, jewellery, and gardening materials for Amway.

Offering me a lift back to my hotel in Hartford, Howe led me into his garage. There were cartons, cartons, everywhere, ready for delivery. Cosmetics. Gardening materials. It looked like the back room of a prairie general store.

"I understand you write novels," Howe said.

"Yes."

"There must be a very good market for them. You see them on racks in all the supermarkets now."

"Right. Tell me, Gordie, do you deliver this stuff yourself?"

"You can earn a lot of money with Amway," he said, "working out of your own home."

Say it ain't so, Gordie.

Gretzky in Eighty-four

NINETEEN EIGHTY-FOUR. Edmonton. One day in March, at Barry T's Roadhouse out there on tacky 104th Street— wedged between welding shops and cinder-block strip joints and used-car lots—the city's amiable sportswriting fraternity gathered for its annual award luncheon. The writers were going to present Wayne Gretzky with their Sports Professional of the Year Award again. "I'll bet he tells us it means more to him than the Stanley Cup," one of the writers said.

"Or the Hart."

"Or his contract with General Mills. What do you think that's worth, eh?"

Bill Tuele, director of public relations for the Oilers, joined our table. "Does flying really scare Gretzky that much?" I asked.

"Nah. It doesn't scare him *that* much," Tuele said. "It's just that if we go bumpety-bump, he staggers off the plane with his shirt drenched."

Gretzky, who was running late, finally drifted into Barry T's. A curiously bland twenty-four-year-old in a grey flannel suit, he graciously accepted his plaque. "Any time you win an award, it's a thrill," he said. "With so many great athletes in Edmonton, I'm very honoured to win this." Then, his duty done, he retreated to a booth to eat lunch. And in Western Canada, where civility is the rule, he was not immediately besieged by reporters with notebooks or tape recorders. They left him alone with his overdone roast beef and curling, soggy french fries.

There had been a game the night before, the slumping Edmonton Oilers ending a five-gave losing streak at home, edging the Detroit Red Wings, 7–6, only their second victory in their last eight outings. Even so, they were still leading the league. Gretzky, juggling his crammed schedule, had fit me in for an interview at the Northlands Coliseum at 9 a.m. Increasingly caught up in the business world, he told me he had recently read *Iacocca* and was now into *Citizen Hughes*. Though he enjoyed watching television soap operas and had once appeared on "The Young and the Restless" himself, he never bothered with fiction. "I like to read fact," he said. "I'm so busy, I haven't got the time to read stories that aren't real."

After the interview, there was a team practice and, following the sportswriters' lunch, he was scheduled to shoot a television commercial, and then there was a dinner he was obliged to attend. The next night, there was a game with Buffalo. It would be the seventieth for the Oilers in the regular NHL schedule but the seventy-second for Gretzky, who had played in two Canada Cup games immediately before the NHL season. There were a further ten games to come in the regular season and, as it turned out, another eighteen in the playoffs before the Oilers would skate to their second consecutive Stanley Cup.

But, at the time, Gretzky, understandably, was in a defensive mood, aware that another undeniably talented club, the Boston Bruins, led by Bobby Orr and Phil Esposito, had promised better than they had paid, faltering more than once in the playoffs. "We've already been compared to the great Boston team of the early seventies, which won only two cups but they still say should have won four," Gretzky said.

I asked Gretzky if he didn't consider the regular NHL schedule, which more than one wag has put down as the longest exhibition season in sport, to be insufferably long and meaningless. After all, it ran to 840 games, from September to April, and when it was over only five of the then twenty-one teams had been cut from what knowledgeable fans appreciated as the real season—the Stanley Cup playoffs. "Well," he said, "this city's not like New York, where there are lots of things to do. In Edmonton in February, we're the only attraction."

When I asked Peter Pocklington, the owner of the Oilers, about the seemingly endless season, he protested, "We're the only show in town. Coming to see Gretzky is like going to watch Pavarotti or Nureyev. What else are you going to do in Edmonton in the middle of the winter? How many beers can you drink?"

The capital of Alberta is a city you come from, not a place to visit, unless you have relatives there or an interest in an oil well nearby. On first glance, and even on third, it seems not so much a city as a jumble of a used-building lot, where the spare office towers and box-shaped apartment buildings and cinder-block motels discarded in the construction of real cities have been abandoned to waste away in the cruel prairie winter.

If Canada were not a country, however fragmented, but, instead, a house, Vancouver would be the solarium-cum-playroom, an afterthought of affluence; Toronto, the counting room, where money makes for the most glee; Montreal, the salon; and Edmonton, Edmonton, the boiler room. There is hardly a tree to be seen downtown, nothing to delight the eye on Jasper Avenue. On thirty-below-zero nights, grim religious zealots loom on street corners, speaking in tongues, and intrepid hookers in miniskirts rap on the windows of cars that have stopped for traffic. There isn't a first-class restaurant anywhere in town. For all that, Edmontonians are a truly admirable lot. They have not only endured great hardships in the past but also continue to suffer an abominable climate as well as isolation from the cities of light. And, to some degree, like other westerners, they thrive on resentments against the grasping, self-satisfied East, which has exploited their natural resources for years, taking their oil and gas at cut prices to subsidize inefficient Ontario and Quebec industries.

Insults, injuries.

For as long as Edmontonians can remember, the biggies were elsewhere. Though they had contributed many fine hockey players to the game, they could only hear about their feats on radio or later see them on television. Hockey was *their* game, damn it, *their* national sport, but New York, Chicago, Detroit, and Boston were in the NHL long before the league's governors adjudged Edmonton not so much worthy as potentially profitable. But in 1984, Canada's hockey shrines were either in decline, as was then the case in Montreal, or in total disrepute, as in Toronto. In those glory days, if easterners wanted to see the best player in the game more than twice a season, if they wanted to catch a dynasty in the making, why, then, they had to pack their fat coats and fur-lined boots and head for Edmonton, home of the Stanley Cup champions and the Great Gretzky himself.

In March 1984, Gretzky the commodity was soaring to new heights of fame and fortune; Gretzky the most famous player ever was struggling, justifiably fatigued.

In a five-week period, Gretzky had been on the cover of *Sporting News*, two Canadian hockey magazines, and *Sports Illustrated* (for the fifth time), and he had shared a *Time* cover with Larry Bird of the Boston Celtics. He had tested his scoring skills against no less a goalie than George Plimpton, and he had been the subject of an article in the *Saturday Evening Post* and an interview in *Playboy*. He had, Gretzky told me, been criticized for submitting to the *Playboy* interview, accused of endorsing pornography. But, as he put it, "You can't please everybody." Actually, the engaging truth is that his interview with *Playboy* was a triumph of small-town Canadian rectitude over that magazine's appetite for salacious detail.

PLAYBOY: How many woman have been in your life?

GRETZKY: Vickie Moss was my first girlfriend. I never dated anyone else.

PLAYBOY: Do you have *any* vices?

GRETZKY: Oh, yeah, I'm human. I do have a bad habit of swearing on ice. I forget that there are people around the rink. It's a problem. I hope I'm heading in a direction where I can correct it, but I don't know if I will be able to.

Gretzky was what athletes are supposed to be, but seldom are—McIntosh-apple wholesome, dedicated, an inspirational model for young fans. He was an anachronism, rooted in an age when a date wasn't a disco, then your place or mine, but rather a movie, then maybe a banana split at the corner soda fountain. He had owned a Ferrari for four years but had never had a speeding ticket. He still phoned home to Brantford, Ontario, to report to his father three times a week. He struck me as nice, very nice, but incapable of genuine wit or irreverence, like, say, Rug McGraw. What he did tell me, his manner appropriately solemn, was that he felt it was his responsibility never to refuse to sign an autograph: "For that person, that kid, it could be the greatest thing that ever happened to him."

Gretzky worked hard, incredibly hard, both for the charities he supported and for himself. He was boffo sales stuff. The hockey stick he endorsed, Titan, leaped from twelfth to first place in sales in thirty-six months. Gretzky also pitched for Canon cameras, Nike sportswear, General Mills Pro Stars cereal, Mattel toys, Travellers Insurance, and American Express. These endorsements were handled by Michael Barnett of CorpSport International out of handsomely appointed offices in an old, converted Edmonton mansion. There was a large portrait of Gretzky in action on a wall in the reception room as well as the essential LeRoy Neiman; and a placard with a quotation from Ralph Waldo Emerson: "Make the most of yourself, for that is all there is of you."

CorpSport International represented other athletes, but for the past four years Gretzky, who then earned an estimated $1 million annually in endorsements—about the same as his salary—had been the major preoccupation of its thirty-four-year-old president. Barnett, a former minor-league hockey player himself, was in daily contact with Gretzky's lawyer as well as the firm that handled his investments. "Though Wayne listens to all his advisers," Barnett said, "he makes his own business and investment decisions. We get some three dozen personal appearance requests for him a month, but he will only speak for charities. Pro Stars cereal advertises the Wayne Gretzky Fan Club on four million boxes. It costs seven bucks a year to be a member, and for that you get four annual Wayne Gretzky newsletters as well as this set of photographs.

"There have been seven unauthorized biographies," Barnett continued. "Wayne gets between two to five thousand fan letters a month. Vickie Moss's mother handles that for him."

Mattel has marketed a Wayne Gretzky doll ("For avid fans, his out-of-town uniform, jogging suit, and tuxedo are also available"), which has led to cracks about the need for a Dave Semenko doll to beat up any kid who roughs up the Gretzky doll.

Late at night, even as he talked buisness with Barnett, Gretzky autographed coloured photographs of himself. Mattel supplied the photographs, which included its logo, but Gretzky, according to Barnett, paid the postal charges, about $2,000 monthly. Barnett also pointed out that, since the Oilers took their first Stanley Cup on May 19, 1984, Gretzky had only six weeks off the ice before joining the Canada Cup training camp, playing in that series, and then moving directly into the NHL season.

And in March, things weren't going well. Gretzky was playing without his usual intensity. I asked saucy, streetwise Glen Sather, president, general manager, and coach of the Oilers, if he was guilty of overplaying Gretzky. "Wayne," he said, "plays something like twenty-two minutes a game. He thrives on work. The more ice time he gets, the better he is."

Yet Gretzky hadn't had a two-goal game since February 19 or scored a hat trick for two months. He would, however, finish the 1984–85 season with 208 points (73 goals, 135 assists). This marked the third time he had scored more than 200 points in his six seasons in the NHL. A truly remarkable feat, this, when you consider that no previous player in league history had managed it even once.

Records.

The Official Edmonton Oilers 1984–85 Guide lists a modest three records under the heading, "NHL Individual Records Held or Co-Held by Edmonton Oilers (excluding Wayne Gretzky)," and there follows a stunning full page of Wayne Gretzky's contribution to the NHL records. Paraphrasing the guide, here are Gretzky's statistics:

"No. 99, centre: height, 6'0"; weight, 170 lbs.; born, Brantford, Ontario, Jan. 26, 1961; shoots, left. He is not the fastest or the most graceful skater in hockey, neither does he boast the hardest shot. But he now holds 38 NHL records."

Of course he would, as was his habit, set or tie even more records in the 1985 playoffs, as well as win the Conn Smythe Trophy for most valuable player in that series. But back in March 1984 all I asked him was, did he feel a 100-goal season was possible?

"Sure, it's possible," Gretzky said. "Somebody will do it. The year I got ninety-two, everything went my way." But he had begun to feel the pressure. "Yesterday you got two goals in a game, tomorrow the fans want three." He has said he would like to retire at the age of thirty, after fifteen years in hockey. "When Lafleur retired, it made me open my eyes," he said.

Lafleur, who quit suddenly in 1984 (temporarily, as it would turn out) at the age of thirty-three after four mediocre years, had scored sixty goals in his best season, 1977–78. "I wasn't surprised he retired," Gretzky said. "You wake up, you're no longer in the top-ten scorers, you think, 'Oh, my God,' and you begin to press. When Lafleur was in his prime, it was a much rougher league, but slower. We get hit, but not as much as in the late seventies."

Danny Gare, the Red Wing veteran who had played against Gretzky the night before, told me, "They don't run against him like they did on Lafleur." Acknowledging Gretzky's enormous talent, he added that it had been more exciting to watch Lafleur. Well, yes, so it was. And come to think of it, the same could be said of Bobby Orr.

When either Lafleur or Orr were on the ice, you never took your eyes off them, never mind the puck. Orr could literally establish the pace of a game, speeding it up or slowing it down at will. Lafleur couldn't do that. He was—in Ken Dryden's felicitous phrase—the last of the river-hockey players, who had learned the game outdoors instead of in a rink, a solitary type, often lost in a reverie on ice all his own. Gretzky was something else again. Sometimes you didn't even realize he was out there, watching as he whirled, until he emerged out of nowhere, finding open ice, and accelerated to score. Other times, working out of a seemingly impossible angle in a corner, he could lay a feathery pass right on the stick of whoever had skated into the slot, a teammate startled to find the puck at his feet against all odds.

It's not true that they don't run on him. The hit men seek him here, they seek him there, but like the Scarlet Pimpernel they can't board him anywhere: he's too elusive. Gretzky can fit through a keyhole. Watching him out there, I often felt that he was made of Plasticine. I've seen him stretch his arms a seeming two feet more because that's what was required to retrieve a puck. Conversely, putting a shift on a defenceman, cruising very low on ice, he seemed to shrink to whatever size was necessary to pass. He is incomparably dangerous behind the opposition's net and unequalled at making a puck squirt free from a crowd.

If, to begin with, Gretzky had a fault, it was his tendency to whine. For a while, all an opposing player had to do was to skate past Gretzky thinking negative thoughts for No. 99 to fall to the ice, seemingly mortally wounded, his eyes turned imploringly to the referee. In Edmonton, this had earned him a pejorative nickname: "The Wayner."

In June, Gretzky won the Hart Memorial Trophy, the league's most valuable player award, for the sixth straight time, this in a year in which he had already won his fifth consecutive Art Ross Trophy, for the NHL's leading point scorer during the regular season. One hundred and eighteen years after Confederation, the only thing out of Canada more famous than Gretzky was the cold front.

For a hockey player, it should be noted, this was a grand accomplishment for, as a rule in 1985, NHL stars had to cope with a difficult paradox. Celebrated at home, they could, much to their chagrin, usually pass anonymously south of the 49th parallel. Not so Gretzky. But for all his fame, he remained something of an enigma, a young man charged with contradictions. Ostensibly modest beyond compare, he had taken to talking about himself in the third person. Speaking of the endless hours he clocked on his backyard skating rink as a child, he said: "It wasn't a sacrifice. That's what Wayne Gretzky wanted to do." Discussing possible commercial endorsements, he allowed, "The thing to look for is . . . is there a future in it for Wayne Gretzky?"

Seemingly self-composed, he didn't fly on airplanes easily. Obviously, there was a lot of inner tension bottled up in Gretzky, and at thirty thousand feet it began to leak. In 1981, trying to beat his fear of flying, he tried a hypnotherapist, but it worked only briefly. Come 1984 he flew with pilots in the cockpit as often as possible, which helped only some, because they had to send him back into the cabin once they began landing procedures, and Gretzky had been known to sit there, unable to look, holding his head in his hands.

Sifting through the Gretzky file, it appeared that just about every reply he had ever given in an interview was calculated to oblige. Again and again, his answers were not only boringly proper but tainted by what W. H. Auden once condemned as the rehearsed response. Under all the superficial sweetness, however, I suspected there was a small residue of bitterness. This, in remembrance of a boy deprived of a normal childhood, driven to compete on ice with boys four to six years his senior from the age of six.

Gretzky, for example, unfailingly went out of his way to pay obeisance to his father, his mentor. Walter Gretzky, a thwarted hockey player himself, a man who was mired in Junior B for five years, was still working as a telephone repair man in 1984. In his brash memoir, *Gretzky*, written with Jim Taylor, he gloated, "Wayne learned to skate and Walter Gretzky built a hockey star." He had Wayne, at the age of four, out in the backyard skating rink well into the dark evening hours, learning to criss-cross between pylons made of Javex bleach containers. Walter Gretzky wrote: "You can just see them thinking, 'Boy, did he push those kids! That's a hockey father for you!' Actually, it was the most natural thing in the world." But in an epilogue to the book, Wayne, recalling that he had been shipped to Toronto to further his hockey career when he was barely a teenager, noted, "There's no way my son is leaving home at fourteen." At fourteen, he added, he thought Toronto was the greatest thing in the world, "but if there was one thing I could do over again, I'd like to be able to say I lived at home until I was eighteen or nineteen."

Wayne was only eleven years old when he began to set all manner of amazing records in minor-league hockey, even as he would later astound the NHL. But in 1984, even as Gretzky was arguably the best player the game had ever known, a much-needed publicity bonanza for the NHL in the United States, he was also, ironically, a menace to the game.

Imagine, if you will, a baseball outfielder, not yet in his prime, who hits .400 or better every season as a matter of course and you have some notion of Gretzky's hockey stature. Furthermore, since Gretzky's sophomore year in the NHL, there had been no contest for the Art Ross Trophy. Gretzky is so far superior to any other forward, regularly winning the point-scoring title by a previously unheard of fifty or sixty points, that he inadvertently makes the other star players appear sadly inadequate. And while the other players tend to tell you, tight-lipped, that "Gretz is the greatest . . . he has all the moves and then some," I don't think they really liked him, any more than Salieri did the young Mozart. Effortlessly, he made most of them look mediocre.

Peter Gzowski, in one of the very few intelligent books ever written about hockey, *The Game of Their Lives*, ventured, "Often the difference between what Wayne Gretzky does with the puck and what less accomplished players would have done with it is simply a *pause*, as if, as time freezes, he is enjoying an extra handful of milliseconds." Gzowski goes on to cite experiments done with athletes by a neurologist at McMaster University in Hamilton, Ontario. Based on this and other research, he suggested that Gretzky, like other super-stars (say, Ted Williams or Bjorn Borg), benefited from motor neu-trons that fired faster than those of mere mortals. Or, put more simply, time slowed down for him. Gretzky also profited from an uncanny ability to react quickly to everybody's position on the ice. "What separates him from his peers in the end," Gzowski wrote, "the quality that has led him to the very point of the pyramid, may well have nothing to do with physical characteristics at all, but instead be a manner of perception, not so much of what he sees— he does not have exceptional vision—but of *how* he sees it and absorbs it."

As Gretzky often emerged out of nowhere to score, so did Peter Pocklington, the owner of the Oilers. The son of a London, On-tario, insurance agent, he parlayed a Ford dealership, acquired at the age of twenty-three, some choice real estate, and a meat-packing firm into a fabled fortune, even by western oil-patch standards. Pocklington got into hockey, he said, because he wanted to be rec-ognized on the streets. In 1984, he not only owned the most talented team in the NHL, a club that boasted such players as Paul Coffey and Mark Messier, but he also had Gretzky tied to a personal-services contract that made him one of the world's highest-paid indentured labourers. It was said to be worth $21 million and to extend until 1999.

In 1981, Pocklington's assets were estimated to be worth $1.4 billion, but the recession got to him, and his holdings by 1984 had reportedly shrunk to a mere $150 to $200 million. Gone, gone, was the $9 million worth of art, the private Lear jet, and the Rolls-Royce. I asked Pocklington about the rumours, rampant at the time, that—such were his financial difficulties—he might be offering his legendary chattel to the nefarious Americans, say Detroit or New York. Looking me in the eye, he denied it adamantly. "There's nothing to it," he said. "You can imagine what they would do to me here if I sold Wayne. It's almost a sacred trust."

From Satchel,
through Hank
Greenberg, to
El Divino
Loco

COME SPRING, I turn hungrily to the sports pages first every morning to ponder the baseball scores, held in the thrall of overgrown boys whose notion of humour is to slip an exploding device into a cigar, drench a phone receiver with shaving cream, or line the inside of a teammate's hat with shoe polish. But, to be fair, a certain corrosive wit is not unknown among some ball players. Asked if he threw spitters, Hall of Fame pitcher Lefty Gomez replied, "Not intentionally, but I sweat easy." Invited to comment on whether he favoured grass over AstroTurf, relief pitcher Tug Mc-Graw said, "I don't know. I never smoked AstroTurf." On another occasion, a reporter asked McGraw how he intended to budget his latest salary increase. "Ninety per cent, I'll spend on good times, women, and Irish whisky," he said. "The other ten per cent I'll probably waste." Then the immortal Leroy "Satchel" Paige once said, "Don't look back. Something might be gaining on you."

Satchel Paige, one of the greatest pitchers the game has ever known, was shamefully confined to the Negro leagues in his prime. Only in 1948, when he was forty-two years old, did he finally get a chance to compete in the majors, signed by Bill Veeck to play for the Cleveland Indians. Paige helped the Indians to win a World Series in 1949, went on to pitch for the St. Louis Browns for a couple of years, and then dropped out of sight.

The film director Robert Parrish once told me a story about Paige that he then included in his memoir, *Hollywood Doesn't Live Here Anymore*. In the early fifties, Parrish was shooting a western in Mexico, *The Wonderful Country*, in which Robert Mitchum was playing the lead. Mitchum suggested that they get Satchel to play a black sergeant in the U.S. Tenth Cavalry.

"Where can we find him?" Parrish asked.

"Why don't you call Bill Veeck?"

Parrish called Veeck and learned that Paige was now with the Miami Marlins in the Southern Association, but he didn't think that Parrish could contact him because he was in jail on a misdemeanour charge and the judge, who was a baseball fan, would let him out only on the days he was to pitch. Parrish called the judge.

"Well," said the judge, "I think we can work it out. Leroy has a sore arm and has lost his last four games. I'll let him out if you'll guarantee he doesn't touch a baseball until he comes back to Miami."

Paige arrived in Durango, Mexico, a week later, accompanied by a beautiful teenaged black girl whom he introduced as Susan. Parrish knew he had a daughter and assumed that's who she was. "Paige . . . stayed with us for six weeks," wrote Parrish in his memoir, "and when it was time to send him back to Miami, Mitchum and I took him to the airport. Susan boarded the small commuter plane, and Mitchum, Paige, and I stood on the tarmac . . . and after a while, Mitchum asked a question that had been bothering both of us since Paige arrived. "Is Susan your daughter?" he asked.

"No," said Paige. "She's my daughter's nurse."

There was a pause and then Mitchum finally said, "But your daughter's not here."

Paige looked at Mitchum and smiled. "How about that?" he said. Then he turned and boarded the plane, still smiling.

The late Hank Greenberg wrote in his autobiography, *Hank Greenberg: The Story of My Life*, of John King, a legendary left-handed slugger who hit .380 in the Texas League but never made it to the bigs because he couldn't cope with southpaw pitching. Once, according to Greenberg, King came out of a restaurant and saw a beggar with a tin cup: "King slipped a quarter into the cup. As he turned around, he saw the beggar pull the quarter out of the cup with his left hand and John went back and grabbed the coin out of his hand, and said, 'No left-handed son of a bitch is going to get any of my money.'"

If my devotion to baseball is an occasional embarrassment to me, I blame it on being a Montrealer. We put up with plenty here. Going into the 1989 season of dubious promise, for instance, Claude Brochu, president of Les Expos and a former Seagrams marketing maven, pronounced that the year would be successful if fans would just increase their consumption and spend $7.25 per game on soggy hot dogs and lukewarm beer rather than the measly $5.50 they grudgingly parted with the previous season. Baseball, once a game of inches, was now a business of pennies. Hank Greenberg's father, a prescient man, understood this as early as 1929, when Hank signed his first pro contract.

"Pop," Hank said, "are you against baseball as a career?"

His father nodded.

"The Tigers offered nine thousand dollars."

His father whistled softly. "Nine thousand dollars," he said. "You mean they would give you that kind of money just to go out and play baseball?"

"That's right."

"And they'll let you finish college first?"

"Yes."

"I thought baseball was a game," his father said, "but it's a business—apparently a very good business. Take the money."

My problem with Montreal baseball is compounded by the fact that in a climate where we are fortunate to reap seven weeks of summer, maybe six, the game is played on a zippered carpet in a concrete container that resembles nothing so much as an outsize toilet bowl—a toilet bowl the cost of which would humble even a Pentagon procurement agent. The ugly Olympic Stadium, more properly known in Montreal as the Big Owe, cost $650 million to build in 1976, *more than the combined cost of all the domed stadiums constructed in North America up to that time.* And this price doesn't include the parking facilities, which set taxpayers back another $70 million. Nor did it take into account the so-called retractable roof, finally put in place in 1988, its reported cost another $80 million. A roof that retracted only erratically come 1989 and already leaked in several places.

Despite these local difficulties, I am not only addicted to the game but also to books that celebrate it: say, George V. Higgins's *The Progress of the Seasons: Forty Years of Baseball in Our Town,* composed in praise of those who came closest to the sun, playing in Boston's Fenway Park. Baseball, writes Higgins, differs from football and basketball in that it is "a game played by generally normal-sized men whose proportions approximate those of the majority of onlookers, and whose feats are therefore plausibly imagined by the spectator as his own acts and deeds."

There is a lot in that, certainly, but also an exception to the rule, the towering six-feet-four Hank Greenberg, who first came up with the Detroit Tigers in 1930 and before he was done, in 1947, had hit 331 home runs in a career that was interrupted by four years of military service in the Second World War. Greenberg, whose lifetime batting average was .313, was twice named MVP. He drove in 1,276 runs and remains tied with Lou Gehrig for highest average of runs batted in per game with .920, or nearly one RBI a game for his career. He is also one of only two Jewish players in the Hall of Fame, the other being Sandy Koufax.

Ira Berkow, who did an admirable job of editing and amending *Hank Greenberg,* an autobiography that remained unfinished when Greenberg died of cancer in 1986, notes that Greenberg's one-time teammate Birdie Tebbetts recalled, "There was nobody in the history of the game who took more abuse than Greenberg, unless it was Jackie Robinson." But Greenberg, a man of immense dignity, refused to either Anglicize his name or flaunt his Jewishness. Instead, he put up with the taunts, though on one occasion he did walk over to the Yankee dugout, which was riding him hard, and challenge everybody on the team.

The racial slurs that Jewish players once heard in the majors were not always devoid of wit. Andy Cohen, a New York Giants infielder who came up to the bigs before Greenberg, tells about one Texas League game in 1925. "I made a good catch and the fans gave me a pretty big hand. Then I heard one guy yell out, 'Just like the rest of the Jews. Take everything they can get their hands on.'"

In 1934, Greenberg, a non-observant Jew, decided that it wouldn't be proper for him to play on Yom Kippur, the holiest day of the Jewish calendar, and became the subject of a poem of sorts by Edgar A. Guest, the last stanza of which read:

Came Yom Kippur—holy fast day world wide
    over the Jew—
And Hank Greenberg to his teaching and the
    old tradition true
Spent the day among his people and he didn't
    come to play.
Said Murphy to Mulrooney, "We shall lose the
    game today!
We shall miss him on the infield and shall miss
    him at the bat,
But he's true to his religion—and I honor him
    for that!"

Another incident, even more famous, came in 1938, when Greenberg hit fifty-eight home runs, two short of Babe Ruth's record, with five games left to play. When he failed to hit another homer that season, a lot was made of the story that pitchers had thrown him anti-Semitic fastballs, racist sliders, and Jew-baiting curves, but Greenberg would have none of it. "Some people still have it fixed in their minds," he wrote, "that the reason I didn't break Ruth's record was because I was Jewish, that the ball players did everything they could to stop me. That's pure baloney. The fact is quite the opposite: So far as I could tell, the players were mostly rooting for me, aside from the pitchers."

Walter Matthau told Berkow that when he was growing up on the Lower East Side of Manhattan, his idol was Hank Greenberg: "Greenberg for me put a stop to the perpetuation of the myth at the time that all Jews wound up as cutters or pants pressers. Or, if they were lucky, salesmen in the garment center."

Years later Matthau joined the Beverly Hills Tennis Club only because Hank Greenberg was then a member.

"For thirty years," said Matthau, "I told a story which I read in the newspapers about Hank Greenberg at a port of embarkation during the Second World War. The story had it that there was a soldier who had had a little too much to drink, and he was weaving around all the soldiers sitting there. He was quite a big fella. And he said in a very loud voice, 'Anybody here named Goldberg or Ginsburg? I'll kick the livin' daylights out of him.' Or words to that effect. Hank had been sitting on his helmet, and he stood up and said, 'My name is Greenberg, soldier.' The soldier looked at him from head to foot and said, 'Well, I said nothin' about Greenberg, I said Goldberg or Ginsburg.' I told this to Hank when I met him at the club. He said it never happened. I told him I didn't care to hear that. I was going to continue to tell that story because I liked it. He said, 'Okay, whatever you say, Walter.'"

The most original and quirky baseball book I have read in ages, *El Béisbol: Travels through the Pan-American Pastime*, by John Krich, is an antic tour through far fields, where Fan Appreciation Day is "*El Día de Los Fanáticos*," the Day of the Fanatics; pitchers must beware of a *robador de bases*; and Roberto Clemente is still worshipped above all.

El Béisbol abounds in vivid set pieces, among them a game Krich attended in Puerto Rico with Vic Power, a slugger with the Cleveland Indians in the late fifties, and Rubén Gomez, a.k.a. *El Divino Loco* (the Divine Crazy), who pitched for the Giants in the first game they played after their move to San Francisco. "Oh, baby," Power told Krich. "My biggest salary in the major leagues was thirty-eight thousand dollars. Now the average Puerto Rican kid wants that for a signing bonus. The kid's mama, she knows too much!"

Pete

Rose

———————

CROUCHING OVER HOME PLATE in Riverfront Stadium one night in September 1984, claiming it in that aggressive manner he has made his own, he couldn't be confused with one of your latter-day California-bred players; flaxen-haired, features finely chiselled, the manner of a man who in the off-season might be doing a guest spot on "Dynasty" or finishing a Merrill Lynch trainee course. Endlessly striving Pete Rose, home at last, at bat for the 15,099th time in his major-league life, was a throwback to an earlier age. If he didn't exist, Ring Lardner might have invented him. If he hadn't been capable of playing ball, then surely the alternative would have been shifting beer cases or working on a construction site. He hit a line drive. A single. "If he had the natural ability of a Johnny Bench," said one of the sportswriters, "he would have had to pack it in long ago. But he never had natural ability. It's all hustle."

Going into the new season, the legendary Rose, player-manager for the Cincinnati Reds, was only 94 hits shy of the game's ultimate statistic: Ty Cobb's record of 4,191 career hits. "All the reporters do is ask me about it," Rose complained by rote. "All I do is answer them. It would be great for baseball if I got it, but I'm not going to jump off a bridge if I don't." But later, his eyes hot, his manner disconcertingly boyish considering his age, he added: "It took Ty Cobb twenty-four seasons. I'm going to do it in twenty-three."

But sour baseball rabbis waiting in the tall grass would certainly howl that Rose had already had 1,982 more times at bat than Cobb and, furthermore, that Cobb's career batting average was .367, whereas Rose's stood at .305. Rose was forty-three years old in 1984, his long-pursued grail within tantalizing sight. He allowed that he now found it harder to overcome injuries, but also insisted: "Medical people tell me I have the body of a thirty-year-old. I know I've got the brain of a fifteen-year-old. You got both, you can play baseball."

Rose, a shrewd judge of his own quotes, watched for my reaction. I asked him if he had any other interests. "Say, politics."

"When Reagan was coming here for a campaign rally he called me from Air Force One; he wanted me to introduce him. I can't do that. Maybe fifty-one per cent of the people are for Reagan, forty-nine per cent against him. I introduce him, forty-nine per cent of the fans don't like me. So Johnny Bench introduces him, he doesn't have to worry about being booed any more. On the podium, Reagan tells them he called me. They made it seem I was sorry I couldn't be there."

In 1984 Rose played for the Expos until August 15. He started out in left field, but less than two weeks into the season his elbow went bad on him. Rose, who could no longer throw more than one hundred feet, was shifted to first base. Then, on July 26, the foundering Expos traded for another first baseman, Dan Driessen of the Reds, because Rose was hitting only .259. So the man who had been three times the National League batting champion, with National League and World Series MVP awards to his credit, and who had connected for two hundred hits a season ten times, was benched by a second division club.

Rose, who had come off an embarrassing .245 season with Philadelphia in 1983, reduced to an aging sideshow for hire, might have gone to Seattle, but opted for the Expos. "They brought me there to teach them how to win," he said, "but I never played for a team that took losing so easy. Gary Carter ran that team. He's okay as long as he goes two for four; otherwise he doesn't work the pitchers.

He's always saying, 'I did this, did you see me do that?' I told him, 'Hey there, kid, I played with Johnny Bench.'" Later Rose, wearing his manager's hat, would say that if the Expos ever wanted to trade Carter, he would be glad to have him. But the Mets got him.

Before I caught up with Rose, my first afternoon in Cincinnati, I met with his agent, Reuven Katz, in a hotel bar. Johnny Bench joined us. "Being a player-manager," he said, "would be awkward for anybody but Pete. When I first came up, he took me under his wing. He always wanted me to hit .300. I told him, 'You hit .300, I'll drive you in.' Nobody else will ever get four thousand hits."

In 1978 Bob Trumpy, a sportscaster for WLW radio, had the inspired notion of declaring Pete Rose a national monument. "He represented the work ethic here," Trumpy said. "He's a role model. Cincinnati belongs to him. He can park his Rolls anywhere, nobody will touch him. He can floor it in one of his Porsches and the cops will look the other way. You can take away all the records, everything, Rose has all the intangibles rolled into one. He's unique. He's an art form, the baseball diamond his canvas. But when he came back here he had to talk to Bob Howsam for an hour and a half on the phone to convince him that he could still play ball. When he left here the fans called in one after another to say, 'I will never return to Riverfront Stadium as long as Pete Rose is not playing.' And they didn't."

Bob Howsam, the amiable club president and CEO, allowed that since the days of the fabled Big Red Machine, attendance had slipped from 2.5 million a season to 1.4 million. "We're more interested in him as a manager than a player," he said. "We'll have to see how well he does."

The truth is that truly gifted players—Ty Cobb, Rogers Hornsby, Mel Ott, and Frank Robinson among them—have not signed the skies with their acumen as managers, an exception being Frank Chance, who won four pennants for the Cubs. Our of necessity, however, Rose had always looked for an edge as a player. He had the advantage of being an astute as well as an ebullient student of the game. A great judge of talent, according to Johnny Bench. Yes, but would he find it difficult to be patient with players of lesser ability or hustle? "I don't expect anybody to play like me," Rose said, un-abashed, "because they can't, they just can't."

On opening day in Cincinnati, on April 8, 1963, at Crosley Field, popular Don Blasingame was no longer at second base, having been displaced by a brash twenty-one-year-old interloper called Pete Rose. Rose had come up to the Reds a graduate of Macon, Georgia, in the Class A Sally League, where he had been known as "Holly-wood," "José Hustle," or "Hotdog." He had signed with the Reds for a $7,000 bonus and scrambled on to win the National League Rookie of the Year Award and, in succeeding seasons, playing in the outfield or at second or third base, just about every trophy on the shelf. In 1975, the year Sparky Anderson's Big Red Machine won a mind-boggling 108 games, Rose led the last real National League dynasty in hits and doubles. Then, in one of the most exciting World Series in living memory, Boston taking the Reds to seven games, Rose hit .370 and was named MVP. Two years later, at the age of thirty-six, he surprised everybody by breaking yet another Na-tional League record, hitting safely in forty-four consecutive games. Then came the diminishing years. He was gone, first to Philadelphia for five seasons and then to Montreal, enjoying only one more vin-tage season, 1979, when he hit .331 for the Phillies.

On August 14, 1984, enduring the humiliation of the Expos' bench, Rose seemed to sniff his magnificent career coming to an end, not with a bang, but a whimper. "It looks like I'm not going to get Ty Cobb's record," he told a reporter, "unless something happens."

The next day the fifth-place Reds, their record a dismal 51–70, announced that they had hired Rose as player-manager, and among baseball fans everywhere joy was unconfined.

"PETE COMES HOME," ran the *Cincinnati Enquirer*'s headline. A playing field in Cincinnati named after Rose. There is also a Pete Rose Drive. Sparky Anderson, who managed Rose for nine years, said, "I told Pete long ago that when he goes to the Hall of Fame he should only take one uniform with him."

A crowd of 35,038 fans, each one awarded an "I Was There" certificate, turned out to hail the prodigal's return on August 17, 1984, and when he stepped up to the plate they remembered when he was young and they were young and there was a Big Red Machine.

Rejoining the Reds had cost Rose a big cut in pay but, he told me, he didn't need the money. Outside of baseball he was earning a million dollars a year, maybe more, largely as the representative of a Japanese firm, Mizuno Sporting Goods. He was also a partner in the Precinct, the best steakhouse in town. "You've got to try it," he said. "It's run by a friend of mine, an expert, he was at Yale. Is that where they teach restaurant management?"

At the Precinct, I drank in the upstairs bar with co-owner Jeff Ruby, a graduate of the Cornell Restaurant School. Indicating all the attractive young women milling about, I asked, "Are they groupies?"

"Don't say that," he said. "We've got a mailman, he's only five feet four, he comes in here. He says all these girls are gold diggers, they won't talk to him. 'Hey,' I said to him, a mailman, 'what are you going to get, a better route?' These ball players are young and their bodies are in good shape and they've got lots of money." Some nights, Ruby went on to say, he enlisted celebrities to tend bar. "The last time Pete did it, he asked me, 'How much did we take in tonight?' I told him, 'Thirty-eight hundred bucks.' 'And how much,' he asked, 'did you take in the night Johnny Bench was here?' 'Four thousand,' I said. Pete pondered that. 'Johnny had better weather,' he said."

Old teammates, Bench and Rose remained friendly rivals. The more thoughtful Bench retired in 1983 at the age of thirty-five. "If you have to hang in there beyond your time for the applause, if your happiness is in the hands of others, you're in trouble. After you quit, though, there's a long time between Monday and Friday."

I asked him about Rose.

"Once his objective was three thousand hits. Then it was Musial's record. He knows all his own stats. In the early days, remember, he wasn't making money. He wanted to become the first singles hitter to drive that Rolls. Now Cobb's record is basically everything to him. Okay. But nobody wants to see him embarrass himself out there or for the pursuit to become blinding. There's so much respect for him."

Rose, who lived out in Indian Hill, a choice suburb, was outside hosing down his Rolls-Royce when I arrived for a late breakfast with him and his new young wife, a former cheerleader for the Philadelphia Eagles. Carol was expecting a baby within a week. All the same, she had cooked us enormous steaks, eggs, and home fries. Pete showed me around the house, which sat on a five-acre lot. There was a TV satellite dish and a large kidney-shaped swimming pool in the backyard. Inside, there were twelve rooms. Marble floors. Three giant TV screens, one on each floor. A sauna. A Roman-sized bath. A trophy room with the line-up card for Rose's first World Series game; the bats he had used in his All-Stars games encased in glass; embarrassingly bad oil portraits of Rose standing at the plate in his prime, and a plaque listing his stats during his forty-four-game hitting streak. There was also a mahogany bar in his sunken living room. "And I don't even drink," Rose said.

Rose didn't see himself as a desperately needed attraction for a team that was going nowhere. An aging star without a vehicle. "There is no dynasty-type team in our division," he said. "It's up for grabs."

Nor did he see himself as a man so absorbed in the game that he had possibly sacrificed his family to it: his first wife, of sixteen years, Karolyn, and their two children, Fawn, nineteen, and Petey, fourteen.

He led me through his ritual interview. "Sure I'm divorced, so are sixty per cent of American men. So why focus on me?" Yes, Koufax had been the hardest thrower he had ever faced, but Marichal was the best pitcher. Cobb's record, he assured me once more, was not an obsession. Captain Ahab, if I had interviewed him, would have said he didn't give a tinker's damn about white whales, it was the amount of oil he brought home that counted. "If I'm hitting, I'll play. If I'm not hitting good, I won't play. Hey, I don't need the money. I'll play as long as I'm useful."

Accompanying me outside after lunch, Rose looked back at his big house in the hills. "They say you can't live good hitting singles." Then we got into one of his Porsches and drove back into town together. "I can't think of anything I'd rather do in summer than play baseball," he said.

Kasparov

———————

T HE GAMES I owe my allegiance to are not cerebral but athletic. Put another way, within most fat, fumble-fingered, middle-aged Jewish novelists there is a slender Sandy Koufax waiting to leap out. Those who can, pitch, those who can't, scribble about it. Hence the baseball novels by Bernard Malamud and Philip Roth, as well as a couple of *goyish* efforts: Robert Coover's wonderful *The Universal Baseball Association, Inc., J. Henry Waugh, Prop.* and Ring Lardner's classic *You Know Me, Al.* In celebration of the latter novel, Virginia Woolf, whom I suspect never chased line drives hit by Vita Sackville-West on the grounds of Sissinghurst, wrote: "Mr. Lardner has talents of a remarkable order. With extraordinary ease and aptitude, with . . . the sharpest insight, he lets Jacke Keefe the baseball player . . . fill in his own depths, until the figure of the foolish, boastful, innocent athlete lives before us."

Alas, the games I'm still addicted to—hockey and baseball—ain't what they used to be. Once hockey was a winter sport, done with long before I had the pleasure of fingering drowned mosquitoes out of my Scotch and water at backyard barbecues. But, as I write (early in June 1993) our fabled Montreal Canadiens have just trounced the Los Angeles Kings, winning yet another Stanley Cup. Unfortunately, the final wasn't pretty. Instead of headmanning the puck, stickhandling it over the blue line, there was far too much dump-and-chase on the part of both teams. And avarice has become the NHL's golden rule: in many areas, advertisements for Speedy Muffler or Coca-Cola are now actually embedded in the ice.

Mercifully there are still no advertisements crocheted into the outfields in baseball parks, but the contests have become punishingly long, the pitchers labouring in slo-mo, and just about every batter pausing to sort out his itchy genitals before stepping endlessly in and out of the batting box. And our munificence helps to shower millions on .235 sluggers and 6–10 pitchers, a new breed of sensitive plants who go on the fifteen-day disabled list if they suffer a paper cut or ingrown toenail.

Nevertheless, these are the games that have captured my boyhood loyalties. I'm stuck with them. But when I was still a shining morning face, bound for a frozen pond with my hockey stick and skates, or for Montreal's Fletcher's Field with my bat and mitt, looking for a game of scrub, I was aware of other kids on my street who were obsessed with a more intellectual game. Blizzards, rain or shine, it has been played for centuries with thirty-two regal pieces on a board with sixty-four squares. While we disputed the comparative merits of Joe DiMaggio and Ted Williams, they replayed the opening moves from championship matches originally contested by François André Danican-Philidor, Paul Morphy, Wilhelm Steinitz, Emanuel Lasker, Jose Rual Capablanca, and Alexander Alekhine.

Chess, the royal game, has always had its impassioned advocates as well as its critics. It is, said Goethe, the "touchstone of the intellect." Or, as Raymond Chandler once wrote, "as elaborate a waste of human intelligence as you could find anywhere outside of an advertising agency."

The origins of the game, wrote William Hartson in *The Kings of Chess*, "are celebrated in a host of romantic legends, but remain obstinately shrouded in the mists of antiquity. The first mention of chess is to be found in Sanskrit texts around A.D. 600, but there is no hard evidence of anyone actually playing the game until the ninth century. By that time, games similar to chess existed in Indian,

Arabic, Islamic and Chinese cultures. Whether they have a common ancestor remains a matter of speculation."

King James I of England, for one, found the game a tad too demanding: "As for Chesse, I think it over fond, because it is overwise and Philosophicke a folly: for where all such light playes are ordained to free mens heades for a time, from the fashious thoughts on their affaires; it by contrarie filleth and troubleth mens heades, with as many fashious toeys of the play, as before it was filled with thoughts on his affaires."

Garry Kasparov, the reigning world champion, is the subject of a compelling biography by Fred Waitzkin, *Mortal Games: The Turbulent Genius of Garry Kasparov*. Until the astonishing Kasparov surfaced (his 1992 international rating of 2,805 is the highest in the history of chess), the greatest player of all time was reckoned to be Bobby Fischer. Fischer won the world championship, taking a sequence of matches against Boris Spassky in Reykjavik, Iceland, in 1972, in spite of the fact that the Commie titleholder was bolstered from beginning to end by troops of grand masters and Fischer had no coaches whatsoever. Given the Cold War climate of the times, this was taken as proof positive that communism didn't work but capitalism did.

For the next twenty years, Fischer, wearing disguises, hid out in squalid rooming houses, complaining that the Jews were out to get him. He had the fillings in his teeth removed, lest he be misled by Jewy radio signals. Then, in 1992, he emerged for a rematch with Spassky, beginning on the remote island of Sveti Stefan and moving on to Belgrade, spitting on a U.S. State Department document that warned he would be prosecuted for playing in Serbia. He won, pocketed a purse of $3.35 million, and then did a flit.

The undeniably brilliant but loopy Fischer is only one of many eccentrics who populate *Mortal Games*. My favourites, certainly, are the Russian émigrés, Rustam Kamsky and his fifteen-year-old chess prodigy son, Gata, who lived in an apartment in Brighton Beach, Brooklyn. Waitzkin writes that in 1990, as a consequence of an article he had written about the pair for the *New York Times Magazine*, Rustam told a mutual friend that "he was coming to my apartment building and would wait for me outside and then stab me to death. Rustam wasn't worried about going to jail, she said, because he had already spent a great deal of his life behind bars and believed that, given the American system of law, he would be sent away for only a few weeks."

Quoted in the *Times* article, Gata's loving dad had said, "Gata didn't become interested in chess. I made him play. I am the person who deserves the credit for my son being a champion. It's not Gata's doing. Talent is not important. Any child can become a world champion . . . The coach has to put his soul into it. To give up his social life. Not to watch television, no theater, no beach. The coach has to completely forget about himself. There are few people like that."

Forget about corked bats, spitballs, hockey sticks with illegal outsize blades, or pucks kicked into the nets. Such transgressions pale beside the dirty work, real or suspected, that prevails in the world of international chess. Bobby Fischer, said an observer, was afraid that if he defended his title against Anatoly Karpov, in 1975, the Russians would have him murdered. During a series of games played in the Philippines in the late seventies between Soviet defector Victor Korchnoi and the then-champion Karpov, Korchnoi charged that Karpov's psychologist, seated in the fourth row, was trying to hypnotize him. Furthermore, it was claimed that Karpov's support team of grand masters was slipping him coded messages by varying the colour of the yogurt he was handed while a game was in progress. Then, in 1984, going into Kasparov's challenge for the championship, a five-month, forty-eight-game marathon against Karpov, it was said that one of Kasparov's trainers was offered $30,000 to reveal the secrets of the challenger's opening moves. Gata's dad was heard from again eight years later. During a tournament in Linares, Spain, eventually won by Kasparov, Rustam warned his boy not to drink from opened bottles of mineral water, because another player had revealed that Kasparov's assistant, Alexander Shakarov, was looking for an opportunity to poison Gata.

Garry Kasparov was born in Baku, in the Soviet republic of Azerbaijan, on April 13, 1963, to a Jewish father and an Armenian mother. His father, Kim Weinstein, died in 1971, when Garry was only seven years old. His devoted mother, Klara, attends most of his chess matches and remains an important influence. He is married, and he and his charming wife, Masha, have a child. Kasparov is a millionaire and is usually accompanied by six bodyguards when in Moscow, where he is a celebrity as readily recognizable as Michael Jordan in the U.S. "When he walks the streets," Moscow police commissioner Arkady Murashov told Waitzkin, "everybody wants to touch him. It only takes one crazy. It's smart for him to have bodyguards."

The overworked accolade chess "genius" certainly applies to Kasparov, and he is far from a one-dimensional man. He is an avid reader. A hockey fan, he was instrumental in easing the passage of Viacheslav Fetisov from the then-Soviet Union to the New Jersey Devils, and the two remain friends. Kasparov is a political animal, an impassioned anti-Communist. He contributes op-ed pieces regularly to both the *Wall Street Journal* and the *European*.

"Garry is one of the brightest political figures in the Soviet Union," said Murashov. "He gains respect among intellectuals here by the day. His one drawback is time. If he were to give up his chess life, he could do anything he wanted in Soviet politics."

On August 20, 1991, on the second day of the coup in Moscow, Kasparov was a guest on "Larry King," along with Jeanne Kirkpatrick and a Russian defector. "The defector," Kasparov later told Waitzkin, "believed that the coup would fail but that it would be a lengthy process. Jeanne Kirkpatrick said it would take forty-eight weeks. I said the coup would be defeated in forty-eight hours." And, of course, he was right.

Kasparov is an avowed enemy of Gorbachev, whom he blames for the Azerbaijani massacre of Armenians, including many loved ones in his hometown. "I would prefer to have him out of the country," he said. "I think the perfect choice for him would be to join the faculty at Harvard."

At the core of the engrossing *Mortal Games* is the exciting account of Kasparov's 1990 world championship rematch against

Karpov, then the challenger, which took place in New York. It all came down to the last game: "On New Year's Eve, Karpov and Kasparov played the highest-stakes chess game of all time. If Kasparov won or even drew game 24, he would get the Korloff trophy, worth about one million dollars, as well as $1.8 million of the prize fund. If he lost, they would divide the Korloff trophy and each player would get $1.5 million of the prize fund. One chess game for eight hundred thousand dollars. But Kasparov had further raised the ante for himself. Before the game, he had decided that, if he won the bejeweled trophy, he would sell it and create a fund for Armenians who were destitute and homeless after the slaughter in Baku."

Eventually establishing a winning position on the board, Kasparov offered Karpov a draw, which most commentators regarded as an act of noblesse oblige.

Politics

Audrey!
Audrey!
Audrey!

An NDP Leadership Convention Diary: November 29–December 2, 1989.

WEDNESDAY, NOVEMBER 29, Toronto. I arrive early for Air Canada's 5:05 p.m. flight to Winnipeg, suspecting it will be overbooked, and I'm right. Distressed delegates mill about the desk, picking up their standby numbers. Gloomy, middle-aged men. Fat ladies, their choice of stretchy slacks ill-advised. But not everybody looking for a seat on AC-195 is, as Ed Broadbent would have it, an "ordinary" Canadian's tribune. There are also two quarrelsome men, obviously sloshed, both wearing plaid shirts, jeans, and pointy cowboy boots.

"I wouldn't mind if a Canadian called me that," one of them says, "but not a fucken raghead. Them fucken ragheads, eh?"

"Yeah."

Once aloft, I turn to the *Toronto Star* clip I have brought with me that features photographs of the candidates, each one, save for Dave Barrett, the image of a high-school principal. The *Star* clipping enables me to put faces to names, a necessary tool, because the only one

I recognize is Barrett, B.C.'s very own Happy Warrior. I have the
same recognition problem watching the Montreal Canadiens on television these days. What with so many injuries, interchangeable rookies
bouncing up and down from the Sherbrooke farm team, I can't tell the
players apart without a program. With the NDP leadership candidates,
however, it is not a question of injuries so much as ice-shy starts (Roy
Romanow, Bob Rae, Bob White, Stephen Lewis) unwilling to lug the
puck when they know damn well that yet again their team is bound to
finish out of the playoffs. So the far from glittering prize will be left on
the table to be claimed by a Jew, a black, or a woman. Whichever it may
be, editorial writers from coast to coast will celebrate the election as a
triumph of multiculturalism or equal-opportunity personhood. Everybody will feel good, especially the sleaze-squad coach B. Mulroney,
Esq. Meanwhile, Simon de Jong is a candidate on the boil, unhappy
with the media: "The press is condemning us as being the 'B' group."

The *Star*'s photograph of the favourite in the race, Audrey
McLaughlin, gives me pause. I suspect something of the good
schoolmarm there, the sort who used to keep us after class to watch
National Film Board shorts featuring Ukrainian folk dancers or Es-
kimo throat singers. I suspect that she would ask me to put out my
cigarillo and that she isn't big on cakes and ale. All the same, she has
to be a spunky lady. Ran a mink farm. Taught in Africa for three
years. Lit out for the Yukon in 1979. Paddles a canoe. But no use
chatting up the delegates on AC-195 because all they do is throw
back yesterday's newspaper columns at you. "It's Audrey's to lose,
but Dave will have to walk on water."

At the convention itself, the majority of the delegates have no
opinion of how their candidates have performed until they have
consulted the next morning's *Globe and Mail*, or have seen Peter
Mansbridge and his gabby bunch pronounce on CBC-TV. At one
point, David Halton ventured that Audrey was supported by "a
mindless bloc of women voters." But the CBC bon-mot prize clearly
belongs to Stephen Lewis. Blessing McCurdy, the black candidate,
on the network of all the people, he said, "In him energy is a beautiful thing. He just has it in spades."

The last time I was in Winnipeg was for the Tory convention in 1983, where goofy Joe Clark, supported by something like two-thirds of his party's delegates, nevertheless resigned and called for a leadership convention, at which point his declared supporter B. Mulroney, Esq., pulled the pins out of his Clark doll, and went to wash the blood off his hands.

At that convention, jolly paymasters, representing either Joe or Brian, were at the airport to greet the huge, thirsty delegation from Canada's distinct society, leading them to cars and hotel suites awash in booze and promises. This time out the thin trickle of sour Quebecers on AC-195 will, like me, have to make their own way to their hotels.

I'm told that the best restaurant in town is Dubrovnik's, but my dinner there is vile. Watery lukewarm borscht. Cabbage rolls re-heated so often the leaves peel like slime. Bob White, huddling at the next table with other union men, is affable enough but refuses to say who he is going to support. I turn to this evening's *Winnipeg Free Press*, its front-page headline reading, "NEW DEMOCRATS DO NOT PARTY, FORMER PREMIER REVEALS": "Howard Pawley has a surprise for Winnipeg eateries and nightspots figuring to make big bucks out of the NDP's leadership convention here this weekend—his party doesn't party."

But tonight, in any event, I discover a number of delegates in the bar of the Holiday Inn, adjoining the convention hall, most of the NDP whoopee-makers sipping coffee. Caffeine-free, no doubt. I settle in with one of the most engaging and intelligent of the lot, Robin Sears, who turns out to be profoundly worried about Quebec. I do my best to reassure him, but add that should Quebec separate I do hope that Anglo dissidents, like East Berliners after the wall came down, can count on being greeted at the Ontari-ari-ario border with $100 bills and glasses of champers, the real stuff, not the indigenous plonk. Bad news. Lorne Nystrom, who was to be convention co-chairman, has been arrested in Ottawa, charged with shoplifting a container of contact-lens cleaner worth $7.79. A forlorn hooker, obviously not a *Free Press* reader, works the bar, the poor girl more

likely to earn a lecture on social redemption than turn a trick. Finally
I take a taxi to my hotel. "It was twenty-six below yesterday," the
driver says, "now it's plus four. It's gotta be all those warm socialist
hearts."

As my room in the Sheraton boasts a VCR, I pause to scan the film
cassettes available in the display case in the lobby. *Playboy Lingerie*;
Night Nurse; *Wild, Wicked and Wanton*. Instead, I dig out my proof
copy of Budd Schulberg's *What Makes Sammy Run?*, recently reis-
sued by Random House.

"Going through life with a conscience," Sammy Glick says, "is
like driving your car with the brakes on."

Thursday, November 30, Winnipeg Convention Centre. Ten a.m.
Damn, I've arrived too late to hear the new puritans declare the
hall a smoke-free zone. Most of the delegates, about half of them
women, are middle-aged and look as though they suffer from
plugged bowels, among other complaints, but if they are charged
with resentments, they have good cause. These are worthy, hard-
working blue- and white-collar workers, paying more than their
share of taxes because they are nabbed at source. No three-martini
expense-account lunches or offshore tax havens for this lot. They
are heirs to our only political party that doesn't have office as its
guiding principle; a party, with some claim to nobility, that has
served long and thanklessly as our nation's conscience, largely responsible for our admirable safety net of social programs; a party that
has seen many of its most innovative ideas denounced by Liberals
who then went on to pilfer them, and that is still stuck in second
gear, spinning its wheels, failing time and again to win more than
its traditional 15 to 20 per cent of the popular vote or to make a
breakthrough in Quebec. If only they didn't appear so grumpy, such
injustice-collectors. Or, put another way, joy is confined on Thursday morning. Refreshment tanks thoughtfully placed here, there,
and everywhere in the hall offer nothing more intoxicating than
cold water—NDP ambrosia.

Most of the delegates seated at the long tables in the hall have important-looking documents set out before them, but something about them immediately puts me in mind of a legion hall and the conviction that their papers are in fact bingo cards. There are hardly any youngsters about. Almost no French Canadians, Jews, blacks, Chinese, Sikhs, or native people. Everywhere I wander, badges and position papers are thrust at me. My favourite badge, happily ambiguous, its intent possibly even saucy, reads TRADE UNIONISTS FOR AUDREY, but fails to proffer numbers. Audrey, I learn, wants to be fair to Canada's First Peoples and is for building a strong party in every region, province, or territory. Loopy Roger Lagassé, running "an environmentally sustainable leadership race," once suggested that all the candidates should ride the same bus in order to produce less pollution. Former probation officer (St. Louis, Missouri, juvenile court) Dave Barrett is committed to a war against pollution, his position supported by Major General Richard Rohmer, Canada's shortest air cadet. Ian Waddell, facing the future, is for Canadian independence and wants everybody to attend his Hawaiian night at the Delta Hotel on Friday. "Bring your Hawaiian shirt (and hula skirt if you have one)!" Simon de Jong (a "Journal" stoolie, and wired, though we didn't know it yet) wants Canada to play a global role, as well as to recycle and "reforestate." Howard McCurdy, a roadshow Jesse Jackson, is for PASSION and all the colours of the rainbow. Steve Langdon wants the NDP to abandon the marshmallow middle for a new radicalism.

Pick up a copy of the *Globe and Mail* and break for a solitary lunch at Oscar's Deli, across the street from the Holiday Inn. The astute Jeffrey Simpson writes, "Seldom have so many delegates at a leadership convention been so weakly committed to so many candidates."

The *Toronto Star*'s Val Sears has arrived. So has Allan Fotheringham. Lysiane Gagnon from *La Presse*. The *Ottawa Citizen*'s delightful Marjorie Nichols. Apologists Hugh Segal and Senator Mike Kirby, intruding manifiosos, both hired to gab away on television, are also there to snoop for their respective parties, but Barbara Frum, another convention regular, is sitting this one out. Most of all, I miss Dalton Camp. The press, myself included, are already bored. Their observations are scathing, as they regale each other with inside Ottawa stories too juicy to print.

The action promises to pick up this afternoon in the so-called bearpit session, wherein the seven suitors—including lovable, huggable Roger Lagassé, the NDP's simpleton out of Sechelt, B.C.— will answer zingers thrown at them by delegates from the floor. Problem. All the candidates, with the exception of Barrett, look as though they would be comfier running a health-food shop than a country.

Later. Alas, the event itself promised much better than it paid. After the inevitable nutters on the floor were heard from—demented shop stewards more eager to make a speech than ask a question—the rest of the session proved insufferably tame. The candidates, incapable of eloquence, served up knee-jerk socialist banalities in response to everything. Pencil poised, I cornered a delegate and asked him what he made of the proceedings so far. He rubbed his jaw, pondered, and then told me: "Speaking frankly, in my opinion, seldom have so many delegates at a leadership convention been so weakly committed to so many candidates."

Finally the bearpit session lapsed into unreality, if not quite cloud-cuckoo-land yet. Impassioned delegates wanted to know if the convention should now recognize the emerging government parties of East Germany and Czechoslovakia or if they should wait, because possibly they were the same old Commies trying to seduce the West in hastily donned social-democratic skirts. In my mind's eye, I saw desperate men sweating it out, waiting by the fax machine somewhere in East Berlin; I espied Vaclav Havel standing by the phone, pleading for silence from the thousands rattling their key chains in Wenceslas Square . . . everybody waiting on the word from the NDP convention floor in Winnipeg. The eye of the storm.

Earlier in the day, I had phoned home to send for my youngest son, Jacob, who is twenty-one years old. He is majoring in history at Concordia, and I feel it's time he saw some in the making. Something else: I can use some lively company.

Six-thirty p.m., Hall B, third floor, Winnipeg Convention Centre. "A celebration," my invitation read. "New Democrats pay tribute to Ed Broadbent."

"Is this going to take long?" I asked Robin Sears.

"If I were you," he said, "I'd get a table close to the bar, but not too far from an exit."

In speech after speech, Canada was never once spoken of as "this country," but only as "this great country," populated, it goes without saying, by "ordinary Canadians." The speakers, including Shirley Carr and Allan Blakeney, were too discreet to mention that Honest Ed, though highly critical of the manner in which Mulroney dispensed patronage, had—like other uncompromising New Democrats before him (Ian Deans, Dennis McDermott, Stephen Lewis) —made an exception in his own case, tumbling onto a very soft pillow, courtesy of the pol from whom all good things flowed. Broadbent, it would be officially announced later in the month, had had his arm twisted and accepted a $100,000-or-more-a-year post to head the new International Centre for Human Rights and Democratic Development, to be headquartered in Montreal. No better place to begin, I thought. After all, I'm a Montrealer, born and bred, and now find my language banned from commercial display outdoors. This, of course, is a shocking violation of my freedom of expression under the Charter of Rights and Freedoms, and has obliged me to take down the sign (an offence to the collectivity) posted on the road leading to my cottage in the Eastern Townships:

FREELANCE ENGLISH-SPEAKING WRITER
NO OFFER TOO SMALL
FREE ESTIMATES ON REQUEST

In the absence of Tom Paine, surely Citizen Broadbent ("the best man for the job," said Audrey M.) can be counted on to put his shoulder to the wheel in his new job and fight for my rights. The NDP may have lost a leader, but the abandoned anglophones of Quebec, or at least what's left of them, have clearly found a champion. Fundamental human rights begin at home, as Ed surely knows.

At 10 p.m., Jake arrives from Montreal in time to join a bunch of us (Val Sears, Charlotte Gray, Chris Young, and Pat Nagle of Southam News, among others) for dinner at Amici's, a decent Italian restaurant, everybody complaining about how little there is to write about so far. A discerning reader of fiction sends a bottle of champagne to me and I have the rare pleasure of seeing Val Sears impressed. "Does this happen to you very often?" he asks.

"Every time my wife and I go out to dinner," I reply. "Actually, it's becoming a bit of a bore. Cheers."

Friday, December 1. Eight a.m. Here at the Sheraton Winnipeg Hotel, where scratchy face towels are the rule. NDP parlance is getting to me. Merely climbing out of bed to brush my teeth, I feel physically challenged. The fully booked Sheraton has been unable to provide a room with two single beds for Jake and myself, but we manage nicely in our queen-size. There is a wee problem, however. Starting this morning, hitherto polite chambermaids have taken to glaring at me, obviously a dirty old man. I plead with Jake to please call me "Dad," *in a voice that carries*, when we run into help in the hall. Doesn't work. I'm afraid they've heard that one before. Later in the day, when I return to our room for a nap, there is a sharp rap at the door and I leap up terrified, expecting it's the morality squad come for me, but it's only my laundry.

"How do you find things so far?" I ask a delegate.

"It's Audrey's to lose, but Dave will have to walk on water."

Bob White, a traded unionist, now sports an Audrey button, having backed down from his own candidacy. The television crews, a menace, are everywhere. Behemoths bearing battery packs, hooligans carrying lights or sound booms, cameramen leading with the elbows, backing into innocent bystanders without apology. The scrum, something I have never seen up close before, is a truly frightening business. Barrett or McLaughlin have only to appear on the floor to be instantly besieged, all but lifted off their feet, by an aggressive mob of TV technicians who precede them, walking backwards, their lights blinding. Wendy Mesley, circling the pulsating pack, finds daylight and squirts through to ask a question. Only Barrett, nobody's patsy, gives as good as he gets.

The Meech Lake debate gets off to a jump-start with a strong statement from Manitoba NDP leader Gary Doer: "We must say yes to aboriginal people, yes to northerners, yes to strong federal programs. And we must amend the Meech Lake Accord." But Doer's ardour is compromised soon enough by a convoluted resolution that ostensibly papers over the split in the party. The cakes-for-everybody resolution recognizes Quebec as a distinct society and acquiesces to the five demands the province wants included in the accord. But hold the phone. At the same time it asks for changes in the unanimity amending clause, safeguards in the federal spending formula, and a recognition of aboriginal peoples, minorities, and women, without making it clear whether these changes are a condition of NDP support or could be brought in at a later date. Even so, the tiny Quebec delegation (74 out of 2,435 delegates) has got the sulks, some of them threatening to go home early. Especially unhappy is Phil Edmonston, who has taken to talking about himself in the third person like Charles de Gaulle. Edmonston, the NDP candidate in the February by-election in Chambly, just south of Montreal, told a reporter: "The party set a precedent two years ago by allowing Audrey McLaughlin to break party solidarity and campaign against the accord. Now let's see what they do with Phil Edmonston."

Meanwhile, NDP staff member Claude Rompré is fulminating. "Do you think this will fly in Quebec? No, Quebec will say the New Democrats are hypocrites. It will be extremely difficult to find people to work for the NDP in Quebec." The difficulty could become insurmountable, so far as one Radio-Canada reporter is

concerned, if the voting were to run late tomorrow night, imping-
ing on the telecast of the Saturday night hockey game. The Canadiens are playing the Hartford Whalers.

Demonstrations on the floor, more dutiful than impassioned
until now, have suddenly become feverish or, as Val Sears puts it, the
voices of reason are now being heard from. Delegates, brandishing
banners, shrieking, "Dave, Dave, Dave! Audrey, Audrey, Audrey!
Steve, Steve, Steve!" In the absence of anything more stimulating
than cold water, the delegates on the floor get their charge out of
television, their fervour or lack of it directly related to the presence
of the cameras. I understand. Slipping out to watch proceedings on
television in the press room, the contest appeared exciting. I wish I
was there.

The pictures lie, but in the convention's case they also reveal
that Edmonston isn't the only New Democrat to suffer from third-
person-speak arrogance. Stephen Lewis, fumbling on TV over his
now-you-see-it, now-you-don't Audrey stance, was heard to say to
Peter Mansbridge: "Stephen Lewis is so discredited now. . . ."

Back on the floor, following the debate on Meech Lake, a concerned delegate stands up to call for a resolution on AIDS, a gesture
that a large number of the socially conscious take as an invitation to
drift out into the hall for more lukewarm hot dogs and unspeakably
bad coffee, not to mention a smoke, out of sight of the clean-air
freaks.

Six forty-five p.m. Show-and-tell time. The first candidate to make
his pitch, cutesy-poo Roger Lagassé, is accompanied on to the platform by a number of absolutely adorable children, not a nose-picker
or drug pusher among them, lugging peace symbols of one sort or
another. Lagassé, who doesn't count, is wildly cheered. Were the
NDP a baseball team rather than a political party, Lagassé would be
their mascot. Next comes CBC's "The Journal" freelancer Simon de
Jong, who warns us that, unless something is done, the planet's tem-
perature could increase by five degrees centigrade within fifty years,

a development I would have thought every Winnipegger, regardless of party affiliation, would cheer to the skies. Then, following a boffo demonstration, union toughs belting out his name, Dynamic Dave skips onto the platform to the tune of the NDP's 1984 election-campaign theme song, "Rise Up," thereby undoing yet-to-come Howard McCurdy, who was set to hit the stage in step to the same ditty. Say what you like about Barrett, he enjoys himself up there. He is charged with appetite. If he doesn't exactly walk on water, as required, he does bring the delegates to their feet more than once, telling them, "Everywhere the Tories go, food banks are sure to follow." Socking it to them, demanding real tax reform, bellowing, "Let the rich pay their fair share," advising corporations to "mail your cheques in now, you owe it."

Next the likable Ian Waddell starts out with a self-effacing joke, hardly a knee-slapper but certainly acceptable, about his early days as an NDP campaigner. Unfortunately it earns him not so much as a chuckle from the constipated delegates and you can sense the air leaking out of his balloon. McCurdy, who follows, starts out on a low note, exploiting a delegate in a wheelchair, making a point of using him as one of his endless run of nominators. McCurdy also declares unequivocally, "Either a black man or a woman will be our next leader," but the next day, following his disappointing showing on the first ballot, he will throw his support to Steve Langdon, possibly mistaking him for an albino in all the excitement.

And, at last, there stands Audrey. Audrey, Audrey, Audrey! No political piker, she starts out by saying, "It's time to get rid of the free-trade deal and Brian Mulroney. The day after the next federal election, I will let Washington know: the trade deal is off."

All at once I feel myself lifted into cloud-cuckoo-land. Let's face it, the day after the next federal election the NDP, honouring convention, will limp home third, lucky to hold on to its forty-three seats.

For the rest, Audrey's speech, the delivery flat, proffers no hitherto unheard music; it is pedestrian, obeisance paid to all the socialist clichés. But when I phone home, I discover that Florence, who has been watching on TV, feels that Audrey came over extremely well, fresh, even sparkly. We do agree, however, that the best speech of the evening was the last, by Steven Langdon, but by that time many of the delegates had quit the hall.

P.S. Stephen Lewis, according to reliable reports, also phoned home and as a consequence did another 180-degree turn on Audrey, remembering that he had, like Antony, come not to bury but to praise her.

Saturday, December 2. High noon. On arrival at the convention hall, I find the top of the escalator lined with delegates chanting Audrey's name.

The first poll reads McLaughlin, 646; Barrett, 566; Langdon, 351; de Jong, 315; McCurdy, 256; Waddell, 213; Lagassé, 53.

Only fifteen minutes are allowed for wheeling and dealing between ballots. More than enough time when you consider that the NDP candidates, an impecunious lot, are without cabinet seats, appointments to the Senate, judgeships, lavish advertising contracts, and other patronage goodies to dispense. Winning the leadership of the NDP, unless the party holds the balance of power in a hung Parliament, is like coming first in the Florida Grapefruit League. Too bad for the rest of us, because there are more dedicated, honourable men and women in the NDP, albeit most of them fumblers, than in the other two major parties combined.

Fifteen minutes is enough for Lagassé to be dropped, Waddell to move to Barrett, and McCurdy to Langdon. Barrett edges closer to the lead in the second ballot. McLaughlin, 829; Barrett, 780; Langdon, 519; de Jong, 289. Then de Jong, an obedient child, flies to McLaughlin, and so does McCurdy. McLaughlin wins 1,072 votes on the third ballot and goes over the top of the fourth with 1,316 votes to Barrett's 1,072. Barrett, with a legitimate gripe (although we do not know as much yet), is a gracious loser. He tells cheering delegates, "We are a united party." McLaughlin agreeds. "Fortunately, we're not starting with a lot of ill will," she says. "We're colleagues.

We're the same party. We're working together. We'll build on that."

But the next morning, Robin Sears tells me, "Families are split. Old friends are not talking to each other."

Then, to the amusement of the rest of us, the shit hits the fan.

Simon de Jong, it turns out, has been wired by "The Journal," entrapping innocents in conversations that were being recorded without their knowledge or consent. Dirty pool, that, and very questionable, even detestably devious, tactics on the part of "The Journal" in the dubious name of making an "accurate historical record of a Canadian political convention," to quote a defensive Mark Starowicz, the producer of "The Journal." Only de Jong, however, was sufficiently stupid—or forgetful, to be kind—to make what appears to be a back-room deal with Barrett even as his hidden mike recorded it for the ages. In exchange for the party whip's job, he would move to Barrett on the next ballot.

"It's yours," said Barrett. "It's a deal."

"Okay. All right. Okay."

But de Jong's mother had the last word. Simple Simon, wired for sound, turned to her and asked, "Where should I go, Mummy? What should I do?"

Some observers feel that Mother de Jong's intervention ("Get thee to Audrey, sonny boy") constitutes interference in domestic politics by a possible agent of the notoriously meddlesome Dutch. But to my way of looking, there is nothing sinister involved. Mother de Jong feared that if Simon bolted to Barrett, the leadership contest could run to a fifth and maybe even a sixth or seventh ballot, keeping her son up way beyond his bedtime. This way Simon can go tucky-byes early.

Finally, Audrey McLaughlin isn't elected leader of the NDP in spite of being a woman but because she is one. No obscure male backbencher, an MP for a mere two years, could have come so far so fast. Still, I wish the lady luck. I wish her luck and a new speech-writer, please.

Bye Bye
Mulroney

M ANY A GOOD MAN, it's true, has been destroyed by booze, but an abrupt lapse into abstinence has led to even more of them unravelling by falling in with undesirable company. Take the case of a couple of one-time Montreal chums, both of whom once fancied the four-hour lunch and, believe me, when a man is so happily engaged he can do no harm to the body politic. I speak of Brian Mulroney and Richard Holden. Just for a lark, Holden, yesterday's merry boulevardier, became the Westmount candidate of a quirky little anglophone provincial protest party, the Equality party, and woke up one morning, in 1989, hung-over and in office in Quebec's National (*sic*) Assembly, put there to fight fatuous language restrictions. Then, on a day of infamy, he abandoned his WASP and Jewish drinking companions *de souche* and joined both the AA and the PQ. That poor, misguided man staggered on to the wagon and fell into the waiting headlock of Jolly Jock Parizeau. Parizeau was so out of touch with English-speaking Quebecers that he thought the acquisition of Holden was a coup. Actually, it was the equivalent of the Montreal Canadiens believing they could clinch the Stanley Cup by reactivating Eddie Shack.

Then there is the far more important case of Brian Mulroney, who also overpaid for swearing off the sauce. Suddenly he, too, was seen in dim company, changing his shirt three times a day to mix with dozy Ronald Reagan, and later the Bushes—inarticulate "out-of-the-loop" George and the menacingly sweet "Bar." These sad associations, at their nadir, led to what was surely the most maudlin and embarrassing public display of the Mulroney decade, our suppliant PM joining Reagan on a Quebec City stage, the two of them insufferably twinkly, to warble "When Irish Eyes Are Smiling."

The Mulroney I had encountered briefly in the early 1980s, late-lunching with him a couple of times, was an entertaining companion, a stylish raconteur whose dark side was revealed only when he mentioned the fumbling Joe Clark, whom he held in contempt even then. A born twister, Mulroney was soon protesting his unequivocal loyalty to Clark publicly, even as, in private, he plotted with his back-room hit men the Tory leader's demise. And, it is worth noting, when the knife was plunged into Clark's back, it did not spurt blood but only lukewarm water, albeit Tory blue. Furthermore, according to reliable report, the stricken Clark did not cry out "*Et tu*, Brian," because even he understood that he was dealing not with the noblest pol of them all but merely with a disgusted professional.

Clark's political obits made illuminating reading. In typically wet Canadian fashion, editorial writers praised him for being honest, decent, hard-working, and, above all, nice, but—come to think of it—a resounding flop at his chosen trade, his last pratfall a constitutional pretzel obviously inspired by Rube Goldberg. My own feeling about Clark's political career is that, while I agree with Bobby Browning that a man's reach should exceed his grasp, it is indecent to overreach by as much as Clark did.

Then, on February 24, 1993 (shortly after Clark had quit the scene, threatening to write), Brian Mulroney, pondering an autumn election in which his troops stood to be decimated if he persisted in leading them, fell on his sword. His passing was undoubtedly mourned most profoundly by Jean Chrétien and his front-bench hooligans. Poor Chrétien. In an age when it had become justifiably contingent for any wannabe PM to be bilingual, he seemed to be in double jeopardy, unable to speak either language adequately. The next to quit the Ottawa monkey house, announcing that he would not be a candidate in the coming election, was the admirably sour John Crosbie. Crosbie, an intelligent and cultivated man cursed with a politically incorrect sense of humour, was unfit for Parliament in the first place by dint of his inability to suffer fools (or shrews) gladly. Mulroney, to give him credit, was a consummate pro, an inspired fibber with the built-in advantage of never once being inhibited by shame. Even on the touching night of his resignation, some Mulroney-bashers would have it that he told yet another whopper when he declared that one of the reasons he hadn't quit earlier, say in 1991, was the Gulf War. "It was vital I stay," he said.

Now it's true that our prime minister's moniker didn't even appear in the index of most histories of that conflict. But, fortunately, I happened to see an advance copy of the then yet-to-be-published *Untold History of the Gulf War*, by Pat McAdam and Sheik Saud Nair al-Sabah. It revealed that the night before an alliance of thirty-one nations (backed by a flotilla of aircraft carriers, squadrons of jet fighters, hundreds of missiles of rare intelligence, and other state-of-the-art military hardware) was about to risk defeat against a starving, ragtag army of illiterate conscripts, an ill wind swept through the ranks. Brian Mulroney was contemplating resignation. Morale crumbled. Then a distressed General Schwartzkopf took a phone call.

"It's Brian Mulroney, sir."

"*The quitter?*"

"No, sir. I'm calling to assure you that I am a man who always makes the hard choices, no matter how unpopular. I want you to know that, in spite of the fact that I'm running at zilch in the polls, which I never read, I'm going to see the battle through right here from Sussex Drive."

"Good man. I will pass the word on to the troops immediately."

Speaking in Ottawa in May 1993, understandably queasy about his place in history, Mulroney warned us that his legacy had already been distorted by reporters driven by "personal vendettas" against him; and then he wrestled yet again with the long and intimidating shadow of Pierre Elliot Trudeau, denouncing the former Liberal prime minister for selling Quebec down the river with his 1982 constitution, conveniently forgetting that, at the time, he had thumped the tub for the package himself. Bobbing and weaving, he ventured that the hoi polloi had turned on him only because he had had the guts to make essential but unpopular decisions. There was something in that, but not nearly enough. Mulroney's necessary free-trade deal with the United States and his imposition of a national sales tax, the GST, had not endeared him to the electorate, but neither did it explain the deeply rooted animus against the man. The morning after his resignation, Terrance Wills wrote in the Montreal *Gazette*, ". . . it's safe to say that a hefty majority of Canadians in any current public-opinion sounding would agree, or strongly agree, with the following statement: Brian Mulroney is a devious schemer and unprincipled liar heading an administration of scoundrels, dunces and thieves."

Dalton Camp, the Tories' wise old man, felt that Mulroney's ostentatious style was a problem. Security requirements he imposed on his office in the 1980s, said Camp, "made it appear more presidential than it actually is. It struck a lot of people as glitzy." Another irritant, said Camp, was excessive hyperbole. "It didn't quite wash in our political culture."

All politicians lie, but few as often, or as mellifluously, as did Sincerely Yours, Brian Mulroney, who lied even when it wasn't necessary, just to keep in shape, his voice, a dead giveaway, sinking into his Guccis whenever he was about to deliver one of his whoppers. Campaigning for the Tory leadership in 1983, Mulroney mocked his chief rival for the job, good Tory scout Joe Clark, for playing tiddly-winks with Quebec separatists. Then Mulroney courted them on bended knee, paying for their endorsements with cabinet seats in lieu of roses, punishing the country with wasting years of acrimonious and failed constitutional haggling, which served only to resuscitate the cause of Québécois tribalism. Before assuming office in 1984, he was adamantly opposed to any free-trade deal, but, once in place at 24 Sussex Drive, he signed one with the United States and another with Mexico. Referendums, he declared, were not the way our folks did things. Then he ordered up one for his second offer of a constitutional elixir, and lost, the country dismissing it as quack medicine. The universality of our social programs, he said, was "a sacred trust," and then he attempted to tamper with them. To be fair, there was one promise the trickster did keep. He said he would deliver Quebec on a platter, without which the famished Tories could not expect to win office, and he did exactly that, but at the cost of a Faustian bargain with the separatists. And, in good time, the most compelling of them, Lucien Bouchard, wiped off the blade that had done in Joe Clark and slipped it between Mulroney's ribs, making for symmetry of a sort. Or, at least, prosaic justice.

There were also a couple of other Quebecers of note caught in Mulroney's 1984 net: Benoit Bouchard and that appealing teeny-bopper Jean Charest, a possible future prime minister. But, for the most part, trolling pool rooms, pizza parlours, and beer halls for likely candidates in 1984, Mulroney netted a bunch of dunderheads and bottom-feeders. The roll of dishonour is worth citing here: Suzanne Blais-Grenier, junior minister of transport, forced to walk the plank after she was caught living it up in Paris at our considerable expense; André Bissonette, the next junior transport minister, fired for doing too well out of a land flip-flop with Oerlikon Aerospace, which just happened to be a company with a defence contract; Roch LaSalle, public works minister, who denied being guilty of influence peddling, but thought it prudent to resign all the same; Michel Côté, supply and services minister, shown the door for failing to come clean about a $250,000 personal loan from a Quebec City free-enterpriser with an appetite for government contracts; backbencher Richard Grisé, caught taking kickbacks from builders, pleading guilty to eleven counts of fraud and breach of trust; backbencher Edouard Desrosiers, also found guilty of breach of trust, but coming out ahead when he was fined only $3,000 for pilfering $5,463 from his parliamentary office budget, and for accepting a $2,000 bribe.

Mulroney soft-shoed into office condemning corruption and then presided over a government tainted by a record number of cabinet ministers who were obliged to resign in disgrace, three in all.

In 1993, at least one Tory senator and three backbenchers were still to be tried in Quebec courts. Senator Michel Cogger had pleaded not guilty to a charge of influence peddling. Backbencher Gabriel Fontaine would be obliged to answer to fourteen counts of fraud, breach of trust, and conspiracy. Two other backbenchers, Gilles Bernier and the aforementioned Richard Grisé, who resigned in 1989, obviously both loving dads, had been charged for allegedly putting each other's kids on their parliamentary payrolls and rewarding them for work they never did.

On July 9, 1984, when Liberal Prime Minister John Turner announced that there would be an autumn election, and went on to deal nineteen patronage appointments to prominent Liberals, Mulroney professed to be shocked. "It's something out of an Edward G. Robinson movie," he said. "You know, the boys cuttin' up the cash. There's not a Grit left in town. They've all gone to Grit heaven."

If he were elected, by gum, things would be different.

"I undertake today that all political appointments will be of the highest unimpeachable quality. I'm going to send out a dramatic signal of renewal in this area of Canadian life."

Then, in what was to become a celebrated television exchange, a sanctimonious Mulroney reproached Turner for acquiescing to those nineteen last-minute patronage appointments, imposed on him by the outgoing Trudeau, by saying, "You had an option, sir. You could have done better."

The next afternoon I happened to run into one of Mulroney's longtime cronies in the bar of the Ritz-Carlton Hotel. "I phoned Brian after the debate," he said. "'Hey, what are you doing to us? What do you mean knocking patronage?' 'Trust me,' he said."

And, once thrust into office, Mulroney did do better than Turner. Undeniably loyal to old pals and big givers, he rewarded them with Senate seats, diplomatic plums, and appointments to federal boards and commissions and immigration courts until there was hardly one Tory piggy who didn't have his snout in the trough. Old acquaintances in favour of flogging joined the parole boards. Those who could spell, or had proved capable of following the plot of the last book they had read (probably their Dick and Jane reader), were invited to serve on the boards of the Canada Council or National Arts Centre, and those who still missed "Don Messer's Jubilee," or had sat through *The Terminator*, found themselves pronouncing as directors of the CBC, the National Film Board, or Telefilm.

The first prime minister of our country to have emerged from the working class, Mulroney courted the rich, luxuriating on their parvenu Florida estates, and dressed as if he hoped to be invited to pose for a GQ fashion spread. Towards the end, when the going got tough, he was suddenly and mysteriously touted—some say by his friend George Bush—as a candidate for the job of secretary-general of the United Nations, but he was found wanting. He was undoubtedly shallow, but, on the other hand, nobody ever accused the then leader of the Opposition, Jean Chrétien, of being an intellectual deep-sea diver. And, at the time, many of us could hardly wait for the Liberal party's deputy leader, Sheila Copps, to settle into a job more suitable to her natural talents, say as coach of an industrial-league bowling team. And the scold who led the New Democrats was something else again. Late in February 1993, in what I can only count as the ultimate *acte gratuit*, she released a policy paper that set out what she would do in office.

Brian Mulroney thrived on applause. Until the country turned so savagely against him, he was obviously having the time of his life. In private, he was redeemed by his far-from-mean-spirited sense of humour about the hanky-panky that prevails in Ottawa. I do not blame him for the free-trade deal, which I supported in 1988 and still support now. I believe his version of the value-added tax, the GST, was defensible, although I regret that books and periodicals were caught in the net, and I wish more of the proceeds were going to alleviating our national overdraft. I also fail to grasp why he was condemned for his famous "it was time to roll the dice" statement. God, as Einstein noted, doesn't play dice, but mere politicians must roll them at one time or another. And for all his blarney, I think

Mulroney is devoted to old friends and was deeply wounded by his breech with Lucien Bouchard. What I take to be his one unforgivable political folly was his reopening of the constitutional can, his payola to the Parti Québécois. When Mulroney was first elected in 1984 the PQ was running at 23 per cent in the polls, starved for funds, all but moribund. Then Mulroney promised to bring Quebec back into the Canadian family, as if, given my province's boarding-house reach, it was ever absent from the counting table. His constitutional meddling spawned a PQ revival. It also visibly aged Mulroney, whose constitutional obsession was, I think, also driven by his pathetic need to outshine Trudeau. "I can get the president of the United States more quickly on the phone than Trudeau ever could," he once said. Ironically, by poking Trudeau in the eye with his recipes for constitutional reconciliation, he awakened the sleeping dragon and brought him out of his lair breathing fire and brimstone. Trudeau published a denunciad in *Maclean's* in which he mocked the need of Quebec's nationalist elites to "falsify history to prove that all Quebec's political failures are someone else's fault" and warned that "the nationalists' thirst will never be satisfied," and that "each new ransom paid to stave off the threat of a schism will simply encourage the master blackmailers to renew the threat and double the ransom." This blast is what probably saved the country from the Charlottetown Accord.

Mulroney's decade was not without its accomplishments. Inflation, which was at 4.4 per cent when he assumed office in 1984, had shrunk to 1.5 per cent in 1993. He was also unlucky. The considerable pain of the free-trade deal and the GST working themselves in during an international recession was hardly his fault.

Of course Mulroney didn't resign for altruistic motives, but only because he faced a humiliating defeat in the next election at the hands of the ostensibly lightweight Jean Chrétien and his Brand X front bench. All the same, his departure was affecting. A man who wanted so desperately to be loved by his countrymen had ended his watch as the most intensely disliked of our prime ministers. Watching "Prime Time" on the night of his resignation, I, for one, was astonished by the depth of the man-in-the-street's rage against him. "I measure him low, very low," said one Quebecer. "On a scale of one to ten, I'd measure him probably a one."

"Fabulous," said a Newfoundlander about the resignation. "It's the best thing that's ever happened to this country. I can't believe he's finally gone."

Even the tributes were thin.

"I shall miss his voice," said Lady Thatcher, as if it was Mick Jagger who had just announced his retirement.

Most embarrassing of all, an obsequious little tailor, who also cuts threads for Shimon Peres and Alexander Haig, was dragged out of the woodwork. "There is not another politician in the world," said Russell Goldberg, "—now this is a big stadium—that dresses as beautifully as our prime minister."

Or is as generous to his friends, he might have added. For, leaving office, Mulroney proved the now all-but-forgotten John Turner a piker. Mulroney quit, trailing an unprecedented rain cloud of patronage. Since December 1992, he had doled out 655 plums, 241 of these in his final two months in office, enabling him to establish an unenviable sleaze record. More than 500 of these handsomely paid appointments to the Citizenship Court, Parole Board, National Energy Board, and so on, went to former gofers, back-room boys and girls, dim relatives of senior Tories, and failed candidates, the most risible going to Mila Mulroney's hairdresser and the hairdresser's wife: Rinaldo joined the Federal Business Development Bank and his wife, Pat, the Official Residences Council. And finally twelve slavering Tories, several of whom used to imbibe with Mulroney at Montreal's Mount Royal Club, the favoured watering hole of the city's most affluent tradesmen and corporation lawyers, were compensated with seats in the Senate, the hack's ultimate perk, comfy beyond compare.

Then, even as this recession-ridden country was still reeling from the shameless display of Mulroney "cuttin' up the cash," we were diverted by what many would come to see as a metaphor for the underlying tackiness of the Mulroney years: our prime minister, only weeks out of office, seemingly settling on a second career as a purveyor of used furniture, some of which was not necessarily his own in the first place. On July 1, 1993, Stevie Cameron, one of this country's most intrepid investigative reporters, wrote in the *Globe and Mail*, "Brian and Mila Mulroney did not have to hold a garage sale when they left their official residences last month: the federal government is buying the things they left behind.

"And that includes the custom-built closets made to house the Mulroney family wardrobe."

Marcel Beaudry, chairman of the National Capital Commission (NCC), which is responsible for official residences, revealed that the Treasury Board had forked out $150,000 for seventy-five items the Mulroneys had left behind, including wallpaper, Persian carpets, shower curtains, light fixtures, a kitchen table, a $12,000 engraved Venetian mirror, and forty-nine flower vases. Beaudry, who had been appointed to his job by Mulroney a year earlier, proclaimed the sale a bargain, saying it would have cost taxpayers $400,000 for new furnishings had the Mulroneys skedaddled, peeling off the wallpaper and ripping out the light fixtures, leaving the new prime minister in the dark, as it were. Because Mulroney could not legally do business with the government, the Treasury Board's cheque was made out to Mila. But—oh oh—she could produce no invoices. Beaudry, who had had the goods appraised at replacement value rather than their worth as used furniture, allowed, "I don't know where any of the stuff was bought." Neither could he distinguish between carpets and duvets, or whatever, that had originally been paid for by the government, which had spent hundreds of thousands of dollars on the official residences, and those purchased by the slushy Tory Canada Fund, which had, during the prime minister's first eighteen months in office, contributed $324,000 towards the furnishings. Confusion was compounded by the fact that many of the items in the National Capital Commission's appraisal were identical to goods bought for the Mulroneys by the Tory Canada Fund. Take, for instance, the case of a pewter floor lamp, valued at $500 by the NCC, but identical to one picked up by the Tory Canada Fund for $50, although a new shade had been made for it. Liberal MP Donald Boudria also pointed out that, as contributions to the Tory Canada Fund were tax deductible, we were paying for some of the Mulroney furniture twice. "Call it an involuntary contribution to the Brian Mulroney retirement fund on behalf of the taxpayer," he said.

What with the country on the boil, outraged by what they took to be mind-boggling greed, the Mulroneys, on holiday in France, were finally heard from. A petulant Mila wrote to cancel the deal:

> . . . After a decade of public service, which I performed with pride and pleasure and during which I neither received nor expected to receive remuneration of any kind for my activities, I am of course disappointed by the suggestion—even from some partisan sources—that I might have sought to profit from this transaction. Accordingly, I have instructed my accountant to return immediately your cheque thereby terminating the agreement between us. . . .

And so, Mila ordained, the furniture would remain at 24 Sussex Drive and the prime minister's summer estate at Harrington Lake until it could be replaced. Then, no doubt, everything save the wallpaper, but including a Persian rug valued at $15,000 and a dinner service for fifty valued at $23,000, would be shipped to the newly acquired Montreal mansion of the electrician's boy from Baie Comeau, a former labour lawyer and Iron Ore of Canada executive, who had obviously, like Hillary Clinton, made many canny investments over his salaried years. The house cost just short of $2 million and was undergoing a $600,000 renovation.

Back in February, once Mulroney had thrown in the towel—instantly retrieved for resale by Mila—it was assumed that a number of Tory cabinet deadweights would compete for the leadership, the winner becoming our nineteenth prime minister. Among the likely contenders were Michael Wilson, or Clark Kent II, and the equally bland male bimbo Perrin Beatty, he who would have had us fork out $8 billion for subs that could have issued parking tickets to rusty Russian tubs while patrolling under Arctic seas. And then Hugh Segal flirted briefly with the race. I first suspected that Segal, *rara avis*, a Tory of wit and intelligence, withdrew after three days because he grasped that, campaigning in Don Getty's big-sky country, he would have been obliged to explain his punch lines—but that proved not to be the case. Counting heads, he shamelessly invoked his family, saying that rather than be PM he wanted to be Canada's best hubby and daddy, which suggested he might soon be joining the cast of "Road to Avonlea."

All but one of the prospective candidates genuflected before the onrushing Kim Campbell, whose rise out of obscurity was astonishing. A first-term MP, squeaking past the post in Vancouver Centre in 1988 with a majority of 269 votes, she became Canada's first female attorney general and justice minister in 1990. Two years later, the first woman to be appointed secretary of defence, Ms. Campbell warned journalists, "Don't mess with me, I've got tanks."

When she declared herself an official candidate, on March 25, it seemed that she was heading for a coronation at the Tory convention. Radiating confidence, she said that she was, at heart, "a Texas line-dancer," and, oh yes, she added, she had once smoked pot *and* inhaled.

Kim Campbell entered the fray trailing *the* photograph and a spunky past riddled with quotes that reeked of arrogance to some, but appeared refreshingly direct to others. The saucy photograph that would be published everywhere, leading the British tabloids to dub her "a sexy, dewy-eyed Madonna," was taken in 1990 by Barbara Woodley for her arty coffee-table book, *Portraits: Canadian Women in Focus*. It showed Ms. Campbell bare-shouldered, holding her judicial robes before her on a hanger, suggesting that possibly the naughty girl had posed starkers. "Seriously," said Ms. Campbell, "the notion that the bare shoulders of a forty-three-year-old woman are a source of prurient comment or titillation—I mean, I suppose I should be complimented."

When Ms. Campbell ran for the leadership of British Columbia's Social Credit party in 1986, coming in last with a mere fourteen votes, she warned delegates against Bill Vander Zalm, the intellectually disadvantaged theme-park proprietor who would go on to become provincial premier. "Charisma without substance is a dangerous thing," she said. Two years later she was still heckling the premier. "I only wish I knew him before his lobotomy," she said. But what was to become her signature quote, figuring in just about every potted biography, including this one, was plucked from an interview she gave the Vancouver *Sun* in 1986:

"As an intellectually oriented person, I like to socialize with people who read the same things I do and have a similar level of education but generally I like ordinary people. I think it's very important to realize that a lot of people that you're out there working for are people who may sit in their undershirt and watch the game on Saturday, beer in hand. . . . I suppose these people would find me as boring as I would find them."

Actually, as I am one of those louts who watches Saturday night hockey on TV, as well as baseball in summer, preferably with a Scotch in hand, this *pensée* gave me pause. On the other hand, as Ms. Campbell was a devotee of Gilbert and Sullivan's splendid operettas, she couldn't be quite as condescending as she sometimes sounded.

Kim was born Avril Phaedra Douglas Campbell in March 1947, and changed her name to Kim during adolescence. Her father, George Campbell, wounded while serving with the Canadian Army in Italy in the Second World War, came home to become a lawyer. His marriage to Phyllis Cook, in 1944, turned out not to be a happy one. As a consequence of a 1957 sleigh accident, Phyllis shattered a hip socket, screws and plates had to be inserted, and, for a time, she was an invalid. Then, in 1959, with Kim and her sister tucked away in boarding school, Phyllis ran off to France with the Vancouver man who would become her husband, the two of them buying a yacht and setting up charters for the rich; Kim didn't see her again until she graduated from high school.

In 1967, Kim, then a student at the University of British Columbia, met her Trilby, the feisty Nathan "Tuzie" Divinsky, a math professor and divorced father of three daughters. He was forty-two,
she was twenty. Her mother didn't care for this working-class Jew,
sprung from Winnipeg's North End, a bona fide chess maven who
claimed to have once played the great Boris Spassky to a draw. "I
found him rude and pushy," she told the *Globe and Mail*'s Stephen
Brunt. "I was very surprised that Kim was attracted to him. He's quite
brilliant. But that doesn't make people likable." Phyllis, who safe to
say doesn't know the words to "Oy Chanukah, oy Chanukah, a yon-
tiff a shayner," recalled a Christmas visit to the family home when
Divinsky, reputedly blessed with a fine singing voice, refused to join
in on Christmas carols. "He sat there like an anthropologist watching
the natives at their curious rites. I never warmed to the man at all."

Nevertheless, Nathan and Kim were soon living together. Then,
in 1970, she went to London to study at the London School of Eco-
nomics, her doctoral supervisor Leonard Schapiro, the renowned
Sovietologist, who took his students on a three-month tour of the
Soviet Union. In 1972, Nathan, on a sabbatical, joined Kim in London and they were married, only to be divorced eleven years later.
Ms. Campbell, who never completed her doctorate, did go on to
earn a law degree. In 1986, she married again in Vancouver and was
divorced again five years later.

In the Owl's Nest, the dilapidated country bar that I favour, out
there in a weedy field on the 243, hard by the Vermont border, only
a few miles from our dacha in Quebec's Eastern Townships, a local
wag said, "If she can't manage two marriages, how in the hell is she
gonna manage the country?"

But in early March she seemed unstoppable, everybody scrambling on board her bandwagon, including a worrying number of
Québécois nationalists who had helped boost Mulroney into power,
and whose hugs she welcomed: dim Guy Charbonneau, bagman
and speaker of the Senate, and the sleek, self-regarding frequent-flier

Marcel Masse, a Union Nationale retread. I had met Masse only once, and he struck me as resembling nothing so much as the quintessential maître d' of the manner of restaurant or nightclub that I wouldn't want to frequent. In her defence, Ms. Campbell said that she could draw a distinction between a Québécois separatist and a nationalist. But, to my mind, if there was a distinction to be made it was between those who wanted all of Ottawa's powers right now and those who were willing to grab them one at a time over the wasting years, providing they also included transfer payments. Ms. Campbell claimed to be a reader of Dostoevsky and Tolstoy, among others. But was she aware, I wondered, that Charbonneau probably thought Dostoevsky was a perogi house in Winnipeg and that Tolstoy was a first-round draft choice of the Quebec Nordiques.

In March, Perrin Beatty, the upwardly mobile communications minister who had already retreated from the race, said "an unprecedented consensus" had formed among Tories that Ms. Campbell was the one to lead Canada into the twenty-first century, "and I agree with that." So, later in the month, when the thirty-four-year-old minister of the environment, Jean Charest, an Eastern Townshipper born and bred, entered the race, the skuttlebutt was that this stripling had obliged out of a sense of duty, at stage manager Mulroney's behest, to lend at least the semblance of a contest to the Tory convention in June. The pundits dismissed Charest as a mere pacer, a Quebecer running for next time, when he would be old enough to shave every day. But he turned out to be an appealing campaigner, fluently bilingual, unlike Ms. Campbell, who was given to stumbling in French considerably less assured than advertised. The pleasingly plump Charest was cuddly as a muppet, with a mop of unruly curly hair, a family man, married to his obviously intelligent and photogenic high-school sweetheart, Michele, with three adorable children. As if that wasn't sufficiently all-Canadian nice, his father had been a professional hockey player. And, oh yes, Charest too had been known to puff on the occasional toke during university days, and in his wild teenage years, he confessed "a little red-faced" to a reporter that he had once run foul of the law and lingered for several hours in the slammer . . . for spray-painting *"Bonne Fête Marie"* on a street as a birthday greeting to a friend.

Kim Campbell, arguably more representative of our discontented times, survivor of a dysfunctional family and twice-divorced, seemed very much her own person as she came charging out of the starting gate, armed with quips. But then she was taken over and processed by the insufferably slick Tory machine, emerging shrink-wrapped, a far too calculating front-runner, dodging difficult questions lest she offend any more "ordinary people" out there. Charest was a clear winner of the candidates' first television debate. Ms. Campbell, invited to pronounce on Quebec's loony-tunes language laws, which at the time still banned the use of English on outdoor commercial signs, among other fatuities, would venture no more than, "I think the worst thing I could do is throw myself in the middle of this debate. . . . It is for Quebecers to decide whether it is good, or the best route to take." In the second television debate, Ms. Campbell, reading from a prepared text, the gospel according to Marcel Masse, promised to shelter Quebec from "arrogant and dominating federalism," that is to say, respect for individual rights, which I once took to be a Tory tenet. But Charest proclaimed that a prime minister must "defend the rights of linguistic minorities everywhere in the country, including Quebec."

The more one saw of Ms. Campbell the less there was, or so it seemed. There was all that meaningless gabble about "the politics of inclusion," which suggested that the rest of us, like it or not, were now part of her Political Science 101 seminar. All at once it appeared that she wasn't running for prime minister at all, but wanted instead to be the loquacious head guide to a democracy theme park.

"CAMPBELLMANIA FIZZLES," ran a May 25 headline in the *Globe and Mail*, but she had already locked up twice as many delegates as her rival—although not enough for a first-ballot victory. An eve-of-convention poll showed that Charest was now the most popular candidate of Canadians in general and Tories in particular. The choice of only 10 per cent of Quebecers in March, he was now favoured by 50 per cent; and in the rest of Canada he had risen from

2 to 35 per cent. Over the same period, Ms. Campbell's support in Quebec had dwindled from 33 to 18 per cent; and in the rest of Canada she had dropped a point from her March high of 27 per cent. Against all odds, Jean Charest had made it a contest.

Pity the sizable contingent of rednecks among the 3,400 delegates and 1,500 alternates jammed into Ottawa's sweltering Civic Centre on Friday, June 11, 1993. That fulminating, beer-bellied bunch came out of the Bible-belt Prairies in Stetsons and high-heeled boots, their enormous wives attired in polyester slacks and sequined blouses, candidates' badges riding their outsize bosoms. Real-estate agents, hardware store proprietors, small-town lawyers, feed merchants, actuaries, insurance-policy pedlars, and car dealers, all convinced that the True, North, Strong, and Free was going to hell in a multicultural handbasket. Why, you can now wear a turban in the RCMP or a dagger in your belt to high school if you're a Sikh. Our kids are being dealt condoms rather than brownies at recess, and you can't take them to a movie any more, all they show is screwing on kitchen tables and in elevators and airplane toilets. The National Gallery in Ottawa is paying zillions of our tax money for twenty-foot-high colour charts called paintings by conmen named Newman or Rothko, probably both Jews. Canada's broke, but it's a proven fact that rug-head welfare cheats are having cheques sent, under three different names you'd have to be a genius to spell, to their winter addresses in Florida. This great land that once gave the world Deanna Durbin and Guy Lombardo is now supposed to be proud of k. d. lang, a dyke *and a vegetarian*, even though she came from cattle country. You know what caused AIDS? God Almighty's disgust.

True, the rednecks would be serenaded throughout the long weekend, at family BBQs and pancake breakfasts, by Toronto suits importuning for Ms. Campbell, and others hustling for Charest or one of the three minor candidates. But they were to be pitied because on Sunday they would have to choose between a la-di-da divorcée, from hot-tub city out there in flaky B.C., a woman who would rather play her cello than watch the Stanley Cup playoffs, and a bloody frog still wet behind the ears who had the nerve to speak English better than most of them did, and reminded them of that bastard Trudeau, who had rammed bilingualism down their throats.

I had been to a couple of earlier Tory conventions, and two things were immediately clear about this one. Joy was confined, and a rattled Tory big machine had gone into overdrive working the floor for Kim. Young Jean, they were whispering in delegates' ears, might be a fine fellow for next time, but don't forget that for twenty-six of the last twenty-seven years our prime minister had been a Quebecer, and the rest of Canada has had it up to here. While the outnumbered Charest people were saying that only their man, already the people's choice in the rest of Canada, could clean the clock of Lucien Bouchard's Bloc Québécois in Quebec and so, look here, it would be self-destructive for our party to go with Kim.

If the polls were right, the BQ was slated to win a majority of Quebec's seventy-six seats in the coming federal election, unless Bouchard was obliged to run against the shining new face of Jean Charest. In his stem-winder of a Saturday night speech at the convention, Charest pleaded with the delegates to turn him loose on Lucien Bouchard.

First, however, we had to endure self-promoter Brian Mulroney's orchestrated tribute to himself on Friday night. In the months leading up to the convention he had embarked on a final farewell tour of the United States and Europe, much criticized at the time for being too costly. And unnecessary. Mulroney countered that he was bound for Europe to deliver a speech on Canadian foreign policy, that is to say, to come out strongly for peace among nations and making a better world for our children. On a slow news day, these *pensées* might have won him a mention on page sixty-one in *Le Monde* and page fifty-three of the London *Daily Telegraph*. Expensive ink, yes, but in those days that preceded the furniture scam I can remember thinking Canadians should be charitable, because soon enough Mulroney would be suffering from photo-op deprivation. But Friday night in Ottawa's Civic Centre we learned the real reason for Mulroney's junket. It had enabled him to solicit and film testimonials to his greatness by George Bush, John Major, François Mitterand, Helmut Kohl, Bill Clinton, and Boris Yeltsin. These tributes were at the heart of a $300,000 home movie that was, at best, merely embarrassing, and, at worst, self-serving and saccharine beyond compare. We learned that Mila was highly regarded by Barbara Bush, Olympic skater Elizabeth Manley, and singer Céline Dion, and oh my gosh she got a kick out of preparing breakfast for her children; and we caught glimpses of good old Brian playing softball and horsing around with his family. There was also a stage show of sorts. Mulroney had vetted every word in the script, but, a consummate showman, aware of the circling TV cameras, he laughed at the jokes he had approved as if hearing them for the first time, and shed tears on cue, his big moment coming when the star of the Toronto production of *Phantom of the Opera* crooned "Danny Boy" to him.

In Jean Charest's Saturday night make-or-break speech, a direct appeal to those delegates who were still uncommitted, he said, "Yes, I am young and vigorous—and so is Canada." And, sticking it to Kim, he added, "I want to be prime minister of Canada and not prime minister of caution."

Kim Campbell, the last of the five candidates to speak, chose to be "prime ministerial," and delivered a bomb that sounded to most observers like a printout of clichés from a master Tory computer. But she did begin to distance herself from Mulroney. "We need a different kind of leadership," she said, "one that responds to the yearning of Canadians for real change in our politics and our politicians."

The informed word in the press room, from those with impeccable inside sources, was that sentimental favourite Jean Charest would take it on the second ballot; but in fact it was Kim, with 1,822 votes to Charest's 1,630. Anxiety-ridden federalists in the Tory's Quebec caucus were not pleased. MP Fernand Jourdenais said, "If we want to keep Quebec in Canada, we've got to do it now, and if we don't do it with Jean, we're gone. The BQ is going to have the edge on us. What's going to happen after the BQ takes fifty or sixty seats in Quebec?"

Certainly it would have come as no surprise if Lucien Bouchard hearing the results had cracked open a bottle of champagne, and Jean Chrétien also had to be delighted. Chrétien, something of a quipster himself, had already adjudged Ms. Campbell "a Mulroney in skirts" who had won herself no more than a summer job.

Come August, Ms. Campbell, Chrétien, Audrey, Bouchard, and Preston Manning had already begun to bore us on the photo-op and sound-bite trail, flipping burgers in an endless run of backyard barbecues in anticipation of the autumn election. Kim, most likely with her fingers crossed behind her back, promised to balance the budget in five years, but was outbid by Manning, who claimed he could manage the trick in four years. Delighting the Liberals, Kim also ventured that there would be no more jobs until the next century, and pronounced the election the wrong time to engage in a serious discussion of our social programs. Audrey, a special case, said she would tear up the free-trade deals and cancel the GST, but guarantee universal day care, full employment, a squeaky-clean environment, and no rain on weekends. All the leaders had to contend with a disenchanted electorate. Following the sleaze that had characterized the Mulroney years, politicians had never been held in lower esteem. A long-in-the-tooth Chrétien had to overcome the general perception that he was yesterday's man. However, he was a far more experienced campaigner than Ms. Campbell, and even as she continued to distance herself from Mulroney, Liberal flacks reminded her that she had once said, "[Mulroney] is an extraordinary leader, an extraordinarily intelligent person with a great passion for this country and he inspires great loyalty. . . ." Lucien Bouchard was hard put to muzzle the most zealous of his no-name candidates, many of whom were consumed with inchoate rage against *les autres*. Preston Manning had to cork the incipient racists in his bottle, many of whom wanted an end to immigration, a ban on French outside of Quebec, and, if only to demonstrate their devotion to "family values," a determination to bring back flogging and the noose.

Instant Prime Minister Kim Campbell's initial attempt to impress the country with the new frugality backfired. She ordered ministers in her new, pared-down cabinet to take taxis, rather than chauffeured limos to the swearing-in ceremony at the governor-general's residence. But as snide reporters were quick to point out, the taxpayers really ended up forking out twice, because the chauffeurs had to sit and wait—on the public payroll.

At the time, my own cherished if unlikely election result depended on Lucien Bouchard not only taking just about every seat in Quebec, but also fielding a number of candidates in the western boonies. Out there, I thought, many would vote BQ because rather than wait for Quebec to separate or get off the pot, they would just as soon kick them out of Confederation right now. And so Bouchard, I speculated, the winner of eighty-five or ninety seats, could then form a coalition with the surging Reform party, and find himself, a sworn separatist, in the nightmare office of prime minister of Canada. The morning after, the premier of Ontario would inform Bouchard that he intended to sue for sovereignty. Bouchard, sobered by his new responsibilities, would tell him, "I was not elected prime minister to preside over the dismemberment of this great country that is the envy of the world. *Va te faire foutre.*"

Alas, it didn't work out that way. Nearly, but not quite.

From the
Ottawa
Monkey House...
to Referendum

O N JANUARY 16, 1994, I flew in to Ottawa from London, to attend the opening later in the week of our thirty-fifth and conceivably last Parliament of Canada as it has been known for a hundred and twenty-seven querulous years. The Liberals, who would warm the government benches after almost a decade in the wilderness, were jubilant, but so, understandably, was the Bloc Québécois, which had elected a sufficient number of MPs to make up the second largest party in the House. The evening of my arrival it was thirty degrees below zero Celsius in the capital. The few pedestrians in the snowbound streets were bundled up, leaning into punishing arctic winds. Passing cars were washed window-high with road salt and slush. But the bars in the Château Laurier and Hilton hotels swirled with roistering Liberal lawyers, advertising agency honchos, and bagmen, cheered by the prospect of a return to the trough. A party apparatchik assured me that lobbyists were no longer in favour. "But that doesn't mean," he said, "that we're going to turn our backs on our friends."

Recognizing that voters had had enough of Mulroney's glitzy style, the Liberals, nicknamed the "Integrity party" by *Frank* magazine, ordained that hair shirts would be the new parliamentary rule. No more free shoeshines or massages for MPs, who also lost their $400 annual allowance for framing pictures. Prime Minister Jean Chrétien's new car would be a Chevy. Lucien Bouchard, not to be outmanoeuvred, turned down the offer of new wheels, settling for a heap that had already done a hundred thousand kilometres. But Reform party leader Preston Manning snookered the other penitents, that virtuous prairie populist refusing the offer of *any* vehicle provided by taxpayers. Manning had already asked his caucus to take a 10 per cent cut of their far from munificent annual salary of $64,000. Canadians, he said, are justifiably cynical about the shenanigans in Parliament. "[It] is supposed to be the supreme democratic institution in this country, and it's been taken and turned into a house of hacks. . . ."

I was brought up in a country-with-a-view, Canada Inc., where, if we suffered from anything beyond frostbite, it was issue-envy. The world always seemed to be happening elsewhere. But now it appeared possible, if far from certain, that riding dark tribal horses we might manufacture a crisis of our own. Playing catch-up we might yet create some interesting history. Possibly, the centre might not hold, Quebec finally opting for independence of a sort. In any event, Canadians were surely in for a playoff-style Parliament, tripping, cross-checking, and spearing inevitable in an endgame anticipated last summer by Jolly Jock Parizeau.

On August 22, 1993, a triumphal Parizeau had addressed two thousand of his party faithful at the PQ's twenty-fifth anniversary conference in Montreal. "Lace up your skates," he said, "pull on your sweaters, buckle up your pads, there's going to be a lot of action. We've seen a little before, but that's nothing compared to what's going to happen. In the first period, we send as many Bloc MPs to Ottawa as possible."

At the time, the three-year-old Bloc Québécois had eight MPs seated in Parliament, seven of them defectors from either Tory or Liberal benches, and only one, Gilles Duceppe, elected on the Bloc ticket in a 1990 by-election. But in coach Parizeau's projected first period—the general election that had been called for October 25, 1993—the Bloc would be sending candidates over the boards to contest all of Quebec's seventy-five seats. And Quebecers would be obliged to vote yet again in a provincial election to be held in the autumn of 1994, the PQ consistently running ahead of the governing provincial Liberals in the opinion polls.

"Some time between next spring and September 25, second period," Parizeau went on to say, "and we take power [in Quebec]. And then, a few months later, a referendum. Our country. Quebec. *Vive le Québec libre!*" he concluded, echoing party-pooper Charles de Gaulle's chant from the balcony of Montreal's city hall, which had sent an unseasonable chill through the country in our centennial summer of 1967.

Parizeau's first period ended in a blowout. True, the Liberals, led by the underrated Chrétien, won a huge majority, taking a surprising 176 seats; but rattled Canadians discovered that in our bizarre new Parliament, the very party that was dedicated to dismembering the country would also fill the office of Her Majesty's Loyal Opposition, our government-in-waiting.

An unabashed Bouchard, who had been a senior member of Mulroney's right-wing cabinet for eighteen months, now did one of his quick changes in the ideological phone booth and presented himself as the champion who would safeguard our country's social programs. "It is a strange paradox," he said, without even the hint of a smile, "that a sovereigntist party from Quebec will be the only party fighting to preserve the main value of Canada."

On January 17, the eve of the new session, more than two thousand Liberals gathered to whoop it up in Parliament's Hall of Honour, their glee constricted by the discovery that drinks were only available from cash bars. The Bloc was dismissed as an aberration, celebrants quick to point out that Bouchard, looking to harvest his province's protest vote, had told Quebecers they didn't have to be separatists to support his party. Why, that duplicitous man, they said, had campaigned on a slogan ("We're giving ourselves real power") that didn't even mention the word sovereignty. I was cornered by a lawyer with runny eyes and the sniffles who had made the two-hour drive from Montreal just to attend the party, and would be risking icy roads to return home later that night.

"You should be home in bed," I said.

"I've got to show the flag, don't you understand? Most of the Bloc members," he said, "come from hick towns and have never been to Ottawa before. Florida maybe, but not here. You wait. Just you wait. They're going to get to like the perks and to start thinking how sweet it would be to serve a second term and qualify for a pension. Give it a year, maybe two, and some of them will discover that Canada ain't that bad and cross to our benches."

Liberals argued that Parizeau's projected second period was still in question. The PQ had yet to win the forthcoming election, the pompous Parizeau himself, with a mere 27 per cent personal support in the polls, a serious drag on the party's popularity. Parizeau, it's true, was not a convincing people's tribune. A rich man's son, a sybarite, given to maladroit off-the-cuff pronouncements, he seemed more like the silent movie banker come to foreclose the mortgage on Charlie Chaplin. Quebecers had never warmed to him. Furthermore, they were a notoriously mischievous lot, fond of giving Ottawa the finger, and, so, even if they did boost the PQ back into office, it was also true that a majority only endorsed independence when they could not be held accountable for their enthusiasm. A wag at the Liberal party said, "Worst case. They do just barely win a second referendum, but, hell, that would only count as a tie." Then, picking up on Parizeau's hockey analogy, he suggested, "Maybe we're in for a best-of-seven referendum series, just like the Stanley Cup finals."

Two hundred and five of the 295 newly elected MPs were rookies, the vast majority of the Bloc and Reform members unilingually

French- or English-speaking. A Bloc MP had already said that English Canadians were as foreign to her as Turks or Greeks, and many Reformers were even less well disposed to what they took to be uppity French Canadians. On the sub-zero morning of January 18, the MPs and distinguished guests in their finery trudged up Parliament Hill to listen to the speech from the throne. The speech, delivered by Governor-General Ray Hnatyshyn in the Senate, MPs obliged to stand in the crowded chamber, was refreshingly succinct, only seventeen minutes long, but it was also anodyne. The new government, turned over old sod, was gung ho for economic growth, job creation, a review of the social security system, and opposed to racism and violence against women or children. It was committed to "integrity, honesty, and openness on the part of those who exercise power on behalf of Canadians," even as Mulroney's 1984 effort had promised to "renew the confidence of Canadians that Parliament is truly the voice of the people." *Déjà vu*, cried the pundits.

Following the speech, I joined John Lynch-Staunton and Jean Charest for lunch in the subsidized parliamentary dining room, which offers a sumptuous buffet for a mere $9.55. Righteous Reformers had promised to take advantage of it only when they didn't have time to hitchhike back to their rooming houses for a can of soup.

The amicable Lynch-Staunton, a Montrealer born and bred, was Tory leader in the Senate, where his debt-ridden party held 58 of the 104 seats, and had its hot hands on a suddenly vital $1.7-million research budget. But the Senate, at best, was a dubious foundation for Tory renewal. The *Globe and Mail* had dismissed it as "an anachronistic and feeble collection of unelected party hacks and political donors."

Jean Charest, having failed to grasp what was once considered a glittering prize, was now stuck with an unenviable burden. Appointed interim leader by the party's shell-shocked national executive on December 14, 1993 (a day after Kim Campbell resigned, or was pushed by the men in suits), his caucus was reduced to a risible two members, and he would now be obliged to persevere in the House as an independent in all but name. He would have to whistle, stamp his feet, or turn cartwheels in order to be given the nod by the speaker to put an occasional query to the government benches. Ahead of him spun years of traipsing through the snow from coast to coast to address meetings of disgruntled party workers at service-club luncheons in legion halls and high-school gyms. He would also have to live with what might have been.

With hindsight, the received wisdom was that the Tories, led by Charest, could have won twenty to twenty-five seats in Quebec, and possibly done well enough elsewhere for his party to form the official Opposition. Obviously still brooding, he wouldn't acknowledge that he might have been his party's saviour. Instead he fed me what had become the considered Tory morning-after-the-débâcle lament. They had won 16 per cent of the popular vote, as opposed to 19 per cent for Reform and 14 per cent for the BQ, yet their seats did not total in the fifties because their votes had been spread throughout the country.

Setting out to rebuild his demolished party one brick at a time, Charest would be hobbled by the legacy of Brian Mulroney. One of Mulroney's friends, who asked not to be identified by name, said that in the weeks following his announcement that he would not run again, he was given to fishing his favourable reviews out of a jacket pocket and thrusting them at visitors. His standby was a *Foreign Affairs* article that stated obloquy was the price a real leader paid for having the courage to take unpopular, but necessary, decisions. "One evening," his friend said, "this guy gave Brian's passing limo the finger. Brian ordered his driver to stop, lowered his window, and asked the guy to step closer. He approached the limo tentatively. 'No, closer,' Brian said. So the guy stepped right up to the open window. 'Go fuck yourself, you horse's ass,' Brian hollered and then drove on. I tell you it was paranoia time around here, just like in Nixon's last days. What was really bugging Brian was his place in history, which he felt was being compromised by enemies in the media conspiring against him."

Mulroney had a lot to answer for. He had, among other things, invented Lucien Bouchard, plucking his old law-school chum, then still a *Péquiste*, out of small-town obscurity and anointing him ambassador to France.

Hardly noticed when Parliament convened for question period on January 19, but surely a harbinger of unacknowledged changes to come in a country where 40 per cent of the population was now of neither French nor English extraction, and was becoming increasingly impatient with the squabbling of our "two founding races," was a statement by Gurbax Malhi, an MP from Ontario. He advised the speaker that "today is the three hundred and twenty-eighth birthday of Sri Guru Singh Ji, the tenth guru of the Sikh religion," who should be remembered for "his belief that all persons are the same though they appear different."

Responding to the throne speech, a grim Lucien Bouchard spoke for almost an hour, shifting from rapid-fire French to English and back again. "Let there be no mistake," the leader of Her Majesty's Loyal Opposition said. "Bloc members will not forget that their commitment to sovereignty constitutes the real reason for their presence in this House. One could say that as far as we are concerned, the pre-referendum campaign has begun." He declared the Canadian family dysfunctional, the country ungovernable, and said the time had come for a split, "a sovereign Quebec becoming a neighbour and friend of Canada."

Then the debate about Canada's future zeroed in on what really galvanizes Canadians in winter: hockey. Roger Pomerleau, a Bloc backbencher who was a stranger to irony, noted the absence of Quebecers on "Team Canada, this country's national hockey team, which will defend Canada's honour in Lillehammer—Quebecers are once again suffering discrimination as a result of racial prejudice and stereotyping."

Pomerleau was troubled by a remark said to have been made earlier by Team Canada coach Daniel Dubé, a Quebecer himself, who had allegedly denigrated his province's players as one-dimensional goal scorers, a calculated insult to the Montreal Canadiens' incomparable defensive stalwart, Guy Carbonneau, among others.

The next day a perplexed Preston Manning was also heard from. "The Prime Minister has repeatedly said that he does not want to reopen constitutional issues at this time and that the priority of his government is jobs and economic growth. Yet yesterday he and other Liberal members were repeatedly drawn into heated exchanges with Bloc members on the constitutional future of Quebec. There are millions of Canadians, including Quebecers, who want Parliament to focus on deficit reduction, jobs, and preserving social services. Is the Prime Minister abandoning his commitment to stay out of the constitutional swamp or is it still his resolve to stick to economic, fiscal, and social priorities?"

From 1976 through 1992, 129,705 English-speaking Quebecers, reacting to restrictive language laws and burgeoning tribalism, quit their native province. A Statistics Canada report, released in 1992, stated that enrolment in English-language schools in Quebec had dropped by 59 per cent in twenty years. Another 1992 study, this one undertaken by the Royal Bank of Canada, found that some 73 per cent of anglophone students felt that within ten years they would no longer be living in Quebec.

In a 1992 book entitled *Quebec Inc.*, Pierre Arbour, a former senior investment adviser at the Caisse de Dépôt et Placement, which is Quebec's $41-billion pension fund management agency, identified the anglophone flight as the primary cause of Quebec's decline relative to Ontario. "In the face of this growing exodus, however," he wrote, "the [PQ] government of Quebec took a passive stance, a stance bordering on outright hostility." Yet in this climate of subtle, non-violent ethnic cleansing, Québécois-style, it is the francophone nationalists who feel oppressed. For twenty-seven of the last thirty years the prime minister of Canada has been a Quebecer, but in an interview published in the Paris weekly *L'Express*, on January 13, 1994, Bernard Landry, deputy leader of the PQ, stated that francophone Quebecers were the last remaining colonial nation in the West. "Basically, we have for centuries been a bit like the firemen at the heart of Chernobyl," he said, "at the centre of the cataclysm, but still standing."

Given the magnitude of the nationalists' grievances, real or hyperbolic, it hasn't always been clear whether they want a new marriage contract or a divorce. Speaking to college students in Montreal in September 1993, Lucien Bouchard said that a sovereign Quebec might share a postal service, army, navy, and air force with the rest of Canada. Earlier Parizeau had declared that he wanted a new state of Quebec to continue to use the Canadian dollar and remain a member of the Commonwealth, a union of English-speaking peoples, and for Quebecers to be allowed to keep their Canadian passports.

When I caught up with Bouchard in his office, he said, "I want a divorce. A friendly divorce." On reflection, he added, "I suppose it will not be sweet. Some people will feel we are breaking up their country, but in the end I hope rationality will prevail. I hope hundreds of thousands more anglophones will not leave if we become sovereign. That would be a bad thing. We need them. The English-speaking community in Montreal was instrumental in building Quebec."

But when the Quebec Liberal government, responding to ridicule from abroad, introduced Bill 86 the previous December, which belatedly recognized the right of the descendants of all people educated in English in Canada to attend English schools in Quebec, and softened the French-only commercial sign laws, Bouchard had said, "Now is not the time to reopen old sores."

Depending on who kept the books, federalism was either ruinously expensive for Quebec, or an economic bonanza. According to Bouchard, Ottawa raised 23 per cent of its revenue in the province but only kicked back 19 per cent. Yet if the bean-counters in Statistics Canada are to be credited, then from 1981 to 1991 Quebec's net revenue gain from Ottawa had totalled $73.1 billion. I reminded Bouchard that Parizeau, generally regarded as a distinguished economist, had once said that sovereignty would cost Quebecers no more than the price of a case of beer a year. He laughed. "The real cost," he said, "is an unknown domain. I am not prepared to say there is no risk."

Meanwhile, I suggested, he did live in an incredibly tolerant country. Imagine, I said, Jefferson Davis being welcomed in his nation's capital city as leader of the Loyal Opposition, and being presented with a million-dollar research budget the better to argue his case of secession. (Davis, he pointed out, had been no stranger to Montreal, and during the American Civil War had stashed Confederate gold in a local bank for safe-keeping.)

Unarguably now the most popular politician in Quebec, the charismatic Bouchard, addressing large gatherings of the faithful, is something of a firebrand, ill-tempered, his impassioned sermons unredeemed by humour. But in private he is soft-spoken, a charmer, capable of laughing at himself. He is a natty dresser, like his erstwhile pal Mulroney, whom some now say Bouchard manipulated from the very onset of their friendship. "The Québécois in Mulroney's cabinet were never real Tories," he said. "We were nationalists."

What, I asked, did he think of Landry's Québécois-as-Chernobyl-firemen statement in *L'Express*?"

"Perhaps he was misquoted," he said.

"I've got it right here."

"In that case, I must say it was somewhat extreme."

The social scientist Daniel Latouche, a former PQ functionary, is one of the authors of an analysis of support for independence: it concludes that, after all these wasting years, a third of Quebecers are committed separatists, the remainder undecided. Since, I asked Bouchard, he had won only 49.5 per cent of the popular vote in the election, and a sizable proportion of that support came from discontented federalists at no risk, how could he expect to win a referendum when everything would be on the table?

"Ah, well," he said, "many *Péquistes* didn't vote for us—maybe as many as federalists who did. Some *Péquistes* feared that if we won considerable concessions for Quebec in Ottawa, it would prove that federalism worked. As things stand, you have a nation and we don't. Quebec is only a minor part of Canada. Independence would enable us to assume responsibility for our own fate."

Did he also favour, I asked, independence for every cultural group that was a minority in their own nation: say, the Welsh, the Basques, the Flemish, the Corsicans, the Catalans, and the Scots, among others.

"That is for them to decide. But in the coming referendum, we will not be asking a question that seeks sovereignty only if the rest of Canada first agrees to economic association. Voters will be invited to answer a straightforward question. Are you for sovereignty or not?"

"What if you lose?"

"That would be a disaster for us."

"Have you a contingency plan in the event that you do lose?"

"A hockey coach doesn't go into the arena with a losing game plan."

"But losing is possible, isn't it?"

"We would then have to reconsider our role here. I can't exclude any option now. But, personally, I might return to private life."

Bouchard has refused to move into Stornoway, the Opposition leader's official residence. Instead, he and Audrey, his Californian wife, and their two children, live in Hull. "Stornoway was too grand for me. I'm ill-at-ease with the lifestyle of politicians. I'm a maverick."

When Audrey was about to give birth to their first child, in 1989, Bouchard had rushed her across the Ottawa River to a hospital in Hull, so that their child might be born in Quebec. Audrey's parents (her father is a former United States marine who served in Vietnam) live in California. "They are real Orange County Republicans," Bouchard told an interviewer from *Maclean's*. "When Alexandre"— his four-year-old son—"comes back [from a visit to California] he's dressed like an American kid. He says to me, 'Daddy, I'm an American,' and he wants to speak English. 'You're a Québécois and I'm American,' he says."

Over the years Jean Chrétien has alienated many of the Quebec bourgeoisie by joking about himself as "a pea-souper" in English

Canada. His garbled French syntax and heavily accented, uncertain English also embarrassed them. Bouchard once dismissed him as a vulgar politician who didn't speak French properly. He reminded voters that the Liberal leader had mocked Quebec's longing to be an international player, saying it amounted to no more than coveting "*un* flag *sur le* hood," a fractured phrase that was also a measure of Chrétien's scorn for sovereigntists.

Going into the campaign, Chrétien, ridiculed as "yesterday's man" by his opponents, arranged to have himself photographed water-skiing, jogging, or lugging cases of beer; however, it wasn't his muscles but his intelligence that was in question. Following his election, but before Parliament had convened, he was still being patronized. On November 22, 1993, a *Globe and Mail* front-page headline marvelled, "CHRETIEN STYLE IMPRESSES CLINTON." Our new prime minister hadn't been caught picking his toes or farting in his first meeting with the American president at the Asia Pacific Economic Co-operation forum in Seattle. In fact, wrote a condescending Jeff Sallot, Chrétien "gets good marks" for his international debut. "Canadian government officials . . . say he quickly grasped the detail and nuance of material in his briefing book. . . ."

If the unassuming Chrétien has an American political hero it is Harry Truman, who also benefited from low expectations on assuming office. Before I was ushered in to see Chrétien, an aide slipped me a report on the latest Gallup poll published in *La Presse* the previous morning. It showed that the prime minister now enjoyed a 57 per cent national approval rating: "*Les libéraux n'avaient pas connu un soutien aussi considérable depuis les jours de gloire de Pierre Trudeau, en 1970.*"

Brian Mulroney, sprung from the working class, overcompensated by favouring cashmere topcoats, stylish made-to-measure suits, and by accumulating dozens of pairs of tassled Guccis. But Chrétien, a casual dresser whose preferred tipple is beer, seemed at ease with his origins. The son of a machinist, the eighteenth of nineteen children, born in Shawinigan, Quebec, he looked like a man capable of changing his own disc brakes or unblocking a toilet. "More civility exists here than elsewhere," he said. "Our cities are safe and of a better quality and our institutions work. I don't subscribe to the notion that the land and the blood must match, but believe in the equality of all the peoples in this country. Our party includes MPs of every colour and faith and that is the real future of Canada." Focusing on Bouchard, who had belonged in turn to the PQ, the NDP, the Liberals, and the Tories, he said, "That man has a certain flexibility, there isn't one party he didn't belong to once. He benefited enormously from a protest vote. He is a bit naive, promising a Utopia in which everything will be cured. But he never dared use the word 'independence.' It was always the ambiguous 'sovereignty,' a word that doesn't even exist in Larousse. Those Quebecers who are most fearful of anglophones tend to live in regions where they probably haven't ever met one. Montreal is paying the price. If there's another referendum, I hope this time they will ask an honest question: Do you want to separate or not?"

"And what if they win?"

"Back in sixty-four, René Lévesque asked me to quit Ottawa and join him in a great adventure. Quebec, he said, would be independent within five years and that was, what, twenty-five years ago? The francophone press has cast me as a villain since Meech. They've buried me many times, but I'm still here."

In 1980, I pointed out, Trudeau had said that if the federalists lost the referendum, he would resign as prime minister. He was mindful of being a Quebecer himself, and said he had no mandate to negotiate separation.

"I'm a positive thinker."

"But have you a contingency plan in the event you lose a referendum?"

"In the end, I'm sure common sense will prevail."

I left Ottawa with the feeling that either Chrétien had a contingency plan, but wouldn't own up to it because it smacked of defeatism, or that his government's policy, should Bouchard put a call

through the morning after a referendum win, was not to answer
the phone.

Speaking to the Canadian and Empire clubs in Toronto in the autumn of 1993, Bouchard had said, "I am well aware of the fact that to
many English Canadians, Quebec sovereignty at best appears to be
illogical and irrational. They feel that Canada is one of the world's
great democracies. So why, they wonder, would anyone want sovereignty for Quebec?"

In the past, Quebecers have marched boldly to the independence
precipice, peered over the edge, and retreated. But next time things
could just possibly be different. The federalists' problem is that their
case is rational, it appeals to the head, but Bouchard's romantic call is
to the heart. Federalists argue, reasonably enough, that separation
would be costly to both French and English Canada, and that any
settlement is bound to be protracted and acrimonious. There would
be no "friendly divorce," but, instead, a bruising battle over the
country's spoils, and division of the national debt, as well as an independent Quebec's acceptable frontiers.

Should separatists prevail in a referendum, it seems to me that the
rest of Canada would not tolerate a prime minister, who was a Quebecer himself, negotiating on their behalf with his native province.
Most likely Chrétien would call a snap election, and then Quebecers
might have to contend with Prime Minister Preston Manning, the
Christian fundamentalist in the prairie woodpile. Manning is canny.
He has succeeded in presenting himself as an aw shucks political
neophyte, our take on James Stewart in *Mr. Smith Goes to Washington*, but the truth is he has been active in politics for years. As prime
minister, he would demand that Quebec accept a status as just another province among equals or cut bait. He has attracted an embarrassing number of rednecks to his crusade. On February 8, 1994, it
was revealed that the constituency association of Werner Schmidt, a
Reform backbencher out of British Columbia, had included in a
newsletter a quotation from Adolf Hitler: "What luck for rulers that

men do not think." Another Reform MP, Cliff Breitkreuz, of Alberta, told a local newspaper he felt that Ottawa was too "Frenchified." The throne speech would have been shorter, he said, had it been read in English only.

In early 1994, the final score of Parizeau's projected third period was still open to question. Meanwhile, in the prevailing uncertainty, Canada, like Leacock's horseman, continued to ride off in all directions. But a month after I left Ottawa, Quebec's Liberals enjoyed a hallelujah day. After having suffered five by-election defeats in a row, they actually won one in Shefford, on February 28, taking a district that the PQ had held since 1981 and whose population is 96 per cent francophone. "The voters have reminded us that the game isn't over until the last period has been played," Parizeau said.

A few days later, Parizeau responded to recent poll results—that now 44 per cent of Quebecers wished to stay in Canada and only 37 per cent favoured independence. On March 2, speaking at a Montreal conference sponsored by the *Economist*, he said, "If you ask me what will happen if we fail again, I will tell you we will try again. . . . Do you really think that an idea as potent as the independence of a country can reach levels like that of 1980, of 40 per cent of the population, and just peter out, vanish? . . . Are you absolutely sure that the idea of an independent Scotland is gone forever?"

Since then, the baffling Parizeau has stated that, on the one hand, Quebecers who endorse the PQ in the coming election are voting for sovereigntists but not sovereignty and that, on the other, he would interpret a win as a licence to begin preparing for sovereignty, and to start talks with Ottawa on the transfer of powers, even though Quebecers would not be making a final decision until they voted in a referendum to be held no later than June 1995.

On May 2, the PQ released a position paper in English: "Quebec in a New World." It warned that an independent Quebec would revive the ban on most English-language commercial signs, restrict entry to English junior colleges (CEGEPS) to Quebecers with a parent who had been to English-language primary school, and demand that small businesses with ten to fifty employees make French the language of the workplace, especially in written materials. However, it also declared the English community an invaluable asset, and promised to retain the right to speak English in the National Assembly and the courts. It also guaranteed the survival of Montreal's two English-language universities: McGill and Concordia. But none of this might be necessary. Five hundred and fifty thousand of Quebec's remaining 760,000 anglophones live in the greater Montreal area. They have already indicated to pollsters that half of them would leave if Quebec separated. The 1993 survey, undertaken by the provincial government's Office de la Langue Française, noted that anglophones "fear being isolated from the rest of Canada if Quebec separates." They anticipate a disastrous economic situation and are fearful of losing their rights and being badly treated.

The most chilling image of the referendum campaign appeared on television on October 25, the night of the big Yes rally in the Montreal suburb of Verdun. A young woman, eyes squeezed shut, held a little fleur-de-lys flag overhead, then began kissing it again and again as Lucien Bouchard thundered on stage. A man who can arouse such all-but-orgasmic fervour in the young is a threat to the social order and would be more safely engaged at home honouring his own agenda, making "white race" babies. Bouchard's summons to Québécoise women *pure laine* to bonk more productively did at least establish, in case anybody out there still had doubts, that the imprint of that vile, racist cleric, the Abbé Lionel-Adolphe Groulx, still haunts the separatist cause. In 1922, Groulx published a pseudonymous novel, *L'Appel de la race*, elaborating on his theme of racial purity. Five years earlier he had already preached the *pure laine* ideal in the monthly journal *Action française, la revanche des berceaux* (the revenge of the cradles). *Plus ça change*, as my grandmother used to say, *plus c'est la même chose.*

Groulx's vitriol, rising out of a spiritual sewer, also touched something in Jacques Parizeau, separatism's second banana. In 1917, Groulx observed that Canada's soul was menaced by "cosmopolitan European immigrants." And seventy-eight years later, as television watchers in the Western world now know, an apparently sloshed, embittered Parizeau, addressing the faithful after their defeat in a referendum squeaker, blamed the ethnics and the money, and talked of revenge.

Nobody booed or hissed. Nobody, so far as I know, walked out of the auditorium in disgust. Instead, responding to Parizeau's bile, the crowd began to roar, "*Le Québec aux Québécois.*" A chant, as I wrote in the *New Yorker* in 1991, that is tribal and does not include anybody named Ginsberg or MacGregor.

Parizeau's billet-doux to Quebec's racially impure was immediately endorsed by France's odious National Front leader, Jean-Marie Le Pen. And a couple of days after the premier's talk of revenge, hooligans began to oblige. Somebody painted "FLQ" on the base of the statue of Queen Victoria outside the McGill Conservatory of Music on Sherbrooke Street. Then, on November 11, a brick, inscribed "Last Chance 101," was thrown through the front window of Café Books, and somebody, using a black marker, wrote on the window "ENGLISH SHIT GO HOME."

There had been an earlier incident late on referendum night. The Parti Québécois's Rottweiler-in-residence, Deputy Leader Bernard Landry, entered the Inter-Continental Hotel, attempting to manage "le check-in," as they say in Paris. Landry turned on two hotel employees—one a francophone, the other of Mexican origin—and raged against immigrants, who had robbed the separatists of a triumph that their scrutineers had worked so hard to make good. A few days later Landry allowed that he had been "animated" but not abusive, and refused to apologize. Then he discovered that there was a video tape of the contretemps and, on second thought, he did offer an apology of sorts.

Landry complained that it was indecent of immigrants to vote "according to their grandmothers' chromosomes." Grandmothers who, maybe sixty years ago back in Poland, Italy, Greece, Haiti, or wherever, dandled grandchildren on their knees and told them, "Promise me when you grow up you won't ever eat with your elbows on the table, cheat at cards, or vote Yes in a Quebec referendum." Our grandmothers failed us. Had they been truly visionary, they would have taught us to make an acceptable referendum X, neither line crooked, neither too faint nor too dark.

Landry, to give him his due, has always been good for some comic relief. In the heat of the referendum campaign, he wrote to the American secretary of state, Warren Christopher, to warn him that Quebecers would take it amiss if American officials continued to support Canadian unity. "If victory eludes the Yes side by a slim margin, as is plausible," he wrote, "those who did vote Yes—a clear majority of francophone Quebecers—will be tempted to assign responsibility to the United States for part of their profound disappointment. I do not know how many decades it will take to dispel that feeling." So far as I know, Landry is still waiting for a reply to his letter.

Parizeau's *cri de coeur* and Landry's vulgar outburst in the Inter-Continental Hotel were both condemned in the French-language press and Lucien Bouchard promptly disowned the slur made by his increasingly embarrassing sidekick (though this did not inhibit Sheila Copps, the Liberals' parliamentary fishwife, from rising in the Ottawa monkey house and pretending that Bouchard had been mute on the issue). It should also be noted that those separatists who truly believe in territorial rather than ethnocentric independence of a sort were horrified by Parizeau's gaffe. Parizeau was denounced by Jean-Marc Biron and other prominent Jesuits. They wrote in the Montreal *Gazette* that Parizeau's remarks "do not represent the sovereignty movement." I'm afraid I disagree. The PQ, as Don MacPherson wrote in the *Gazette*, is "a political party founded by old-stock French Canadians to address their own grievances and advance their own interests. . . . As a government, it has often advanced francophone interests at the expense of non-francophone ones. The most obvious example is the French Language Charter, also known as Bill 101.... At worst, [the PQ] has treated non-francophones as scapegoats or a threat against which francophones must be protected—by PQ sovereignty, of course."

Although some in the PQ insist that the term "Québécois" embraces all those who live in the province, that concept, to my mind, is a public-relations fib. A chimera. Going back to René Lévesque, never mind the Abbé Groulx, there has been too much damning evidence to the contrary. When René Lévesque appointed Robert Boyd head of Hydro-Quebec, he hastily pointed out that in spite of his Anglo-sounding name Boyd was a bona fide Québécois, that is to say, of *pure laine* origin. More recently, the ineffable Pierre Bourgault warned that there would be trouble in store for non-francophones if their vote deprived "real" Quebecers of independence, a sentiment endorsed by the former Tory cabinet minister Marcel Masse. Then, in February 1995, Bloc Québécois MP Philippe Paré accused "immigrants" of getting in the way. "Couldn't they, if they don't want to contribute to the Quebec solution, avoid putting on the brakes by voting against us?" Another Bloc backbencher, Gilbert Fillion, declared, "Who's to say that at some point two years from now, they won't wind up in Toronto, these people?" And Bloc MP Suzanne Tremblay snarled at Joyce Napier, a Montreal-born reporter, that, judging by her accent, she probably wasn't "a Québécois at the start."

The truth is, the goodwill of pure-of-heart separatists notwithstanding, their movement is essentially xenophobic, and an independent Quebec would not be a healthy environment for non-francophones.

Immigrants to this country, whether Norman peasants, dispossessed Scots, Irish fleeing the potato famine, *shtetl* Jews, poor Ukrainians, Greeks, Italians, Chinese, Koreans, or Portuguese, came to these shores to escape tribalism and discrimination. Our grandparents or great-grandparents, wherever they came from, were mostly dirt poor. If anybody's blood in this country is blue, it's not owing to their progenitors but is a consequence of the climate. And that includes the *pure laine*. Together we eventually forged a civil society where everybody was equal, at least in their democratic rights. But now, after all these years, tribal conflict is threatening to undo us; and, to the amazement of people in less fortunate lands, this incomparably rich, still nearly empty country, everybody's second chance, may soon self-destruct, splitting into two acrimonious parts. And if that happens, there will certainly be another mass exodus from Montreal, and the only ethnics left in town, "getting in the way," will be the poor and the elderly.

Three or four years from now, when Bouchard, adding up his humiliation points, pronounces it time for Referendum III, the separatists could win by default. Since the first referendum, in 1980, at least 150,000 of *les autres* have quit the province, and over the next few years another 50,000 unwelcome anglophones and ethnics, maybe even more, could easily vote with their feet. The PQ's policy of genteel, non-violent ethnic cleansing may yet win them a country with a depleted but uniform population, where the only surviving English-language sign would read For Sale.

That young woman at the Yes rally, kissing the flag in such a state of ecstasy, strikes me as a metaphor for Quebec now. This province, once Church ridden, has embraced a new faith: nationalism. And in the shape of Lucien Bouchard it enjoys the presence of *un chef*, the strongman the Abbé Groulx once longed for: a veritable Dollard des Ormeaux redux.

But as things stand, the PQ, now Bouchard's chariot, is not so much a political party, its members sharing an ideology beyond independence, as it is an umbrella of convenience that would splinter into three or more parties following separation. These would range from the far left to the extreme right. The irresponsible left, tied to the unions, would promise day care, full employment, whopper pensions, and winning lottery tickets. A ring-a-ding francophone Utopia, although there is no candy in the provincial store. On the extreme right, we could count on enduring the nutters of the St.

Jean Baptiste Society, those luvvies who, in 1938, delivered to Parliament a petition signed by nearly 128,000 of its members opposing "all immigration and especially Jewish immigration" to Canada. Today the St. Jean Baptiste Society is composed of such linguistic zealots that it would surely call for a limit on the number of English-language TV and radio stations serving Quebec, and possibly even seize cans of alphabet soup that failed to include *accents graves* and *aigus*. Something else. Right now the largely Jewish-owned clothing industry employs something like fifty thousand people in Montreal, but some manufacturers are already looking at other sites for their factories in Ontario and Vermont. The day after a Yes vote in Referendum III many of them would pack up, swallow their losses, and move on to more hospitable climes, which could cost Montreal at least thirty thousand jobs. Then union leaders would surely complain that *les maudits Juifs*, who had prospered in the city, were deserting the new state. Certainly it wouldn't acknowledge that it was Jewish energy that helped to create a viable economy in Montreal, and that the Jews had departed only after they had been made to feel unwelcome in the city that had once been their cherished home.

And so, should separation come, I do expect a revival of racial strife in Quebec where, as demonstrated by Parizeau and others, it has never lurked far below the surface.

The separatists in Referendum II did not have to cope with Pierre Elliot Trudeau, whose scorn they justifiably feared. Instead there was only Jean Chrétien at home in Ottawa and a Liberal front bench made up of footnotes. And, oh yes, there was also Preston Manning and his band of bumblers. In an I'll-show-those-bastards Rambo mood, a Reform party stalwart advocated that MPs belt out "O Canada" every day in the House. Alas, this might have necessitated the lyrics being projected on a screen, so that his bunch could follow the bouncing tennis ball, as in the community singsongs in the cinemas of my childhood.

The federalist campaign, even before it was overcome by panic in the final week, was astonishingly inept—the indefatigable Jean Charest, doing his Canadian passport shtick everywhere, a shining exception to that rule.

Charging cocksure out of the starting gate, the federalists began to fumble and contradict each other, tripping over their bromides, once Lucien Bouchard, having disposed of Parizeau like a used Kleenex, geared the separatist campaign into overdrive. Clearly, whichever ad agency was responsible for the federalists' TV spots ought to be tarred and feathered and driven out of Ottawa on a rail. Their lack of verve and imagination was beyond belief. Instead of ducking Bouchard they should have tackled him. They could have shown footage of that latter-day Messiah who, after his swearing in as a Tory cabinet minister in 1988, said, "I don't like the word 'separatist.' You know it is a loaded word. It's not the reality. You know many people voted yes [in the 1980 referendum] for negotiation. . . . I feel since Quebecers have decided in a democratic way that their future is within the federation . . . it is the duty of the francophone Quebecers to make it work. . . . I am very proud to be a Canadian. I showed the flag in Paris for Canada . . . I proved it possible to be a committed Canadian and a Quebecer at the same time."

Honouring another of Parizeau's gaffes, they might have flashed on screen every night, without comment, a live wiggly lobster being plunged into a pot of boiling water. They should have played my favourite Parizeau TV sequence: in an effort to remake that pompous man's image, he is shown on his estate near Knowlton in the Eastern Townships, not so much habitant as squire, wearing a snazzy tweed cap and stylish topcoat, seated unconvincingly on his tractor with modishly attired farmerette Lisette. He turns the key in the ignition, pumps the pedal, and smiles lamely as the tractor won't start. This, with the caption "SEPARATISM IS A NON-STARTER" would have appealed to Quebecers' sense of humour. Instead, the what-Canada-can-do-for-you TV spot that turned up again and again showed a man being rescued from drowning at sea by a helicopter, hardly a Quebecer's typical experience.

And then, whichever adviser allowed Jean Chrétien to appear on national television—which meant that Bouchard, the far more capable advocate, had to be granted equal time—ought to be strung up by his thumbs for a week. Chrétien's broadcast to the nation was a disaster. Looking sickly, a loser, he appeared not as Canada's champion but like a supplicant. And he emerged from the campaign a diminished leader who panicked in the last week, making nebulous promises to Quebec about distinct-society status and a renewed constitutional veto. Back to square one. Back to the discredited Mulroney's Rube Goldberg constitutional fiddles.

CBC-TV's "The National Magazine" also let me down. Mind you, I have a problem with Hanna Gartner. Whenever she appears on "The National Magazine," fidgety, twinkly, her direct, wide-eyed stare into the camera somewhat crazed, I automatically retreat a couple of feet lest she actually leap out of our TV set to demand my attention; and then along came her interview with Bouchard.

Rarely have I seen such an inadequate, ill-researched, no-brainer of an interview with such an extremely vulnerable politician. Bouchard, posturing as Mr. Clean, was not asked about the millions that his sponsor Mulroney had manured his Lac-St-Jean riding with in 1988 in order to ensure Bouchard's election in time-honoured Duplessis fashion. He was not questioned closely about how it was that a former Tory cabinet minister could be born again a social democrat, just as the separatists were desperate for union support in the referendum. There was no suggestion that a man who had been a Liberal, a PQ member, and a convincing Tory before founding the Bloc Québécois in his own image might be a hustler with his eye on the main chance or, to be kind, a tad confused. Bouchard wasn't asked how a man born into a working-class family in the boonies, who had risen to become our ambassador to France, an MP, a cabinet minister, and a leader of Her Majesty's Loyal Opposition, could parade as a victim of anglophone prejudice and feel humiliated, as he claimed, every day before dusk. As Bouchard went on to say that French Canadians are a people and that it is therefore natural for them to have a country, I waited for Gartner to inquire if Bouchard also favoured nationhood for the Cree, who are also a people. But no. Instead, at any moment, it seemed the adoring Gartner would ask Bouchard what his favourite flower was, and whether he had given Audrey chocolates for Valentine's Day.

On the other hand, Bouchard's free ride was nothing compared with the idiocy of Gartner's chit-chat with the CBC's national reporter, Francine Pelletier, the evening after Parizeau's *bon mots* about ethnics and money.

> PELLETIER: Jacques Parizeau is not a racist. I know everyone wants to call him a racist. It's the thing to do often in terms of——
> GARTNER: No, people aren't calling him a racist. They're saying what he said was racist.
> PELLETIER: Yes, well, very often they mix up the two.

I don't mix them up. *In vino veritas.* If you talk like a racist, you are a racist, pure and simple.

Following this exchange, Gartner and Pelletier sailed off into cloud-cuckoo-land.

> PELLETIER: Jacques Parizeau has been around for thirty years . . . and that first generation of nationalists . . . when they got up to fight for this, there were no ethnic minorities to speak of.
> GARTNER: So he's not out of touch.
> PELLETIER: Yes. . . . Because if Quebec had remained the *pure laine*, uniform society it was thirty years ago, they probably would have won it by now. . . .

Pelletier, who has covered Quebec politics in the past for both Radio-Canada and *La Presse*, knows better, even if Gartner knows nothing about Montreal. In 1965, the population of Montreal was 2,109,509. Far from being a uniform francophone society, this figure included 101,466 of Italian origin, 73,062 Jews, 26,347 Polish,

27,873 Germans, and 11,849 Asians, not to mention 462,260 anglo-phones of British, Scots, or Irish origin.

On an earlier segment of "The National Magazine," Pelletier ventured that Parizeau was an honest man. Tell us the *Reader's Digest* is a cornucopia of original ideas, say you would buy used furniture from Brian Mulroney without doubting Mila's price tags, but don't pretend Parizeau is a man of honour. A wily old pol, yes, an enormous ego, certainly, but honest, no.

A trained economist of undoubted intelligence, Parizeau, a couple of years back, assured Quebecers with a straight face that independence would cost each of them no more than the price of a couple of cases of beer a year. Then, when the sovereignty campaign started to falter in the early going, Parizeau, elbowed by Bouchard, suddenly advocated the offer of a partnership with the rest of Canada. However, in a television interview released after his resignation, he revealed, "For a long time, I have started from the principle that that thing would never happen."

Parizeau has been known to suffer other lapses into candour. The *Globe and Mail*'s Graham Fraser reported after the referendum that Parizeau had once said privately, "We are elected by idiots. In Quebec, 40 per cent are separatists and 40 per cent are federalists—and 20 per cent don't know who is prime minister of Canada. And it's that 20 per cent that makes and breaks governments."

Actually, 30 per cent idiots is more like it. For, according to consistent poll data, that was the percentage of Quebec Yes voters who believed they could become "sovereign" and still remain in Canada. Put another way, our country came uncomfortably close to being undone by the votes of Parizeau's village "idiots."

What with the polls predicting just about an even split in the vote in the days leading up to the referendum, dread was rampant in Montreal. Rich and middle-class people, francophones among them, emptied their bank accounts and safety-deposit boxes and transferred their savings and stock portfolios to Ontario. As the Canadian dollar teetered, there was a stampede to convert into American currency. Even the poor in the Eastern Townships, where I live, were scared. Snowplough drivers, house painters, and barmaids of my acquaintance lined up at the banks in Mansonville and Knowlton to withdraw their meagre savings and stuff them under a mattress. Currency speculators made money out of our misery. And prominent among them was the politically motivated Caisse de Dépôt et Placement du Québec, *la machine à milliards*, which bought Canadian dollars on the cheap, propping up the buck, and came out ahead by a declared profit of $7 million.

In the last days of October, confusion was the rule in some quarters.

Item: The troubled CEO of a Montreal factory that makes train wheels, CN its major customer, told me that he had spoken to his workers, explaining that if the Yes side won, their jobs would be at risk. The plant would have to move. One of the men on the floor corrected him. "He held up his paycheque," said the CEO, "and pointed out the deductions for provincial and federal tax. 'If the Yes side wins,' he said, 'we will no longer have to pay federal tax. I will take home a bigger paycheque.'"

On referendum eve, old people stood in line for hours to claim Canadian passports, lest their citizenships be withdrawn on November 1. Many of us thought they were overreacting, but, astonishingly, it turned out that their apprehensions were justified. Pushy little Bernard Landry, that compulsive penpal, had sent notes to all the embassies in Ottawa, advising them: "When the Quebec National Assembly will have proclaimed the sovereignty of the new state the moment will have come to recognize it, without putting in peril relations with the rest of Canada." A Bloc MP wrote to francophones in the Canadian Armed Forces instructing them that they should be ready to transfer their allegiance to Quebec. And, according to my information, federal customs officers at the Quebec borders and airports were told to be ready to withdraw and be replaced within twenty-four hours. We were on the verge of a banana-republic putsch. This in a country where, in many cities, you can still get a ticket for jaywalking.

Post-referendum Montreal was deeply depressed and ridden with anxiety. Interestingly enough, René Lévesque never frightened anybody in Quebec, but the perpetually seething Lucien Bouchard had some people terrified. The man whom separatists celebrate as a saint, many of *les autres* continue to fear as an irresponsible demagogue. A twister. A clear and present danger to this province's already severely tested, fragile social fabric.

Item: In Toronto, after the referendum, I ran into a friend from Montreal. "I was born here," he said, "of Greek origin, and I've never been so scared stiff in all my life. I'm fifty-five years old. Fluently bilingual. So what? You work and you work all your life and suddenly everything I've managed to accomplish is at risk. The day after the vote I phoned our real-estate agent in the Laurentians and said I wanted to put our cottage up for sale. She burst into tears. 'I've had forty-five calls today,' she said, 'from people who want to sell, and I haven't got a single buyer on my books.'"

A real-estate agent I ran into in Winnie's Bar in Montreal claimed that just about every house on the West Island was up for grabs. "In Westmount," she said, "people want to sell their homes, move the cash out of the province, and rent an apartment while they hang around to wait and see." She had closed a Westmount sale, she said, with a two-tier contract. "The price was six-fifty, but if the Yes side won, it was five-fifty."

An insurance broker I know told me that many of his clients have acquired pieds-à-terre in Alexandria or Cornwall, Ontario, so that they can easily shift their business addresses out of Quebec. "Meanwhile," he said, "everything is on hold. Nobody is investing."

The separatists tried blackmail. In the early running, long before the official campaign had begun, Finance Minister Jean Campeau warned that if the No side won, he would be obliged to increase provincial sales tax by a percentage point. Next it was intimidation, with Messrs. Bourgeault and Masse threatening trouble if the racially unclean frustrated the wishes of the *pure laine* Québécois. They tried to win by stealth, contriving a murky question with the intention of confusing, not daring to ask Quebecers outright, "Are you for independence, Yes or No?" because they already knew the answer to that one. They first bowdlerized then hid their own damaging studies commissioned by the restructuring minister, Richard Le Hir, at a cost of $5 million, because they clearly indicated the punishing economic cost of separation. Upon taking charge of the foundering campaign, Bouchard said, "I don't want to hear anything about the Le Hir studies. Those are not my studies. That's the past for me. That's the past campaign."

Then there was the vote itself. The separatists had failed to send out ballots to many Quebecers temporarily resident in the rest of Canada, the U.S., or overseas, justifiably fearful that they would have voted No. Scrutineers worked to rule in advance polls in anglophone or allophone districts of Montreal. All too typical was the experience of an old friend of mine, now confined to a wheelchair, who had to wait two and a half hours to vote and finally returned home without filling out the ballot. Other scrutineers, all of them appointed by the PQ, were instructed by their coaches to cheat shamelessly at the anglophone polls in Montreal, pronouncing thousands of No ballots spoiled, as the Xs were adjudged too faint or too dark.

They threatened, they lied, they cheated, and still they didn't win, although they did come nerve-rackingly close. And now four, maybe five, years down the road, we are going to have to endure Referendum III, and no doubt another question calculated to confuse. Next time out, however, whatever ethnics or money that remain here should insist on international observers from more advanced democracies to oversee the shenanigans. Observers from, say, Nigeria, Haiti, or Bosnia.

Previous Publications

Books And Things

"Mr. Sam" first appeared in *Saturday Night*, July/August 1992 under the title, "Speakeasy of Sam Bronfman". "The Reichmanns" first appeared in *The New York Times Book Review*, February 9, 1997. "Lansky" first appeared in *The New York Times Book Review*, October 1991 under the title, "Little Man; Lansky, Meyer and the gangster life". "Woody" first appeared in *Playboy*, December 1991 under the title, "Let's hear it for Woody". "Just Find a Million Readers and Success Will Surely Follow" first appeared in *The New York Times Book Review*, June 10, 1990. "Mencken" first appeared in *GQ*, June 1990 under the title, "Henry down with the heils". "Morley Safer's Vietnam" first appeared in *GQ*, May 1990 under the title, "Morely Safer's poignant Odyssey". "Supersex" first appeared in *GQ*, November 1993 under the title, "Token Sex". "Saul Bellow" first appeared in *National Review*, August 1, 1994 under the title, "King Saul". "Sexual Harassment" first appeared in *GQ*, September 1994 under the title, "Duck! Reflections on Sexual Harassment". "The Innocents Abroad" first appeared in *New Criterion*, May 1996.

Going Places

"Germany 1978" first appeared in *Weekend Magazine*, March 10, 1979 under the title, "Jew in Germany". "Safari" first appeared in *Signature*,

February 1983 under the title, "Africa the great adventure". "Marrakech" first appeared in GQ, October 1985 under the title, "Here's looking at you Abdeslam Aarab". "Sol Kertzner's Xanadu" first appeared in GQ, August 1994 under the title, "Bloody Marys in Xanadu". "Egypt's Eleventh Plague" first appeared in GQ, April 1993 under the title, "Florence of Arabia". "London Then and Now" first appeared in GQ, April 1985 under the title, "My London Then and Now". "Pedlars Diary" first appeared in New Criterion, January 1998.

Sports

"Eddie Quinn" first appeared in Maclean's, November 19, 1960 under the title, "In wrestling all the Indians are chiefs". "Gordie" first appeared in Inside Sports, November 30, 1980 under the title, "Howe Incredible". "Gretzky in Eighty-four" first appeared in The New York Times Sports Magazine, September 29, 1985 under the title, "King of the New Canada". "From Satchel, through Hank Greenberg, to El Divino Loco" first appeared in GQ, July 1989. "Pete Rose" first appeared in The New York Times Sports Magazine, March 31, 1985. "Kasparov" first appeared in GQ, September 1993 under the title, "Cerebral brawn".

Politics

"Audrey! Audrey! Audrey!" first appeared in Saturday Night, April 1990 under the title, "No Deals Please". "Bye Bye Mulroney" first appeared in Saturday Night, June 1993 under the title, "Hail Brian and Farewell". "From the Ottawa Monkey House . . . to Referendum" first appeared in The New Yorker, May 30, 1994 under the title, "Postscript".